Ancient Worlds
Modern Reflections

Ancient Worlds, Modern Reflections

Philosophical Perspectives on Greek and Chinese Science and Culture

G. E. R. LLOYD

CLARENDON PRESS · OXFORD

OXFORD

UNIVERSITY PRESS

Great Clarendon Street, Oxford OX2 6DP

Oxford University Press is a department of the University of Oxford.
It furthers the University's objective of excellence in research, scholarship,
and education by publishing worldwide in

Oxford New York

Auckland Bangkok Buenos Aires Cape Town Chennai
Dar es Salaam Delhi Hong Kong Istanbul Karachi Kolkata
Kuala Lumpur Madrid Melbourne Mexico City Mumbai Nairobi
São Paulo Shanghai Taipei Tokyo Toronto

Oxford is a registered trade mark of Oxford University Press
in the UK and in certain other countries

Published in the United States
by Oxford University Press Inc., New York

First published 2004

British Library Cataloguing in Publication Data

Data available

Library of Congress Cataloging in Publication Data

Data available

ISBN 0–19–927016–3

1 3 5 7 9 10 8 6 4 2

Typeset by SNP Best-set Typesetter Ltd., Hong Kong
Printed in Great Britain
on acid-free paper by
Biddles Ltd., Norfolk, King's Lynn

CONTENTS

PREFACE

For much of my working life I have been engaged in the study of ancient societies, Greece and more recently China, especially, attempting to understand their world-views, why they took the form they did, and how and indeed why they changed. My principal investigations fall broadly into the category of the history of ancient science. But reflecting my education in Cambridge and my early contact with such denizens of the Department of History and Philosophy of Science there as Mary Hesse and Gerd Buchdahl, I have always assumed that it makes no sense to divorce the history of science from its philosophy, nor to try to do the philosophy without the history.

Philosophy enters my work in two ways, first in the form of ancient philosophy of science, primarily though not exclusively Greek philosophy of science, and secondly in the guise of modern philosophical concerns, about what science is, the debate between various brands of 'realism' and 'relativism', the analysis of truth, and many other questions. This book is an attempt to do two things. The first is to confront more directly than I have done previously the fundamental philosophical issues of what it is to study science in ancient civilizations, and in so doing to make a contribution to those modern philosophical debates. The second is to reflect, again more explicitly than I have done before, on how ancient history can be brought to bear on some of the crucial social and political problems of today's world.

Under the first heading, I here tackle head-on such questions as these: how far is it possible to arrive at an understanding of ancient societies? Is it possible to talk meaningfully of 'science' or of its various constituent disciplines, 'astronomy', 'geography', 'anatomy', and so on, in the ancient world? Are logic and its laws universal, or in what sense is that, or must that be, true? Is there one ontology—a single world—to which all attempts at understanding are directed? Do the notions of truth and belief represent reliable cross-cultural universals?

In each case the answer does not take the form of a simple yes or no, but consists in the clarification of the issues and the removal of the confusions that have bedevilled their discussion. Those clarifications can, indeed, be brought to bear on ongoing philosophical debates, for however much scientific practices have changed, even the history of ancient endeavours offers materials, so I wish to claim, that are relevant to issues we continue to discuss. One way of coming to terms with the evident variety in the investigations into the external world in different times and places is by way of identifying their different styles, an idea I take over and modify from Crombie and Hacking. The two most detailed studies in this book, in Chapters 8 and 9, are concerned with the styles constituted by different interests in, and uses of, classification and exemplification. Styles of enquiry are, to be sure, subject to different constraints from artistic or literary styles, or even styles of philosophizing. But the notion can help to do justice both to what the enquiries in question have in common—they are, after all, directed at what is, in some sense that needs explicating, the same subject matter—and to where and why they differ.

Under the second heading, of the lessons that can be derived from the study of ancient societies for today's problems, I here offer three examples. The first is to do with higher education—the present role of the universities and their future responsibilities. The second concerns the question of the universal applicability of the discourse of human rights and human nature. The third relates to the strengths and more particularly the weaknesses of democratic institutions at national and at international level.

But before I embark on these studies, I should first set out the four principal assumptions that guide my methodology, though these will need elaborating in particular contexts in due course. My first methodological principle is that we should, so far as possible, use actors', rather than observers', categories in our historical studies. We should certainly not impose our own preconceptions and expectations on them. Rather, our first task is to try to grasp how the ancient investigators themselves understood their work, their ideas, goals, and methods. We shall see in Chapter 1, however, that implementing that principle runs into difficulties and poses philosophical problems of its own. Nevertheless the ambition to recover ancient perspectives is both a cornerstone of my methodology and one of its strategic goals.

Secondly I sign up to the belief that there are no theory-free observations in science, and no theory-free descriptions in the history of science. It is all the more important, in the latter case, to make the theoretical preconceptions explicit. The recognition that theories and values are inescapable does not mean, of course, that we can adopt just any framework for our work. Quite the contrary. We must be all the more vigilant in examining them for prejudice and bias, whether or not those spring directly from modern presuppositions. Moreover we can and should make maximum use of the differences we can observe in the degrees of theoryladenness, even though at the minimum end there will still be no statement with zero theoretical load.

Thirdly we cannot expect definitive answers in science or in history of science. All conclusions are subject to revision, though to be sure some, in science especially, are clearly more robust than others. But that in turn does not mean that there is no possibility of testing and evaluating theories and interpretations. There are still viable senses to the notions of objectivity, truth, warranting, even though none of these yields an absolute, definitive, result.

Fourthly my historical studies of the origins and development of the literal/metaphorical dichotomy have convinced me of the dangers of its use. Univocity is a limiting case, not a norm to which most terms should be expected to comply. Rather we should recognize that every term can exhibit a degree of what I call semantic stretch. But so far from aggravating such problems as the indeterminacy of translation, we can see that this enables us to establish the continuity between translations between natural languages and interpretations of one another's own idiolects.

To those accustomed to old-fashioned positivist resolutions of the problems, these four principles may seem to offer an unpromising basis for investigations in the history of ancient science. But to my mind they provide far sounder grounds for that work. They enable us to refine the sense in which the phenomena are the same, and yet may also be different, for different ancient investigators across different ancient disciplines. This helps us to escape the sterility of much of the debate between realist and relativist or constructivist positions, and to get round the impasse that opposes correspondence and coherence theories of truth as mutually exclusive and exhaustive alternatives, as well as allowing us to avoid the extravagances of the strong thesis of the incommensurability of belief systems. We can identify, I shall insist, appropriate standards of verifying and justifying in different intellectual endeavours, science, philosophy, history. They are never definitive, but always subject to revision (principle 3): but they are adequate for provisional judgements, the only kind we can expect to make. The demand for certainty, incontrovertibility, incorrigibility, is one that we can trace to its historical origins, just as we can do the same for the dichotomy between the literal and the metaphorical, and the fact that we can see the contingent nature of their development in a particular historical conjuncture helps to liberate us from any obligation to treat them as necessary components in any well-grounded investigation.

The ideas developed in this book have their origin in seminars and lectures that I have given, in different natural languages, in different parts of the world, at different times, and they owe much to the constructive criticisms of my audiences on those occasions as well as to those of my Cambridge colleagues, at History and Philosophy of Science, Classics, and the Needham Research Institute. It is my pleasant duty to acknowledge these debts and those to editors who kindly agreed to publish earlier versions of the talks that I gave.

Chapter 1 derives from my participation in a conference on the problems of 'The Principle of Charity in Interpretation' that was organized by Isabelle Delpla at Nancy in November 1998. Some of the ideas it contains figure in the chapter entitled 'Comment ne pas être charitable dans l'interprétation' included in the conference proceedings, Delpla 2002.

Chapter 2 owes much to my 1999 British Academy lecture entitled 'On the "origins" of science', a version of which I later gave, on the invitation of Liu Dun, as a Zhu Kezhen lecture in the Institute for the History of Natural Science in Beijing in September 2001.

Chapter 3 elaborates points that I presented to a Dibner conference on Chinese science organized by Karine Chemla and Kim Yungsik in November 2001, some of which were included in the chapter I contributed to volume ii of the Enciclopedia Italiana *Storia della scienza* published that year.

Several of the arguments from Chapter 4 and Chapter 7 were first put forward in a conference organized by Jessica Rawson at Merton College, Oxford, in September 2000 entitled 'China and the West: One World or Two?'

Chapter 5 addresses a problem that formed the topic of my contribution to a colloquium on 'La Vérité dans les sciences' at the Collège de France in October 2001. The French version of my lecture, translated by Janet Lloyd, figures in the volume that stems from the colloquium, edited by Jean-Pierre Changeux and Jacques Bouveresse.

Chapter 6 develops arguments that I put to a conference on 'The Processes of Belief' organized by Fernando Gil in Lisbon in July 2002, the proceedings of which are forthcoming.

Chapter 8 elaborates arguments from the Marett lecture I delivered at Exeter College, Oxford, in April 1997, a version of which is forthcoming (ed. Olson).

Chapter 9 develops material that stems from my contribution to a special number of *Extrême-Orient Extrême-Occident* in 1997 on example in Chinese thought, edited by Karine Chemla.

Chapter 10 originates in a lecture I gave under the auspices of John Vallance at Sydney Grammar School in February 2002 and under those of Kato Morimichi at Tohoku University, Sendai, in October 2002.

Chapter 11 stems from a contribution to a set of seminars on human nature organized by David Cannadine at the Institute for Historical Research, London, in November 2000.

Finally Chapter 12 develops arguments that I proposed in a chapter in a Festschrift for Jacques Brunschwig entitled *Le Style de la pensée* (Paris, 2002).

I should like to thank my hosts and audiences on all those occasions, as also the anonymous referees for Oxford University Press, for their helpful and constructive comments, while absolving them all, as is customary, from any responsibility for the form the end result takes.

G. E. R. L.

1

Understanding Ancient Societies

How can we hope to understand societies that existed long ago? Is what we think we understand about them merely the reflection of our own ideas and preoccupations? The problems are particularly severe versions of the general difficulty, much discussed by philosophers and anthropologists in the 1950s and 1960s, of understanding alien cultures. Today's field anthropologist can at least cross-question the people he or she is studying, to check whether his or her interpretation of their ideas and behaviour is along the right lines, and at least sometimes they will confirm that it is, though whether that is simply out of politeness or deference remains an open question. For the student of ancient societies, by contrast, most of the evidence has long been in. Occasionally a new Greek papyrus is found in the sands of Egypt or wrapped around a mummy: far more often silk scrolls or bamboo slips come to light in Chinese tombs. But the point holds as a generalization, and besides, we certainly cannot question any of our ancient subjects. I shall be returning to the problems of the bias and lacunae in our sources at the end of this chapter.

While the problems of the range of evidence are serious, those of the conceptual framework within which interpretation can proceed are even more so. The difficulty can be put in the form of a dilemma. On the one hand are the risks of distortion if we use the conceptual tools familiar to us. In the case of the history of science, especially, that has led to both anachronism and teleology. To talk of the ancients' chemical theories, for instance, is bound to distort what they were doing, since chemistry as we know it today is a product of the eighteenth and nineteenth centuries: I shall be dealing with the problem of talk about science as such in the ancient world in the next chapter. But teleology is even more pernicious, in that it assumes that the ancients aimed to approximate to modern ideas—and as they did not get there, they must have failed miserably. But of course they could not see into the future.

Like ourselves, they were doing the best job they could in dealing with their own contemporary issues.

On the other hand, if the reaction to that first difficulty is to insist that we use the conceptual framework of our ancient subjects, how is that possible? We are used to pointing out that certain ancient concepts, Chinese *qi*[1] or *yin yang*[1], Aristotelian *to ti en einai*, or Greek *logos* more generally, are untranslatable. Up to a point we can tolerate transliterations in a study interpreting the ancients. But that interpretation, sooner or later, has to render the ancients' ideas, not just singly but in complex wholes, into English. An interpretation of Aristotle that proceeded entirely within the framework of Aristotelian discourse—in ancient Greek indeed—would be no interpretation, but at best a replica of some ideas of his.

So the dilemma stands. We cannot, on pain of distortion, impose our own conceptual framework. Yet we have to.[1] The problems of interpretation are particularly challenging when we encounter what seem to be irrational or absurd beliefs and practices in the society we are studying. The reported Nuer notion that twins are birds (Evans-Pritchard 1956), and the Dorze one that the leopard is a Christian animal (Sperber 1975), became famous in anthropological and philosophical debate. But it is easy to suggest similarly extravagant statements, from ancient Greece or China—and indeed from our own society and time. What are we to make of Plato's claim that the Idea of the Good is 'beyond being' (*Republic* 509b), or of the statements in *Zhuangzi* (2: 27, cf. Graham 1989: 178 f.) that 'no thing is not that, no thing is not this', and again that neither the assertion that it is nor again the assertion that it is not is permissible? But then every day in modern Christian churches the belief that God is three *and* that God is one is solemnly repeated.

There are three reactions to this general problem that are tempting, but misleading. The first is to postulate different mentalities as the source for the apparent unintelligibility of certain ideas or behaviour: the second is to claim that that reflects incommensurable belief systems; the third is, on the contrary, to invoke a principle of charity in interpretation that, so far as possible, makes others' statements turn out to be true—by our standards.

The mentalities postulate would offer a quick—all too quick—resolution to the problems. The apparently absurd beliefs merely reflect a

---

[1] This was the subject of a series of exchanges between Winch, Macintyre, and others, see Wilson 1970, and cf. Horton and Finnegan 1973, Hollis and Lukes 1982.

different mind-set: the idea has been applied not just to so-called 'primitive mentality' but also to early modern Europe (Vickers 1984) and to China (Granet 1934*a*, 1934*b*). Yet this will not do. Since I engaged in a detailed critique of the whole idea of mentalities in my 1990, I can be brief.

The gist of my critique can be summed up in four points. (1) First the notion of mentalities at best merely redescribes the phenomena it is supposed to explain, and is itself no explanation of them. (2) Secondly, it blocks, rather than furthers, explanation, by psychologizing the issues, by postulating a cast or casts of mind that, if they existed, could not in any case be investigated independently of those phenomena. (3) Thirdly, the questions of how a mentality is acquired, and how one could ever be modified, remain utterly mysterious, whether we are speaking of individuals or of whole groups. (4) Fourthly and finally, some of the advocates of mentalities attribute a plurality of mentalities to the same subject, and that is incoherent, for how does the individual in question switch between one and another?

The second interpretative strategy I mentioned comes in different forms and it is only the extreme version that is vulnerable to the most obvious objections. The idea that different systems of belief are incommensurable was introduced by Kuhn (1970, cf. especially Feyerabend 1975) to underline, among other things, the difficulty of identifying common criteria to adjudicate between them. The history of science provides plenty of examples where the status or interpretation of crucial concepts—such as mass, force, weight—has changed, thereby making any direct comparison between them problematic. Yet in the strongest form incommensurability suggests that different systems are, strictly, mutually unintelligible. In that form, the hypothesis is open to severe empirical objections.

We can indeed say that Ptolemy's view of the world is, in certain crucial respects, radically different from that of Copernicus. Yet Copernicus of course had a fair understanding of Ptolemy. He did not think of Ptolemy's theories as dealing with a different set of issues from his own: he thought of them as in certain respects inferior solutions to the problems he tackled himself. Again no field anthropologist has ever returned from the study of a culture announcing that he or she could understand *nothing*. When the Buddhists, or the Jesuits, first came to China, it was not as if all communication between them and their hosts was impossible, however frequently misunderstandings, whether wilful or inadvertent, arose.[2] In general, any commentator who diagnoses two strictly incommensurable belief systems is implicitly claiming to be able to understand both sufficiently to be able to make such a diagnosis—and what is to stop the adherents of one or other system arriving at that level of understanding?

Thirdly there is the principle of charity in interpretation, which again has been advocated in different forms by Quine, by Davidson, and others. Delpla 2001 provides a survey of the history of, and variations in, the use of some such principle (cf. Delpla 2002). Sometimes the principle just covers the interpretation of logical connectives in different languages: I shall be returning to the problem of alternative logics in Chapter 4. More often it is extended to apply also to beliefs, where in one version the aim is to make others' statements come out true, so far as possible, in our terms. Obviously when an alien informant uses the term 'gavagai' in the presence of a rabbit, but not when there is an ostrich, it is more economical to suppose that he or she may be saying something about rabbits. Not that we can ever be certain that the substance (as we call it) is meant, rather than, say, the appearance or the process, the rabbit-event-slice, or even the mass of rabbit-hood in the world. In that form the radical sceptical challenge cannot be met. Translation and interpretation are always going to suffer from a certain indeterminacy.

But further limitations on the principle of charity, if construed as a rule with universal applicability, can be illustrated with examples that do not involve translation between different natural languages. We can use our own not so uncommon experiences to extract certain guidelines for the interpretation even of ancient beliefs. Part of what I have to say concerns paradox, part deception, part learning.

The principle was often invoked, in the debate I referred to, in relation to exotic beliefs, attitudes, modes of behaviour, statements, the fruit of ethnographic fieldwork among the Nuer, the Dorze, or whoever. But it is all very well to diagnose strangeness in others. We should bear in mind that we are pretty strange ourselves. Our own society, our own language group, provide plenty of similarly puzzling items—not that the idea of a language group is at all hard-edged. Indeed who

---

[2] The arguments of Lloyd forthcoming are that misunderstanding between Ricci and his Chinese hosts was not inevitable, and further that Ricci was as partial in his grasp of ancient European ideas as he was of contemporary Chinese ones.

counts as belonging to 'our society', and in which contexts, is equally problematic.[3]

However, our own familiar European theology, poetry, philosophy, and science all yield examples of paradox. One of the more obvious scientific instances is that of the wave-particle duality of light. Here it is a matter of the student coming to see how it is that light exhibits some of the features of waves, some of particles, and seeing indeed how these can be combined. It is not that this is paradox for paradox's sake. But that may be the case elsewhere.

Let me return to the Trinity. What are we to make of the doctrine that God is three and God is one? When an attempt at interpreting this was made by Hobbes, the outcome was instructive.[4] Hobbes initially registered considerable bafflement and then suggested that perhaps what was meant was that the three, Father, Son, and Holy Ghost, were each representations of the same person. One might have thought that that was quite a sensible suggestion, but it got him into deep trouble, and he had to back down. No, the theologians insisted, it is not the case that God is one person, with three representations, but three persons—three persons and yet still one. In some contexts, in fact, paradox is there not to be resolved, but to be insisted upon: it may, for instance, underline the very special nature of talk about God.

We should not underestimate the varieties and usefulness of different modes of paradox and of apparently irrational behaviour. Some such behaviour may be sanctioned as conventional. At weddings in Christian churches, the bride and groom should be sprinkled with confetti, never mind that it does not ensure in fact that they will be fertile. Not to do so would somehow not be right, not as it should be, not felicitous.[5] Some puzzlements are fun or entertainment, verbal conjuring tricks, play. Many paradoxes may be more or less intellectual teases, like some of the insolubilia of the medievals. One such goes back to the Liar paradox of Greek antiquity. I, the person speaking to you, am lying. If I am telling the truth, I lie. If I lie, I am telling the truth. Some have the not unimportant function of arresting attention, as we can illustrate from both ancient Greece and China. Heraclitus is recorded as having said that 'the

---

[3] Anderson 1991, especially, has insisted on the work of the imagination in the construction of what is to count as a community.

[4] I owe this example to an intervention by Quentin Skinner at a seminar on the history of philosophy at Cambridge.

[5] Tambiah 1973 developed the contrast between felicity and efficacy as alternative, and complementary, goals for 'magical' acts.

kingdom is the child's', and quite what he meant may have been as difficult to fathom as it has ever since remained for modern commentators.[6] A similar point may apply also to some citations from Hui Shi and from Gongsun Long. The latter was famous for the White Horse paradox (the white horse is not a horse), where our Chinese sources also record some typically deflationary responses. In one story, when a man tried to get past a customs post on his white horse with the claim that it was not a horse, the customs officer would have none of it.[7]

Most poetic discourse, whether or not exploiting paradox, invites the exploration of multilayered, potentially inexhaustible, meanings. 'The expense of spirit in a waste of shame is lust in action', as the Shakespeare sonnet begins. Once we see that waste may be a play on waist, that spirit may be used of semen, and that expense may be ejaculation, we recognize that this may be sexual lust, but that is certainly not all that it is. Poetry is, no doubt, exceptionally open-ended. But closure of meaning is a crass assumption to make with most prose too.

Again some puzzling statements, some rituals, are designed to stress the distance between the outsider and the insider, between the apprentice and the master, to emphasize the superior knowledge that the cognoscenti have or the special character of what it is knowledge of. You may not understand the astral plane at first, but when you have been initiated into the coven, with the appropriate ritual, you will come to understand, indeed you will come to visit it, to be more familiar with it, even, than with the common-or-garden world that surrounds you. I am here talking not of Azande witches, but of witchcraft practised in London in the 1980s, studied by Tanya Luhrmann (Luhrmann 1989), whose analysis brings to light obvious parallels with the notion of empty concepts studied in the Fang by Fernandez (1982) and more recently by Boyer (1986, 1990).

Different responses are appropriate for the different modes of puzzlement with which we may be faced. The principle of charity dictates that we must assume that the message sent will be intelligible. Only if

---

[6] Guthrie 1962: 478, for instance, explores various ways of making sense of Heraclitus Fr. 52, but eventually admits defeat.

[7] This is the story told about Ni Yue in *Hanfeizi* 32. The work of Hui Shi in the fourth century BCE and Gongsun Long in the third is discussed by Graham 1989: 76 ff., 82 ff., for instance. The extant text known as the *Gongsun Longzi* has often been thought to be, in the main, a forgery of between the fourth and seventh centuries CE, though the chapter on the White Horse paradox has been accepted as authentic. I should, however, stress that the relationship between this material, the Mohist canon, and the *Zhuangzi* writings is the subject of considerable ongoing controversy: see C.-Y. Cheng 1997, Johnston 2000 and forthcoming.

it is intelligible, Davidson insisted, can disagreement be meaningful. Now with any complex message, if we are not in possession of the fullest contextualization, who was communicating with whom and against what background of what assumptions and conventions, we are liable to make mistakes. That has not stopped outsiders from diagnosing what must be going on, among the Nuer or the Azande: but most of that is mere armchair speculation. When we do have more of the context, in the case of our own cultures (and others, if we work hard at it), we may still be at a loss, but at least have a surer grip of the conventions. But the experience of our own culture, in optimal communication situations, teaches us that intelligibility may take different forms. Sometimes it is not content that is being communicated at all. The statements may look like propositions, the words may seem to convey a straight message, in our own natural language, which requires no translating, no decoding. But that is not the point. Rather, in many of the situations I have described, we have to recognize that the language use is *designed* to mystify, to deceive, to mislead, to exploit, to convey a claim to superiority. In such cases the message is the mystification.

No doubt Quine and Davidson themselves were well aware of the richness of the possible illocutionary and perlocutionary force of certain types of speech acts. In the anthropological debate, some of Tambiah's early studies on magic, particularly, drew heavily on Austin's work.[8] But to look to the decoding of the *content* of the problematic or puzzling statements may, on some occasions, be to look in the wrong direction. Humans are not the transparent, honest, cooperative creatures they would need to be for the principle of charity to be universally and straightforwardly applicable in that manner. Davidson claimed that we have no option but to assume intelligibility as a general rule (Davidson 2001a: 238 f.). But, to insist on the obvious exception, unintelligibility is sometimes deliberately cultivated. The only way the principle applies in those cases is at the meta-level, when we can recognize unintelligibility as the intelligible phenomenon it is. At the primary level, we do not need, in fact we can do without, the assumption that there is a direct content there to be decoded.

When deception is in play, charity may be a distraction. But it may be premature, when we have resources for learning. Puzzling and paradoxical statements may and do pose acute problems of interpretation:

[8] Tambiah 1973: 220 ff. uses ideas derived from Austin 1962, for instance, and cf. also Tambiah 1990: 73 f.

but they also represent an opportunity. We cannot, of course, exactly put ourselves in the position of an ancient Greek or Chinese audience, when they first encountered the strange language of Platonic metaphysics, or an Aristotelian treatise on logic, or the *Dao De Jing* or the *Zhuangzi* or *Huainanzi*. But just as their incentive was to come to understand what these texts had to say about the world, about knowledge, about values, about themselves, so ours is similar. We are introduced to perplexing new ideas. Initially we may be quite baffled—until we come to have some inkling of their significance. That opens up new possibilities for us, not that our interpretation can ever be definitive, nor that arriving at some understanding implies in any sense *agreeing* with the ideas to which we have been introduced.

Of course we need some assumptions to start building bridges, from which interpretation can be developed and greater understanding won. The possibility of bridgeheads has, indeed, to be assumed: indeed how could it be denied without solipsism? Is that an a priori assumption? Against saying that, we might invoke the point I made earlier when I urged that the ethnographic evidence has yet to come up with a society with which communication is impossible, however many misunderstandings may and do arise.

We are likely to start from (it could be said to be more economical to start from) our own ontological assumptions, to enter the field assuming that rabbits are more likely to be named than rabbit-event-slices. But if we should concede that, it does not mean that we have to *stay* with those initial assumptions, as if they were unrevisable. Rather, we can modify them as we achieve greater understanding. Did we not do that repeatedly as we learnt science at school? Indeed did we not also revise some of our own basic assumptions about the world as we studied works of great literature, from *King Lear* to *War and Peace*? Similarly in the field of pragmatics, we should no doubt start with the assumption that we are not normally going to be wilfully misled and that those who are communicating with us are serious about that. But that too has to be subject to revision. In the process, we may learn more about being misleading, about being misled, about play, than we perhaps bargained for.

The double-bind is obvious. On the one hand in some way we have to make sense of our subjects in our terms, for our audiences. I usually speak English, of course, when discussing the Greeks or the Chinese, though as I noted, like other commentators, I often simply incorporate certain key terms from each language untranslated. I gave *logos* and *qi*[l] as examples, to which many others could be added.

Yet on the other hand our primary obligation is to make sense of our subjects in *their* terms, to allow them their voice, their differing viewpoints on fundamental issues. To be sure I cannot consider myself as one of them: I cannot even identify fully with my modern audiences or readership. But then I am not exactly identical myself with the person I was twenty-five years ago, if we are speaking of what I know or believe.

That is where the opportunities arise, both for expanding our notions on the subject of ontology and in matters to do with pragmatics. We may think of the insights that have come from the careful investigation of the differing views on time, space, causation, number, colour, sound, that are found in different cultures, ancient and modern. Some such differences are, to be sure, more fundamental than others. Those within the experience of time, for instance, between a purely quantitative view and one marked with qualitative differences, for example between sacred and profane time, appear to be deeply entrenched (Leach 1961). Yet even in the case of colour (to which I shall be returning in Chapter 7) we have come a long way from the studies of Berlin and Kay (1969) who assumed—and set out to prove—that all colour vocabularies follow set rules for the acquisition of terms for hues, when it is now understood that in many natural languages, it is not hue that is salient, so much as luminosity, and where many terms in the colour vocabulary do not *primarily* connote colours at all (Lyons 1995).

We may be at a loss to explain, in general terms, how such learning can occur, how new insights into underlying ontological questions can be gained. It may seem that it *cannot* happen, as if *either* other ideas will be reduced to our own, *or* they will remain forever unintelligible. Yet to that the reply is twofold. First that it actually does happen. Secondly that it is essentially no different from the processes of learning that we have constantly been engaged in, since childhood, in our own society, in all its diversity, acquiring and using our own natural languages. Even if we have no algorithm for this, there is much to be said for reflecting on where all of our own experience of learning begins, to make the most of what those reflections suggest, as we confront the more arcane problems of understanding the exotic. Of course the difficulties increase, as we find that we have to acquire further languages, ancient ones such as Greek and classical Chinese, as well as modern, though while that is obviously hard work, it is equally obviously not impossible, even if perfect fluency is always going to escape us: it does in one's own mother tongue, does it not? But if that means that the problems mount up, so too do the potential rewards—since one can learn more about the parochial quality of some of our most cherished assumptions.

Those are the opportunities. Yet we must be clear as to the barriers to full understanding that exist. Let me now return to the problems of the nature of the evidence available to us. There is the double difficulty of bias and of incompleteness. The texts that have come down to us have been selected—in some cases many times over. They have been handed down in complex but clearly defined processes of transmission and at each stage decisions have been taken by individuals, known or unknown, named or unnamed, to preserve or not to preserve.[9] We can only guess at the contents of what was not transmitted. Where we have references to no longer extant texts, we may suspect that the reporting is not always fair. Rather, we often know for certain—because the authors doing the reporting tell us—that it is downright hostile.

So the first bias is in the transmission. And the second is that the vast majority of our evidence takes the form of literary texts. They can be supplemented, for sure, with the inscriptional evidence (texts of a different kind) and by other archaeological data. But what we gain insight into is, overwhelmingly, the products of the privileged literary elite. It is indeed hard to resist being mesmerized by them—to remember just how exceptional most of the individuals in question were in their own culture. How far what they believed was shared by other people is, in most cases, an unanswerable question. The ideas, reactions, preoccupations, attitudes, of the disadvantaged majority of the members of those ancient societies are mostly beyond our reach or at least a matter very largely of pure guesswork. What did the slaves think of slavery, or young brides of child marriage? The gap between the ancient historian and the modern ethnographer is particularly large in such domains.

We have to bear these problems constantly in mind as we engage in studies of detailed texts and issues in subsequent chapters. The proposal of this introductory discussion is that with two principal exceptions, understanding ancient societies is not radically different from understanding our own contemporaries. The past is certainly not a country we can visit. We cannot go and see for ourselves how ancient institutions functioned, what attendance at the Athenian assembly felt

---

[9] What is preserved in the archaeological record is, of course, subject to other forms of bias, but to bias nonetheless.

like to the various participants, what the experience of working in the Chinese Astronomical Bureau amounted to for the officials concerned, or the nature of the hopes and fears of individuals who jockeyed for position in the entourages of Greek tyrants or Chinese emperors.

That is the first exception—not that presence in a society, visiting it, attending the Commons or the High Court or even a university or a research laboratory, is any guarantee of success in understanding what is going on. Then the second exception is that ancient languages are of course no longer spoken, though to describe them, conventionally, as 'dead' is rather to neglect the fact that their range of resonance is no less than that of contemporary English or Chinese. But otherwise, the problems of interpretation we encounter are in principle similar to those we always face, even if in practice we are so much more restricted in the evidence available to us where the ancient world is concerned.

I would claim, furthermore, that the strangeness of ancient ideas can be turned to advantage. We can study bewilderingly diverse worldviews. I shall explore, in Chapter 7, in what sense there is a common ontology underpinning them all. We are confronted too with apparent differences in modes of reasoning. I shall ask, in Chapter 4, whether or in what sense there is a common logic underlying all human rationality. What sense, if any, does it make to talk of alternatives in the matter of reasoning itself? Can we, in this context, redefine and redeploy the notion of divergent styles of enquiry? The ambition is to use history to help resolve the philosophical problems associated with the dichotomies of realism and relativism, objectivity and constructivism, truth as correspondence and truth as consistency. Throughout we shall be coming to terms with, and hopefully learning from, unfamiliar ideas. Some will undoubtedly defeat explanation. All the interpretations offered are in the nature of provisional conjectures to be tested in further enquiry. But the ancients can, and should, be used as a resource for new understanding of the world, of the capacity of humans to understand, and of ourselves. That is the strategic aim of this set of studies.

2

Science in Ancient Civilizations?

Is there science in the ancient world? The issue has been the subject of much heated debate in recent years.[1] One side to the question is definitional: what do we mean by science? Another is substantial: what were the actual investigations that were pursued? The next chapter will deal with the taxonomies of the learned disciplines in ancient Greece and China. Here I shall deal with the general definitional problem. All descriptive terms carry, potentially, an evaluative charge and this is particularly strong where 'science' is concerned, given the place it occupies in today's world. Besides, the question of the applicability of that term to ancient societies is a classic instance of the methodological problem discussed in Chapter 1, namely that of the conceptual framework within which we can discuss ancient ideas. In no ancient language was there a term that exactly corresponds to 'science', even though they generally have rich vocabularies to talk of knowledge, wisdom, and learning. So it might be thought that our term is in every case inappropriate to a study of their enquiries. As we shall see, however, the issue is more complicated than that.

Two further considerations might, nevertheless, be invoked to suggest that we should give a short answer to our original question by simply denying that what we find in the ancient world is indeed science. The first depends upon stipulating that science must deliver truth and then observing that very few of the results of ancient investigations would now be held to meet any such criterion. We have records of a considerable variety of cosmological and physical systems, atomist and continuum theories of various types in ancient Greece, various systems of correspondences and correlations, as well as other theories, in ancient China. But we would not now accept any of these as straightforwardly

---

[1] A special number of *Isis* was devoted to this issue in 1993, but it has been a topic of recurrent debate between constructivists and objectivists of different types. Cunningham and Wilson 1993 offer a characteristically trenchant statement of the problem.

true in their original forms. No modern scientist needs to start with them for the purposes of his or her own research. Even if they may be of historical interest, that is just what they are.

The second arises from the recognition of the enormous differences between the investigations carried on in any ancient civilization and those we are used to today. The institutions within which scientific work is now conducted, the research laboratories, are of a complexity and sophistication that are without parallel in earlier centuries: and that makes a fundamental difference.

But there are two main difficulties for the hard line that has it that there was nothing that could count as science before, say, the late nineteenth century. The first is that, on any story, modern science draws on and uses earlier ideas, even if not ones already adumbrated in remote antiquity. The emphasis on the discontinuities of work in recent times runs the risk of discounting some important continuities, in the studies that become astronomy, optics, harmonics, geology, anatomy, physiology, just to mention some of the more obvious subject areas as we label them.[2] Even when the most up-to-date science does not need to refer directly to earlier ideas, they belong nevertheless to the same field of enquiry in so far as they tackled the problems of understanding presented by the same general phenomena. Besides, quite when what we should recognize as 'modern' science begins has been the subject of controversies including those that focus on the issues of the so-called 'Great Divide'.[3] However, the recurrent temptation there has been to make short work of identifying the supposedly crucial contributions of different individuals or groups in different enquiries in the seventeenth, eighteenth, or even early nineteenth centuries. In any case, the idea of a sudden breakthrough by which truly modern science can be recognized is chimerical. The problem of demarcation then remains.

But the second more fundamental difficulty relates to defining science in terms of results, the delivery of truth. Science is developing today as fast as it has ever done and that means not just that new fields of research are opening up, but earlier views have to be modified. We do not know, we cannot even guess, which parts of what is currently

---

[2] The risks that go with the use of those labels will, however, be discussed in Ch. 3.

[3] The literature on the issue of the Great Divide is extensive, but among the most important contributions are those of Gellner 1973, 1985, and Goody 1977. I return briefly to the problem below.

accepted as the best science may need to be abandoned by the end of this century.

That means that science can hardly be defined in terms of the correctness of the results, for they are always open to revision. We should delineate science rather in terms of its goals or aims. These certainly include understanding, explaining, predicting (and many would nowadays add controlling, by exploiting the knowledge gained for human ends). Yet of course it is not just understanding in any domain, nor just any type of explaining or predicting, that will be characteristic of science. We can and do explain social phenomena. We can understand, for instance, why 25 December is a special day in the calendar for Christians and we can even begin to explain why that date was chosen as the day on which Christ was born (though the answer is quite complex). Certainly we can predict with some confidence that there will be certain celebrations, on that day, in Christian homes. But none of that, on any construal, counts as science.

The alternative to defining science in terms of results is to see it rather as a matter of the ambition to arrive at some understanding of the phenomena of the external, non-social world—of the natural world, we are tempted to say, in the European tradition, though we have good reason to be wary of how applicable the term 'nature' is in general.[4] Even so a complication that immediately arises relates precisely to that distinction I have just drawn between the social and the external, or non-social. In most ancient civilizations the microcosm of human society forms a seamless whole with the microcosm of the human body and the macrocosm of the heavens.[5] All three were believed to be part of a single dispensation, all three indeed exhibiting the same essential structure or exemplifying the same principles. So the gap that we recognize between the study of human social relations and the phenomena of the external world does not necessarily correspond to one marked by the investigators we are studying. Nevertheless, for the purposes of our analysis of the modes of understanding, explaining, and predicting that were cultivated, we can distinguish these, in part, according to the different subject matter under investigation. Among the phenomena that were the object of some sustained investigations were, for instance, the

---

[4] The difficulties of applying the term 'nature' outside the context of European traditions stemming from the Greeks are surveyed in Lloyd 1991: ch. 18, Lloyd and Sivin 2002: ch, 4, and cf. ch. 11 below.

[5] Cf. Lloyd and Sivin 2002: chs. 2 and 5 especially.

movements of the heavenly bodies, the phases of the moon and eclipses of the sun and moon, the functioning of the human body, the classes and behaviour of animals, the kinds and uses of plants—and many other examples can be given, not that we can or should attempt any definitive list of ancient enquiries, let alone one that reflects the hierarchies of different subject areas in modern science.

There might still be the objection that to concentrate just on aims and goals is to be altogether too generous and permissive. Surely, it might be urged, those goals, in relation to the subject matter in question, have to be pursued in the right manner. Surely science is unthinkable without the or a scientific method. But to that it may be countered that quite what the scientific method or methods consist in is itself intensely problematic. We cannot assume that there is a consensus on this issue in principle. Moreover in practice the methods adopted by today's scientists are in many cases very different from the neat schema of the hypothetico-deductive experimental method, as that is taught in schools. That schema plays an important pedagogic role, in introducing the pupil to certain model practices, but it is an idealization. It is one that certainly does not capture the complex processes by which a researcher decides his or her next moves in following up their hunches, getting round the difficulties, devising new protocols to crack the problems.

Yet—the objection would still continue—do we not need some criterion to mark off the sciences from what used to be called the pseudo-sciences, where that label indicates a reluctance to include them in whatever is to count as science? Do we not need to draw a line between astronomy, say, and astrology, between chemistry and alchemy, and the rest? The first issue here relates to the contrast between good and bad science, on the one hand, and that between science and what is not science at all, on the other. Here too we come back to the issue of permanently valid results. The whole story of the development of science down the centuries, including in the twentieth, is as much a history of failures as of successes. Yet those failures still rank as science (I should say) if they meet the basic requirement of aiming at understanding, explaining, and predicting 'natural' phenomena. In the debates between Big Bang and continuous creation, between catastrophism and uniformitarianism, between oxygen and dephlogisticated air, even between geocentricity and heliocentricity, there were eventual winners and losers. But those debates only became easy to adjudicate with the benefit of hindsight. For at the time, the arguments and evidence for and against the alternatives appeared, to many, well balanced.

But with regard to astrology in particular, at least, a further issue needs to be raised, precisely picking up the key question of the kind of understanding that was sought, and what it was related to. Predictions were (and still are) certainly attempted, on the basis of the study of the stars or of planetary positions, at birth or conception or at whatever time was considered relevant. But while the data used belong to the world of celestial phenomena, the conclusions (based on what were often claimed to be tried and tested correlations) concerned the fortunes of human beings or of whole countries. Astrology can thus be contrasted with astronomy not so much in terms of the phenomenal evidence used, as in those of its goal. It aims to understand and predict not the heavenly phenomena themselves, but what they foretell for humans.

In any ancient enquiry we have to assess a variety of factors, the data that were appealed to, how they were collected or assembled, how they were interpreted and the grounds offered for the system of interpretation, and the nature of the conclusions and what they related to. The answers to all those questions will contribute to how we should evaluate the enquiry itself. The verdict is quite often not a simple one. A further complication with some modes of what look like predictive judgements is that the function they serve is not so much to foretell the future, as to advise, or to allow a course of action to be decided impersonally in a way that does not implicate any individual in the success or failure of the enterprise.[6]

Thus far I have discussed the problems at a very abstract, general level. But now let me turn to a concrete case study to show how the recommendations I have proposed work out in practice. Perhaps the best examples to take to illustrate both the quality and the diversity of ancient investigations are those to do with the study of the heavens, where we can also follow up some of the points I have just made with regard to astrology.

The history of Mesopotamian study of the heavens, opened up preeminently by Neugebauer and the subject of exciting new studies by such scholars as David Brown and Francesca Rochberg, enables one to

---

[6] The different functions that may be served by talk that overtly offers predictions concerning the future are surveyed in Lloyd 2002: ch. 2, drawing especially on the contributions of Moore 1957, Park 1963, Bascom 1969, and other anthropologists.

trace certain key developments.[7] The omen text series, known as *Enūma Anu Enlil*, put together some time between 1500 and 1200, but incorporating even earlier work, contains, on the one hand, a mass of empirical data relating to heavenly phenomena of various types (for example the appearances and disappearances of the planet Venus in the famous Venus tablet referring to the reign of Ammiṣaduqa around 1600) and on the other, predictions concerning such matters as harvests, warfare, and political revolutions.

But then from some time around the mid-seventh century (as Brown has argued) there was a shift both in what was being predicted and in the confidence of at least some of the predictions. Phenomena such as the first and last visibilities of the planets, lunar and solar eclipses, came to be rigorously classified and indeed (within limits) predictable. A clear difference opened up between a style of prediction that focuses on the good or bad fortune that will result *if* a celestial phenomenon occurs, on the one hand, and, on the other, one that predicts such celestial phenomena themselves. The hunt was then on to establish further regularities in the phenomena, even though it was not just in the heavens that they were sought. Much less predictable phenomena, such as storms and lightning and hail, were also the subjects of attention. Success in some areas did not lead to a concentration purely on them. Moreover the discovery of certain regularities in celestial phenomena did not lead, in Mesopotamia, to those phenomena no longer being considered ominous. That may seem surprising, until we reflect that to many of our own contemporaries a Friday falling on the thirteenth of the month is considered bad luck, however unavoidable and predictable that occurrence may be.

Some of the same features recur also in the investigation of the heavens in ancient China. The Chinese distinguished between *lifa* and *tianwen*. The first is conventionally translated 'calendar studies', but it included other computational work as well, for example in connection with eclipses. The second is the study of the 'patterns in the heavens', essentially qualitative in character, but including both cosmography and the interpretations of celestial phenomena thought to be ominous. As in Mesopotamia, these studies were a matter of state importance, indeed of personal concern for the ruler (after the unification of China by the Qin in 221 BCE, the emperor). He was considered responsible not

---

[7] See especially Neugebauer and Sachs 1945, Neugebauer 1975, Rochberg 1988 and forthcoming, Brown 2000.

just for the welfare of the state, but for preserving harmony between the heavens and the earth. So it was evidently very important for the emperor to know, in the first instance, that the calendar was in good shape. If it got out of step with the seasons, there were first of all dire practical consequences, but what was more important, ideologically, was that any such discrepancy—like any other inauspicious celestial omen—might be interpreted as a sign that his mandate from heaven was under threat.

With such important matters at stake, the emperors, from Han times onwards at least, instituted an Astronomical Bureau, staffed with considerable numbers of officials whose work included not just calendar regulation but the scrutiny of the heavens for *any* sign that might be thought to carry a message, for the emperor, his ministers, state policy, or whatever. Here too, as in Mesopotamia, empirical phenomena were observed, recorded, classified, and interpreted with great care and determination. Chinese records of novae, supernovae, and sunspots are, for instance, the most complete we have down to the seventeenth century.[8] Nor was the work just descriptive, of course. Important advances were also made in determining more accurate cycles of lunar and solar eclipses, for instance, though, unlike in Mesopotamia, once lunar eclipses, in particular, were predictable, they attracted much less attention as omens. However, in general, as was also the case in Mesopotamia, the phenomena in the heavens were not studied just for their own sakes but for the messages they were assumed to convey.

Like the Chinese, the ancient Greeks too differentiated between different branches and goals of the study of the heavens, even though calendar studies did not take on so important a political role. While we hear of work on the determination of the relations between the solar year and the lunar month dating from the late fifth century BCE, that did not lead to the adoption of a uniform calendar throughout the Greek world. In the classical period, and indeed down to the imposition of a standard calendar by the Roman Julius Caesar in 62 BCE, each Greek city-state had its own luni-solar calendar, with different names for the months and with the decisions concerning such matters as the appearance of the new moon and the need for an intercalary month in the hands of different magistrates in different states.

---

[8] See for example Xi Zezong and Po Shujen 1966.

Moreover we must be careful with the interpretation of the terms *astronomia* and *astrologia* themselves, from which of course our own 'astronomy' and 'astrology' are derived, through Latin intermediaries. Those two ancient Greek terms were often used interchangeably, of any account of the stars. However in the opening chapter of his astrological treatise, the *Tetrabiblos*, Ptolemy clearly distinguishes between two types of predictive study. On the one hand there are predictions concerning the movements of the heavenly bodies themselves (in our terms, astronomy) and on the other the use of those phenomena as the basis for predicting events on earth (astrology). He claimed that astrology was based on tried and tested experience. But the contrast with astronomy was not simply that astrology is conjectural, while astronomy can lay claims to demonstration, but also in terms of what the predictions were about.

From the Hellenistic period onwards, the Greeks drew heavily on Babylonian data (which became more readily accessible after the conquests of Alexander in the 330s BCE). But they also undertook observational work on their own account. Yet much of their interest was devoted not to observing and recording, nor even to interpreting signs from heaven, but rather to the construction of geometrical models by which to demonstrate the movements of the sun, moon, and planets. A late report has it that Plato suggested to the astronomers the task of explaining the apparently irregular movements of the sun, moon, and planets by reducing them to combinations of regular, circular, motions.[9] We cannot confirm that Plato played the catalytic role that that suggests—and indeed it has sometimes been considered unlikely. But it is certainly the case that from the fourth century BCE onwards the history of Greek astronomical model-building is one of successive attempts at such a reduction.[10] First there were the concentric models of Eudoxus, Callippus, and Aristotle: then the eccentric/epicycle model devised by Apollonius, used by Hipparchus for his lunar theory especially, and elaborated by Ptolemy into a fully worked-out quantitative system for all the planets as well.

[9] At *In Cael*. 488. 19 ff. Simplicius cites Sosigenes as evidence for this recommendation of Plato's, and it is possible, though far from certain, that Sosigenes himself was drawing on the history of astronomy composed by Aristotle's associate Eudemus.

[10] The best brief introduction to the complex history of Greek astronomical models is Neugebauer 1957, even though with regard to Eudoxus in particular important recent studies have considerably modified the picture there presented: see Mendell 1998a, Yavetz 1998, Bowen 2001.

Yet as is clear from other remarks in Ptolemy, especially, the regularity that was thereby shown to exist in the heavens was considered as a sign not just of predictability and intelligibility, but also of order and of beauty. Plato had already suggested, in the *Timaeus*, that the study of the regularities in the heavens could help one regulate the movements of one's own soul—and so become a better person.[11] Ptolemy describes the ethical implications of the subject in which he was the leading expert of his day in even more high-flown terms: 'Of all studies, this one especially would prepare men to be perceptive of nobility both of action and of character: when the sameness, good order, proportion and freedom from arrogance of divine things are being contemplated, this study makes those who follow it lovers of this divine beauty and instils, and as it were makes natural, the same condition in their soul.'[12] Like so many who have engaged in the study of nature, and not just in the ancient world, he saw that activity as valuable for more than just intellectual reasons.

This brief account could and should be much elaborated, and many other examples of detailed ancient studies could be given. But it is enough to show first that sustained enquiries were undertaken into heavenly phenomena in all three ancient civilizations. In all three, secondly, it was believed that aspects of those enquiries were relevant also to human affairs, since the heavens sent messages that bore on human destinies, not determining their fate, but rather sent as warnings that the wise should take into account. At the same time, in all three, the closest attention was paid to what was happening in the heavens themselves—even if many of the exceptional events noticed by the ancient Chinese passed unremarked by the ancient Greeks, in part, no doubt, because of their expectation that the heavens should exhibit exceptionless order. The regularities in the movements of the heavenly bodies came to be more fully understood and to be predictable, eclipse cycles were determined, the calendar regularized, the patterns of planetary motions plotted, sometimes by using purely arithmetical methods, sometimes also by geometrical ones.

The primary goal was often that of gaining some insight into what was in store for the ruler, for the state, for private individuals. But it would be as mistaken to treat the study of the heavens, in all three

---

[11] Plato, *Timaeus* 47bc, 90d.   [12] Ptolemy, *Syntaxis*, I 1, Proem, 7. 17–24.

ancient civilizations, as *just* 'astrology' (in our terms), as it would be to ignore that it was partly that. Both the variety in the studies undertaken and their complexity are, then, important. So far as complexity goes, we see that investigations carried multiple implications. While they were stimulated in part by a desire to look into the future, the payoff was—sometimes—greater understanding of the phenomena. When, for instance, the Mesopotamians hoped to establish correlations between signs and outcomes, what they actually discovered included unforeseen regularities in the signs themselves.

But then as to variety, we have to pay attention to the different courses that the history of the study of the heavens took in the three societies we have considered. While certain aspects of those studies recur (an interest in the calendar, in predicting eclipses, and so on) the precise ways in which the problems were defined, the methods used to resolve them, the definitions of the subjects themselves, all exhibit certain important differences. The important lesson that this suggests is that there was no one way in which the study of the heavens *had* to develop, no one privileged route that the emergence of astronomy as we recognize it had to take.

Most of the generalizations on offer about the way in which science itself developed similarly fall foul of the actual complexities of the historical records of the various types of detailed studies undertaken at different periods and in different parts of the world. Attempts to account for the Great Divide that separates pre-scientific cultures from ourselves suffer from oversimplifying either the explanandum or the explanatory factors invoked to account for it. What exactly *was* that 'Great Divide'? Was there at some point a radical breakthrough, heralding the start of modern science? When exactly did that occur, and why? Did it occur at the same time, and for the same reasons, in different areas of science? The tempo and modes of development of astronomy differ appreciably from those of chemistry and again from those of the life sciences, and that may already be taken to suggest that different factors were at work in each case. Many would focus on the seventeenth century, the period of the so-called scientific revolution. Yet the changes that occurred then, whichever branch of enquiry we take—astronomy, physics, anatomy, physiology—are in every case more complex than the term 'revolution' easily allows for. While a political revolution is indeed marked by drastic change in the seat of power and authority, the prime movers in the new ideas of the seventeenth century all adopted and adapted a good deal from their predecessors, even when they cited them primarily to disagree.

Most of the methodological and conceptual points brought into play to resolve the problem—once it has been posed in the dichotomous terms of pre-science and science—turn out to serve at best as very partial explanatory factors. The appreciation of the power and the utility of experimentation is often held up as one crucial development. But while that can indeed be argued in some fields, experiment is irrelevant, indeed impossible, in most aspects of the study of the heavens. Again another favoured idea is that everything depended on the mathematization of physics, and that too has a limited force, though we should recognize that some attempts to apply numbers to things belong rather to the domain of the fanciful and did not advance understanding (cf. Lloyd 2002: ch. 3).

Meanwhile the bid to invoke external considerations, value systems, or religious factors such as the Protestant Ethic generally fail to account for the specificities of the unequal tempo of development across different enquiries. So far as the ancient world goes, Farrington suggested that the key move was secularization, or 'leaving the gods out'. While some Greek natural philosophers did, indeed, restrict explanations to purely naturalistic causes, our rapid survey of Greek, as well as Mesopotamian and Chinese, studies of the heavens shows that, in all three cases, detailed empirical investigations were compatible with the belief that the heavenly bodies are divine.

True, the studies for which we have evidence in the ancient world from Greece, China, Mesopotamia, Egypt, India, all clearly depended on a high degree of literacy—in a section of the population at least—and on an economic surplus reflecting both a robust technology and a moderately complex social organization. But even if we can offer some bland generalizations concerning necessary conditions, that does not take us far. To make any progress in understanding it is essential to follow that up by investigating their diversity in each case—to correlate, for instance, the uses of literacy and the types of social institutions with the actual enquiries undertaken in each ancient society. The problems themselves need in fact to be reformulated, not in terms of science versus pre- or proto-science, but rather in terms of the specific characteristics of the investigations that different combinations of external and internal factors appear to have favoured.

We shall have further occasions to insist on the actual complexities that confront the historian of ancient enquiries, complexities that stand in the way of attempts at grand generalizations, about how science started, how it developed, how indeed it had to develop. But let me end this discussion with a summary of my argument. Evidently there was no science as we know it today in ancient civilizations. Yet there were analogous ambitions—in relation to understanding, explaining, predicting a wide variety of phenomena. The task of the historian is to investigate the forms that those ambitions took, what stimulated or inhibited their growth, how the ancient enquirers themselves evaluated their work, how self-conscious they were about its status and goals and about the correct methods to be used. That series of questions takes us to the subject matter to be discussed in the next chapter, namely the varying taxonomies of the learned disciplines that we find in ancient Greece and China, and their differing maps of the interrelations of the various studies that they undertook.

3

Carving out Territories

Even a modest acquaintance with investigations into the physical world
in more than one pre-modern society is enough to reveal very great
diversity, in the concepts and theories used, in the methods deployed,
and most fundamentally in the way the subject matter itself was construed. It is true that much of that diversity tends to be masked in history of science that stays within the conventional categories with which
we are now familiar. Readers of such histories are informed about what
'astronomy' was done, or 'physics', or 'anatomy', or 'physiology', or
'zoology', or 'botany', or 'medicine', in China, Babylonia, Egypt, India,
Greece, or wherever. But in every case those terms are more problematic than is generally allowed for, when applied to the investigations
that we actually find.

The issues that this raises are continuous with those I have sketched
out already. Within what conceptual framework can we study ancient
investigations? What can we learn from the different ancient mappings
of the enquiries they undertook? If those enquiries developed differently in different ancient cultures, how is comparison still possible?
How can we begin to account for the divergences? Why—to ask a naive
question—do we not find more uniformity in the study of the heavens
and the human body (for instance), given, first, that the subjects investigated—the stars and our physique—are essentially the same, and
secondly, that human cognitive capacities the world over, and through
history, may be presumed not to differ substantially?

I shall begin with some remarks about the problems of using some of
our own familiar terms—derived from Greek or Latin—and then use
Chinese classifications of the enquiries they undertook to underline the
importance of their distinctiveness. However, the Greek data in turn
will serve to dispel any illusion that Chinese investigations were pecu-
liar or particularly disadvantaged in adopting their own, un-modern,
conceptual maps of the disciplines in question. I shall then turn to the

implications of those findings for the possibilities of comparison and of explanation.

We may start with three points about the Greek term *phusike* from which our own 'physics' is derived. First it covered the whole of nature, including animals and plants, for 'nature' is the primary sense of the term from which it stems, namely *phusis*. Secondly, the introduction of that term in the classical period had, in part, a polemical function—it was, as I have indicated,[1] more an invention than a discovery. The so-called natural philosophers, the *phusikoi* or *phusiologoi*, used it to define the subject over which they claimed particular expertise. Traditional wise men, prophets, and poets were sidelined as dabbling in what could forthwith be dismissed as the 'supernatural', the 'magical', the 'superstitious'. They assumed divine intervention in such phenomena as earthquakes or lightning or diseases, and that, according to the natural philosophers, was a plain category mistake, since they all belong to nature and have natural causes. Thirdly, to defend their view of *phusike*, treatises devoted to that subject, such as Aristotle's, deal very largely with what we should call philosophical problems, to do with causation, infinity, space and time, and so on. Greek *phusike* bears almost no resemblance to the work currently done in physics laboratories.

The same applies to the term from which we get 'mathematics'. Greek *mathematike* derives from a verb, *manthanein*, that covers learning in general. Although what we can call the mathematical studies of Euclid and Archimedes—as well as the rather different work of Hero or Diophantus—certainly fall within Greek *mathematike*, so too do other fields of investigation. The term was regularly applied both to what we call astronomy and to astrology, for instance, where we have already noted that the corresponding Greek and Latin terms for those specific studies can be used interchangeably, even though they were also sometimes used to mark the distinction between predictions of the heavenly movements, and predictions on their basis of events on earth. But the astrologer was a *mathematikos* just as much as the astronomer (and it was usually the same individuals who pursued both studies).

The Chinese definitions of the subjects they were concerned with, and of their interrelations, differ both from the modern, and from the ancient Greek, views. Take the example of the study of *di li* ('earth

---

[1] Cf. above Ch. 2 n. 4 with the reference to Lloyd 1991: 18.

patterns' or, better, 'terrestrial organization').[2] Many modern scholars have looked for, and failed to find, a science of geography in pre-modern China, where what that summons up are studies devoted to exact topographical descriptions, if not also to the mathematical solution of the cartographic problems of planar projection of a spherical world. But largely because of their expectations of what the subject should comprise, they have overlooked the extensive materials in the traditions of writing represented by the treatises on *di li* and on *zhou jun* ('provinces and commanderies') in the dynastic histories. Those categories overlap, though the emphasis is sometimes on terrestrial organization, sometimes on administrative units, as the contrasting titles suggest. The variation between these two, it has been suggested, may reflect the political situation at the time of composition. The term *di li* tends to be used at times of comparative unity, while in periods of disintegration *zhou jun* is more usual.

Whether or not that argument is accepted, it is abundantly clear first that the treatises contain much material of crucial political significance (to do with population, wealth and taxation, communications), secondly that they reflect cosmological thinking (notably in the matter of microcosm–macrocosm correspondences and the parallelisms between terrestrial and celestial mappings), and thirdly, that they also contain detailed descriptions of the characteristics of different regions and of the customs of the inhabitants. Evidently such treatises cannot be dismissed as just 'ideology', even though they contain distinct ideological elements. Nor can they be identified as just 'geography', even allowing that that term has not just a narrow, but also a very broad, acceptance. But the moral to be drawn from the discrepancy between Chinese and Western categories—here as so often elsewhere—is not the negative one, of the alleged lack of pre-modern Chinese 'geography', but the positive ones, of their recognition of the importance of *di li* and *zhou jun* and of our need to take them on their own terms to investigate what each comprises.

[2] I draw here on the studies of Vera Dorofeeva-Lichtmann, especially her 2001. In her earlier study, Dorofeeva-Lichtmann 1995, she analysed the components of the *Shanhaijing*, the Classic of Mountains and Seas, which itemizes no fewer than twenty-six itineraries across China and neighbouring regions. This too poses problems of categorization. On the one hand, the text sets out detailed information concerning the various provinces and zones of China and gives the impression of accuracy with its references to specific distances ('120 *li*, ["leagues"], to the south-west', or '200 *li* to the north'). On the other, it is concerned to identify the deities that inhabit the various regions and the sacrifices that should be made to them.

Similar points apply also to some of the generic terms used in Chinese classifications of groups of related subjects.[3] Take, for instance, the category of *shu shu* ('calculations and methods'), where we can detect the influence of the scholar-bibliographers Liu Xiang and Liu Xin in the centuries either side of the millennium. The six sub-classes of *shu shu* comprise: (1) *tianwen* (the patterns in the heavens, including star catalogues and divination by the stars and by meteorological phenomena); (2) *lipu* (including not just calendrical studies, but also work in harmonics, on genealogies, the study of the gnomon, and treatises on calculation); (3) *wuxing* (five-phase theory, that is the study of the interactions of wood, fire, earth, metal, water, and what is associated with them, though those five are thought of not so much as substances as processes and as modifications of *qi*[i]: moreover this area of study also covers calendrical astrology and sexagesimal hemerology, the sixty-day cycle determined by the sequences of combinations of Heavenly Stems and Earthly Branches); (4) *shigui* (milfoil and turtle shell divination); (5) *zazhan* ('miscellaneous prognostic procedures', including dream divinations, auguries, and rituals), and finally (6) *xingfa* (the study of significant shapes, including both those of geographical location and physiognomy).

The evident mismatch between these categories and those we might be tempted to apply is striking. To start with, *shu shu* spans a number of different subject areas that fall either side of the division that we might tend to stress, between 'mathematics' and 'physics'. Again divination and prediction figure in various sub-classes, and not all their forms are included in the category of *shu shu*. The *Yijing* or Book of Changes and the works dealing with its interpretation do not figure under *shu shu*, but in another main category of works devoted to the classics. Again, military prognostication comes under a third category, namely that of writings on *Yin* and *Yang*[i]. Nor is it the case that everything encompassed by the rubric *shu shu* incorporates some predictive element, for star catalogues and treatises on harmonics do not necessarily do so.

Furthermore it is important to note that *wuxing*, five-phase theory, appears as a sub-class on its own. From a comparative perspective, it is striking that five-phase ideas take over this particular area of study, rather, that is, than being just one option, among several, for the

---

[3] For recent discussions of the categories to be found in the *Han Shu* 30, compare Harper 1999: 821–5 with Kalinowski forthcoming.

discussion of the problems in question. While there was plenty of variation as between different detailed elaborations of five-phase correspondences, they were not in competition with other theories in the way in which, in ancient Greece, atomist theories rivalled continuum ones. *Wuxing* was not just one of several rival, radically divergent, doctrines: rather it provided a common language within which variations could be proposed and applied.

We should not be deceived by the relative permanence of Chinese nomenclature into exaggerating the continuities in the underlying concepts and studies themselves. As Kalinowski (forthcoming) again has illustrated, the Han classification itself underwent substantial modification, as for example first in the twelfth century and then again more notably in the eighteenth. At that point, reflecting one of the marked shifts in perspective that occurred, *shu shu* came to be contrasted with *tianwen suanfa*, where the latter covers astronomy and mathematics, while the former is devoted just to divination.

Given that the original Han classification of *shu shu* served bibliographical purposes (not that Liu Xiang and Liu Xin should be treated as *mere* bibliographers), that may be a source of some distortion. The inclusion of the sub-class *zazhan*, miscellaneous procedures, may reflect an ambition to be comprehensive. Bibliographers, after all, have to put books somewhere. But we can confirm, in several cases, that it was not just the names of the disciplines, and their place in some general taxonomic scheme, that run counter to Western expectations, but also their contents and methods.

Mathematics provides a particularly striking example, since we might suppose that it would be very largely uniform and invariant across cultures. Yet we can identify substantial differences between China and other traditions not just in some of the problems investigated, but also in methods and basic aims, where the contrast with ancient Greece is especially remarkable. The *Nine Chapters on Mathematical Procedures* (*Jiuzhang suanshu*) and its commentaries, especially that of Liu Hui in the third century CE, provide valuable evidence on the point. The problems relate to the determination of areas and volumes, the solutions to equations with several unknowns, and so on, and several belong to types that might well be encountered by administrators in the day-to-day conduct of their business. Thus far we may compare other mathematical traditions where there is a similar focus, at least on the surface, on practical problems: ancient Egyptian and Babylonian arithmetic, for instance, or the discussion of problems of mensuration in Hero of Alexandria (see Høyrup 2002).

Yet the strategic goals of the *Nine Chapters* are certainly not adequately captured by treating it as a practical manual. We shall be coming back, in Chapter 9, to analyse how concrete examples are used to illuminate general problems, one of the distinctive features of the style of mathematical reasoning it displays. But for now let me focus on the evidence in the commentator Liu Hui concerning how he saw its aims. As Karine Chemla has pointed out in a series of studies (Chemla 1988, 1990*a*, 1990*b*, 1992, 1994, 1997), Liu Hui often draws attention to the point that the procedures used in different contexts are the same. He uses such terms as qi^{II}, 'homogenize', $tong^{I}$, 'equalize', and a further $tong^{II}$, 'make to communicate', not just to name elements within specific procedures, but also to remark on similarities *between* them. His concern is to make clear what he calls the *gangji*, the guiding principles, that run through all the procedures used (Qian Baocong 1963: 96. 4).[4]

True, he thereby makes explicit what is usually left implicit in the original text on which he is commenting. But his remarks yield an important insight. Where, in the ancient Greek tradition exemplified by Euclid, the goal was to deduce the whole of mathematics from a single set of indemonstrable but self-evident axioms, such an ambition was quite foreign to Chinese mathematics right down to modern times, that is until after the translations of Euclid undertaken by the Jesuits and their followers. In China, the goal was not axiomatic-deductive demonstration, but to grasp the general principles and persistent patterns that run through and link the whole of mathematics. That does not mean there was no Chinese interest in proof. On the contrary, the validation of algorithms is a recurrent concern, to show that they are correct. By their application, as Liu Hui puts it, the values cannot have changed—and so truth is preserved.

The first lesson to be drawn is that proof-theoretical interests take different forms in different mathematical traditions, and the second that so too do the strategic concerns of 'mathematics' as a whole. The Chinese experience shows that sophisticated mathematics does not

---

[4] The two terms $tong^{I}$, to equalize, and $tong^{II}$, to make to communicate, are both used in different contexts in the *Nine Chapters* themselves, e.g. I 18, 99. 4 and 7, VII 14, 206. 11–12, although these and the third key term, qi^{II}, 'homogenize', are not there explained and defined as they are by Liu Hui at I 9, 96. 1 ff. His term *gangji* is used outside mathematics of the guiding principles in, for example, moral or political matters. See, for instance, *Xunzi* 6: 9–10, Knoblock 1988–94: i. 224, and cf. *Shiji* 130: 3290. 3.

presuppose an interest in axiomatization, either in its ancient Greek, or its modern, sense. The Greek ambition, to provide incontrovertible deductive demonstrations of the whole of mathematics, depended crucially on the axioms—whose status was, however, on occasion, anything but self-evident, as the famous dispute on the parallel postulate dramatically illustrates.[5] But the Chinese, free from any such ambition, pursued a quite different, but equally strategic, goal, that of correlating the diverse procedures used in different areas of mathematics in order to reveal their unity.

Similar points can be made more briefly with regard to some of the differences between different traditions of the study of health and disease ('medicine') and of what things are made and how they change ('physics'). In the former case the differences are not just a matter of different styles of therapy practised in different cultures. Acupuncture and moxibustion happen to be distinctive of traditional Chinese medicine. The relative importance of dietetics, cautery, venesection, the use of drugs, and so on varies both as between different pre-modern cultures, and indeed as between different traditions within one and the same culture. But these are of minor importance compared with differences in the conception of *well-being*, which it is the goal of any therapeutic procedure to restore. However, notions of well-being reflect, and in turn vary with, conceptions of the human body, where again the contrast between ancient Greek and Chinese ideas reveals the distinctiveness of each. Thus where the Greeks generally focused on the study of structures and organisms, in China the emphasis was more often on processes, on interaction, on resonances. *Gan*, for instance, picks out not, or not just, the organ—the liver—but the functions associated with it and the part they should play in the balanced economy or, as it was often put in Han times, the bureaucracy of the body.

Analogously in general accounts of change, the fallacy of treating the notion of *wuxing* as if that were an attempt at an element theory in the Western sense is now generally recognized. That mistake stems from the Jesuit project of interpreting indigenous Chinese ideas as merely

---

[5] Euclid included the parallel postulate among his starting assumptions, though he no doubt considered it to be no mere hypothesis, but true of the world. However, some later Greek commentators, including both Ptolemy and Proclus, protested that it should not be a postulate, but a theorem proved within the system. All ancient attempts at proof were flawed, though, since they assumed the point at issue: they were circular. As is well known, it was an attack on its status that led, eventually, to the discovery of non-Euclidean geometries, in the work of Lobachewsky, Riemann, and others.

inferior solutions to the problems resolved in their own physical theories, at the time still based on the four Aristotelian simple bodies. But while, on the Aristotelian picture, the elements are the irreducible, and in themselves unchanging, components of which everything else is made, the five phases undergo constant change. The emphasis is, again, on the resonances between interdependent phases of ongoing processes. The obvious moral of that story, too, is that the understanding of physical events and changes in China—Chinese physics if some care to call it that—was fundamentally different from that favoured for many centuries (but no longer today) in the West.

My argument in this chapter thus far has been that there are important basic differences in the definitions of individual disciplines and in the understanding of the relations between them, as between different cultures and especially as between ancient China and Greece. But that raises the problem of whether or in what sense comparison is still possible. Do the data I have thus far rehearsed not undermine the very idea of comparative history of scientific investigations, the question I raised and answered in a qualifiedly affirmative way in the last chapter?

I have already emphasized two points that separate ancient studies from modern ones. First neither Greek nor Chinese has a term that exactly corresponds to science, and in neither, to be sure, do we find anything like modern science as that is practised in sophisticated laboratories today. However, if we return to the two main positive points we adduced before, they remain valid, even if their interpretation can now be nuanced. These points were first the shared ambitions, to understand, explain, and predict, and secondly the focus of those ambitions on phenomena that are, at least in some sense, the same. Let me now elaborate both those points, before turning to further difficulties they may appear to generate, in relation to how we can begin to explain the apparent diversities that we actually find in the manner in which ancient ambitions were realized.

I have remarked on the different modes that understanding can take. Some forms require the explananda to be brought under a general rule, which the particulars can be seen as instantiating. But sometimes understanding is sought, and found, by observing or postulating similarities or parallelisms or correspondences, where the reasoning may not invoke a generalization from which both items can be deduced, but depend directly on analogies. Explanation and prediction, in turn, may take different forms, and I am not now talking about their subject matter, what they are about—for that evidently ranges over the whole of human experience—but of what is expected of an explanation or the basis on which a prediction can be made. Thus change can be accounted for in terms of cycles of resonating processes or in terms of the effects of efficient causes on otherwise static substances. Similarly predictions of the movements of the heavenly bodies can be based on arithmetical models incorporating observed regularities, or be deduced from geometrical ones.

One point of comparison is, then, provided by those shared ambitions. But the phenomena that were the goal of understanding and explanation were also, I said, in a sense, the same. Among the topics that we find investigated in several ancient cultures are, as I noted, calendrical issues, the lengths of the solar year and the lunar month, the movements of the planets, eclipses, then again the human body and the way it functions, health and disease, animals and their behaviour and modes of reproduction, the kinds and powers of plants and minerals, the modes of interaction and mixture of things of different kinds, sometimes also harmonies and what distinguishes them from discordant sounds.

Of course none of those descriptive terms that I have just used can be construed as entirely neutral. To talk of eclipses, for instance, as a topic for study already presupposes an understanding of the difference between different possible reasons for the darkening of the sun or moon. The nature of the interest in the phenomena in question is far from uniform across cultures. The primary, and ulterior, motivations of the investigators vary, as did their own ideas (and those of their audiences) about what constitutes an adequate account. Sometimes the phenomena are conceived as natural, sometimes as divine, sometimes as both at once. Most enquiries have more or less prominent moral, even political, overtones and implications: the acquisition of knowledge is frequently pursued with its possible eventual practical applications in mind. The ambition to understand, and the phenomena that were there to be understood, provide points of contact that allow comparison to proceed, even while what comparison reveals is, as I have emphasized, at points highly diverse.

But if the comparison of ancient investigations is possible, and yet we find considerable differences in the forms those investigations took, the next question is how we can begin to account for those differences. Why, I asked simplistically, if the ambitions are similar, and what was there to explain was in a sense common, do we find such diversity in different ancient cultures in the studies they cultivated and in the ways they cultivated them? We enter speculative territory here, and I shall limit myself to some comments on the *types* of consideration that do or do not seem helpful. As we noted before, many of the economic, technological, and cultural factors that might be or have been invoked provide at best necessary, not sufficient conditions for the development of sustained investigations. No doubt an economic surplus is necessary to allow specialists to carry on such work; and substantial collections of astronomical data are inconceivable without highly trained scribes to record them. Yet none of that helps to account for the *specificity* of the enquiries undertaken in different ancient civilizations.

To make any progress here we have to follow up the background to the values that generated the ambition to understand in the first place. That means examining the social and political contexts within which the investigators worked. Our agenda must include such questions as where the enquirers came from, the echelons of society they represented, the types of career that were open to them: what kinds of association did they form or what institutions did they belong to? Who were their audiences, whether auditors or readers, and what were the conventions governing the typical occasions of communication or the exchange of ideas?[6]

One striking difference that immediately distinguishes ancient China from Greece relates to the degree of involvement of the state in the enquiries in question. That stretched far beyond the context of technology, where economic and other practical interests were at stake. I noted that imperial interest in such fields as *tianwen* and *lifa* led to the setting up of impressively long-lasting Bureaux designated for their study. The emperors also helped to stimulate research and to encourage the systematization of knowledge in other fields such as the *bencao* traditions—covering pharmacopoeia and the study of plants more generally.[7] Even when the state did not set the agenda (as it often did) the career opportunities and structures of advancement open to members of the literate elite ensured that much of their output was represented as serving, directly or indirectly, the interests of the state. The preferred audience they addressed, whether or not formally in the form of a memorial to the throne, was often the ruler or his ministers, and this

---

[6] Lloyd and Sivin 2002 go into these questions in greater detail than can be attempted here.

[7] See Métailié 2001*a*, 2001*b*.

had certain repercussions, not just, obviously, on the style of presentation of results, but also on the content of what was presented.

The contrast with Greece is very striking. First the possibilities for patronage were far more restricted: in the classical period there were no state institutions offering employment for those engaged in research, and even in Hellenistic times, where the Alexandrian Museum was something of an exception, the extent of the support it provided was very limited. In any case it declined in importance after the first three Ptolemies whose reigns spanned a mere 100 years or so—compared with the 2000-year existence of the Chinese Astronomical Bureau. Greek doctors earned a living by treating the sick, and Greek astrologers by casting horoscopes: but in general Greek intellectuals made their way by teaching. Teaching was, to be sure, an important activity of Chinese intellectuals too, but in Greece it was the prime key both to reputation and to livelihood. Besides, Chinese pupils often had the expectation of eventually entering the imperial civil service, and in the state-run academies that was what they were trained for, even though that training consisted primarily in a grounding in the classics.

In Greece the way you made a name for yourself generally involved risks of a rather different kind from those facing hopefuls who wished to persuade Chinese emperors of their intelligence and usefulness. The format for the presentation of Greek ideas was often the public lecture or debate, which might be followed by question and answer sessions. These were held on such occasions as the Olympic or other pan-Hellenic games, but crowds would gather whenever a teacher proposed a performance. We know too that the debates in question were sometimes adjudicated by the audience who decided who had won the argument, even when the subject matter was quite technical—as in medicine or cosmology. The emphasis in such a situation was on fluency and effect. With that in mind, there was a considerable development of interest in, and the teaching of, rhetoric—the art of persuasion. That was needed not just in intellectual contexts, but also frequently in practical ones, to win arguments in the law courts and political assemblies. Neither of those institutions had any parallel in China:[8] but both formed a fundamental part of the experience of Greek citizens in the classical period, even if the importance of political debate declined when

[8] In Greek law courts, verdicts and sentences were in the hands of 'dicasts'—ordinary citizens chosen by lot—who acted both as judge and as jury. Chinese interests in persuasion, as we shall see in Ch. 4, took a rather different form from those of Greek rhetoric.

the city-states lost much of their autonomy first in the Hellenistic period and then under the Romans.

The ways in which that Greek experience affected the types of investigation we considered before are complex. At first sight it might seem as if Greek axiomatic-deductive demonstration, in mathematics, was worlds away from the rhetoric of the law courts. So indeed it was. Yet it was precisely the sense of the inadequacy of *mere persuasiveness* that acted as one stimulus to the development of a model of reasoning that would do far better, that would not just convince the audience at the time, but that would yield the truth, indeed guarantee it. Demonstration securing incontrovertibility was, to be sure, the ultimate weapon in persuasion, but it presented itself as the antonym of the merely persuasive. First Plato and then Aristotle insisted on the contrast, and both constantly refer to the rhetoric of the law courts and the political assemblies as a *negative* model, of a style of reasoning that would not do for the highest mode of philosophizing.

Euclid himself does not give any indication of why he adopted the axiomatic-deductive mode of mathematical reasoning we find in the *Elements*, and the extent to which he was influenced by earlier mathematics on the one hand, and by the philosophies of Plato and Aristotle on the other, is the subject of ongoing and probably insoluble controversy. What is clear, however, is first that that mode of reasoning shared the goal of incontrovertibility that Aristotle identified as the ultimate aim for philosophy: and secondly that once the *Elements* had shown the way, proof in what came to be called 'the geometrical manner' was enormously influential as an ideal in many other quite unrelated domains. They included both theology (as in Proclus' *Elements of Theology*) and medicine (where Galen sought to cultivate geometrical-style proof even in anatomy and physiology). We can be sure, also, that it was, in Ptolemy's view, the incontrovertibility secured by arithmetic and geometry that provided the grounds for his claim for the superiority of mathematical astronomy over the study of nature—for he says as much in the first book of the *Syntaxis*.[9]

Yet if factors such as these provide a clue as to why what we may provisionally call certain different styles of enquiry were developed in certain cultures, it is as well to end with three reservations. First there were

---

[9] Ptolemy, *Syntaxis* I 1, Proem 6. 17–21: 'Only mathematics, if one attacks it critically, provides for those who practise it sure and unswerving knowledge, since the demonstration comes about through incontrovertible means, by arithmetic and geometry.'

plenty of exceptional individuals in both Greece and China whose careers did not follow the standard patterns and who adopted their own idiosyncratic investigations. They always ran the risk of being marginalized and ignored—by their contemporaries and by future generations. The rediscovery, and in a sense rehabilitation, of the first-century CE sceptical philosopher Wang Chong in modern times illustrates both the scope for individualism, in China, and the dangers that went with it. Greek individualists often exploited that characteristic to make a splash (the Presocratic philosopher Heraclitus is one example, and Empedocles another). But in Greece too, many theorists received less than their due recognition and suffered as a consequence. Among the many whose writings were not transmitted, but only commented on and criticized by others, were the original fifth-century atomists Leucippus and Democritus.

We must distinguish, secondly, between the judgements the ancients themselves made, of different investigators and of different investigations, and those we implicitly or explicitly make in our comparative analyses of ancient work. Evaluation, I said, is inevitable, while anachronism and teleology, I added, must be avoided. The temptation to offer global generalizations about the way science *had* to develop should be resisted and in any case any such programme comes unstuck in the face of the considerable actual variety we find in the successes and failures in different subject areas, in different times and places, in different civilizations. Neither Greek nor Chinese socio-political institutions and values proved an unmixed blessing, and neither Chinese nor Greek ambitions delivered unqualifiedly successful results.

Thirdly, in the matter of the direction of explanation, as between social institutions and intellectual end-products, the influences were not all one way, from the former to the latter, for they also evidently worked in the reverse direction. Greek political debate on the question of the naturalness of slavery had, to be sure, no practical impact whatsoever. But Greek political theory did have a practical outcome, for instance on such occasions as the founding of new colonies. We know that a number of philosophers and sophists were consulted, for example, when the city of Thurii was established in the fifth century BCE. Similarly, and more prominently, in China, while the major cosmological syntheses of the late Warring States and Han, the *Lüshi chunqiu, Huainanzi*, the memorials of Dong Zhongshu, and the earlier parts of the *Chunqiu fanlu* may all be seen as reflecting already existing values and ideologies, all contributed substantially, in their different ways, to the development and consolidation of the ideal of the unified state under a ruler who, as mediator between heaven and earth, should, in principle, be the guarantor of the welfare of 'all under heaven'.

I began this chapter by insisting on the different routes that the development of sustained enquiries into different natural phenomena took in different ancient civilizations, and the different intellectual maps into which those enquiries were fitted. Comparison, I argued, is still possible, given the shared general ambition to understand, and the focus on some of the same explananda if we define these in general terms. While the perception and understanding of eclipses may vary, we can be confident enough that those phenomena constituted part of the subject matter to which attention was devoted.

At the same time the diversity of the developments that took place reminds us, in the first instance, that there was nothing inevitable about the way in which they *should* occur, no one privileged route leading to modern science. There was more to the stimulus to enquiry than *just* a general desire to understand. The investigators occupied their different niches in the societies to which they belonged: they had their personal ambitions and preoccupations; they adopted, or reflected critically upon, the values of their society, and made their conscious or unconscious decisions on the difficult questions of how to hold and persuade their audiences. These are among the factors that may be seen as influencing the distinctive character of different ancient enquiries.

While the institutions of science have nowadays been transformed, in two respects we may say that nothing much has changed. Scientists still have decisions to take about persuading their peers, and are still under pressure not to step too far out of line, even while the premium on originality is so high. Many a scientific reputation has had to be revised retrospectively to redress the imbalances of the reception by contemporaries. Moreover in the matter of endorsing or of criticizing the values of the society to which they belong, they carry an even greater responsibility than their ancient predecessors as science itself opens up undreamt of possibilities for manipulating change. Since the atomic bomb, especially, we have become all too painfully aware of the dangers of the argument that the scientists' job is just to pursue fundamental research and that has nothing to do with how the results are used. On the contrary, scientists' responsibilities have to include the ethical evaluation of the research programme itself. With much work on the frontiers of knowledge, whether it be genetically modified foods or the cloning of embryos, there is an inevitable tension in that the very same individuals and groups who are intent on forging ahead are among the people on whom policy-makers must rely for advice about the very real risks of doing so. I shall be returning to those issues in Chapter 12.

4

A Common Logic?

The explicit analysis of argument forms has a history that goes back to Aristotle. He was the first to explore the validity and invalidity of chains of propositions in abstraction from the question of the truth or falsity of individual premisses. He insisted, further, that the laws of non-contradiction and of excluded middle are axioms presupposed by all intelligible communication. If someone is inclined to deny the law of non-contradiction, that principle cannot be demonstrated (that is what it is to be an axiom—to be an indemonstrable self-evident truth), but he or she can be refuted *ad hominem*. If one indicates something, anything, that presupposes the very principle that the doubter wishes to challenge.

Aristotelian syllogistic focuses on relations of class inclusion and class exclusion between terms. It was the Stoics who proposed a new and more general analysis in terms of propositions as such, and since then the study of formal logic has undergone several major shifts, including, in recent years, the proposal of alternative logics, intuitionist logics (e.g. Dummett 2000, Prawitz 1980), relevance logics (Read 1988, 1994), so-called fuzzy logics (Zadeh 1987, Haack 1996) and other systems that deny bivalence or the principle of non-contradiction or both (e.g. Priest and Routley 1989, Putnam 1975*a*: ch. 9, 1983: ch. 15). I shall have more to say about that later.

The first question that this chapter addresses is how far, or in what sense, the findings of formal logic can claim universal validity. The first, naive, response would have it that whatever logical system we adopt, it *has* to be universally applicable. On that view, one of the criteria by which such a system has to be judged is, precisely, whether it can be applied to all human communication. The denial of the universal applicability of logical rules implies a radical incommensurability between different conceptual frameworks. That has indeed been some people's reaction to the apparent diversity in systems of belief attested in different cultures, ancient and modern, across the world. But it is an exaggerated reaction. As I pointed out in Chapter 1, it faces first an empirical and then a logical objection.

Empirically, there is no human society with which communication has proved to be totally impossible, however hard mutual understanding—always imperfect, to be sure—may sometimes be to attain. Logically, if indeed we are confronted with a conceptual scheme that is incomprehensible in our terms, then we cannot, by definition, make any sense of it. It was one of the strangenesses of Lévy-Bruhl's notion of a primitive mentality that he claimed that it depended on a different logic of participation that implied the breach or suspension of the law of non-contradiction. Yet how, in that case, he thought communication was possible is a mystery.

But if radical incommensurability precludes any further enquiry— and yet other societies *invite* further investigation—that does not answer the question of the universal applicability of logic. That question is badly in need of clarification, and this can be undertaken in two parts, one of them quite straightforward, but the second appreciably more complex, and that takes us to the heart of the problem.

In one sense the answer to the question of whether there are alternative logics must be a simple yes. As already pointed out, competing analyses have been and continue to be offered of the formal rules that govern truth conditions, consistency, and strict validity. It is not that I have any brief for those alternative systems, those that deny the principle of bivalence or the principle of contradiction, or that allow for fuzziness. If anything, it would seem to me that the standard view, that preserves both those principles, has had the better of the arguments so far. Yet even if the technical arguments were to be resolved in its favour (and since formal logicians are pretty tenacious arguers, I have some doubts that a *resolution* is exactly likely), that would still only be a resolution at the level of formal logic.

But then the far more difficult problems relate not to the issues within formal logic themselves, but to its applicability to actual, informal, reasoning. Or, if it fails to be applicable, then what rules should be held to give the best account of such reasoning? In practice, as we are all aware in our own experience of reasoning, and as any historical survey amply testifies, *apparent* breaches of formal rules, including of the principle of non-contradiction itself, occur quite frequently. But then they are far more likely to be (as I pointed out in Chapter 1) challenges to interpretation. Self-contradiction is a concept that applies in the first instance to well-formed formulae, wffs for short. But we do not often communicate in well-formed formulae, except when we are doing logic for instance. We do not even very often communicate by means of complete propositions. Much is left implicit in the statements we make, including in the links between them. Besides, the meaning we convey is not just a matter of what we say, but of how we say it, let alone one also of our body language.

Those remarks apply particularly to ordinary conversation. But they are relevant also to philosophy and science. Any departure from strict univocity undermines the validity of deduction. Yet most philosophy and science employ terms with very considerable semantic stretch. Not only do they not have, and are not given, strict definitions: but the richness of the philosophy and science often makes the most of that considerable stretch. To insist on clear definitions may be an appropriate challenge in limited contexts: but all metaphysics and most creative science depend on the exploitation of more than just the literal applications of the key terms.[1]

What we need for the purposes of an analysis of the reasoning we actually normally use is not so much a formal logic, as an informal logic—where pragmatics has, of course, already made considerable progress (Levinson 1983 gives a clear overview). The work of Grice and his successors, such as Sperber and Wilson 1986, has begun to set out some of the ground rules governing communication. The suggestion that some principle of cooperation needs to be implemented for successful communication to take place looks to be eminently well founded, though the precise relationship between that and the principle of relevance made central by Sperber and Wilson is controversial.

That does not, emphatically, mean that *all* communication is successful, within members of the same society, or even of the same group within it, let alone between members of different societies. But we can hope to gain a better idea of the variety of modes of communicative exchange that make a difference to *what* is being communicated and *how*.

An example relating to vagueness will help to illustrate the point.

---

[1] I have explored in other studies the usefulness of the notion of semantic stretch, and in particular the advantages it offers over an analysis that insists on the dichotomy between the literal and the metaphorical uses of terms. On the semantic stretch interpretation, *all* terms exhibit more or less stretch: see Lloyd 2002: ch. 5, drawing on Porzig 1934.

Vagueness is, of course, a vice in any candidate for the status of a well-formed formula on the traditional view. Vagueness is a sign of *failure* in that context (see e.g. Putnam 1983: ch. 15). But vagueness can reflect aspects of the relationship between the persons between whom the communication takes place: it can be a sign of politeness. Again, in an explanation it may be neither a flaw in propositional form, nor yet a matter of politeness, but rather a sign of hesitancy, concerning the scope or the limitations of the explanation put forward.

Similar points can be made also with regard to consistency. A couple of examples will show how both Greek and Chinese authors were aware of this. In a famous attack on the traditional belief that the sacred disease is caused by the gods, the writer of the Hippocratic treatise *On the Sacred Disease* (ch. 1) criticizes those who claimed to be able to cure it by charms and purifications on the grounds of inconsistency. They claim particular piety, and yet their practices take away the power of the godhead and imply that *humans* can constrain the gods. Of course the purifiers themselves, if they had had a chance to reply (which they do not, in our text), could have said that their procedures merely enable the gods to restore the health of their patients. In this, and no doubt a number of other ways, they could have defended their position against any charge of inconsistency, though some of those defences might have struck their opponents as purely ad hoc.

Then in classical Chinese thought, too, the question of inconsistency was discussed, sometimes, in terms of the story of the manufacturer of lances and shields who advertised the former as being able to penetrate *anything*, the latter as being able to withstand penetration *by* anything.[2] What would happen, someone asked, if one of his lances struck one of his shields? This example became one of the standard ways in which the notion of inconsistency was recognized and labelled. Again, if one speculates about the original claim, while taking 'anything' in a strict sense in both statements leads to inconsistency, the claim can easily be rephrased to preserve consistency at the price of abandoning that strict sense and allowing exceptions to the universal claim that it apparently makes.

We may now pause to take stock of the implications of this analysis for the work of a comparative historian. The question 'is there a common or a universal logic?' must be disambiguated if we are not to be led

---

[2] The story occurs in one version in *Hanfeizi* 36: cf. Harbsmeier 1998: 215 ff.

into confusion. It is a simple observation of the ongoing disagreements among formal logicians to say that they are indeed debating alternative logics. Even the question of whether, in this debate, there must be just the one eventual winner is itself controversial. Yet formal logic does not deal with actual speech acts with all their resonances and multilayered complexity, but rather with what is abstracted from them, for the purposes of studying validity, invalidity, and so on. Formal logic examines statements that meet the criteria of well-formed formulae and dismisses those that do not. It demands univocity in the use of terms, and ordinary communication notably falls far short of that requirement.

Pragmatics, on the other hand, sets itself the task of investigating the forms of reasoning actually found in ordinary communication. The aims here too are to arrive at certain universally applicable principles, cooperation, relevance, and the like, to understand conversational implicature, and so on. Yet the crucial difference is that the *ways* in which they are applicable are context-specific. There are as many different modes of cooperation as there are different relationships between individuals or groups engaged in communicating with one another. Pragmatics shares with formal logic the aim to arrive at certain general rules, yet in the case of pragmatics, since these relate to actual communicative acts, they must be as varied in their applications as those acts are.

The difference between the two types of study is brought out most vividly by considering how they deal with apparent breaches of abstract principles such as the law of non-contradiction. The formal logician will point out that adherence to the denial of such a law leads to anything following from anything—precluding any further formal study of chains of reasoning whatsoever. The pragmatist will look to the context or circumstances in which the apparent breach occurs to see what purposes were being served. Was this a statement designed deliberately to shock? Or to mystify? Or otherwise serve notice to an interlocutor that this was no ordinary subject of conversation? Or has indeed a mistake been made?

We have no call to postulate alternative logics such as were associated with the hypothesis of primitive mentalities: indeed to do so would be to preclude understanding, not enable it. The rules we need to make sense of the pragmatics of communication are an ongoing subject of specialist study. In a way they provide the beginnings of a common *in*formal logic, which there is no reason to believe does *not* apply to all natural languages.[3] Yet, as explained, the rules vary in the ways they apply in different contexts.

Communication breaks down if canons of relevance and cooperation are not observed: but what counts as such depends, in part, on the subject matter and the interlocutors. As for formal logic, that too is an ongoing specialist study: but with one major exception that we shall come to shortly, it is not one that has much bearing on the problems of interpretation that the historian faces.

We must, then, pay due attention to the variety of ways in which we may make sense of communicative exchanges. Some statements defy explanation initially, but only initially. Some paradoxes, I said, deliberately pose a challenge—which has to be met by using one's imagination, with no guarantee of success, although there never *is* any such guarantee in any interpretative exercise. Some statements are deliberately mystificatory, and we may or may not be able to define the kind of mystification we are faced with. In some cases, as I noted in Chapter 1, the only intelligibility we can grasp is at a second level, recognizing the unintelligibility of the statement as the unintelligibility it is. We are often in no position to diagnose the sense that underlies the apparent nonsense. When it comes to some of the complex explanations that have been offered to resolve deep problems in understanding the world, we may be hard put to it to come up with an account of precisely what is being claimed, let alone of why, although sometimes it is not a matter of anything being claimed *precisely*. Yet that does not necessarily mean that nothing significant is being stated.

The preceding deflationary account offers a resolution or clarification of some of the problems that have followed from some applications of the notion of alternative logics. I mentioned the exception to my generalization about the usefulness of formal logic as such for the interpretative work of the historian. This is a matter of the difference it may make when certain distinctions deriving from formal analysis become explicit and are available to interlocutors in their comments and challenges on the statements they are discussing.

---

[3] The differences between pragmatics, semantics, and syntactics are crucial. Both semantics and syntactics exhibit large surface differences across different natural languages. That point may be agreed whatever view we take about the deep structures postulated by Chomsky and his followers. But pragmatics aims to set out the rules that govern communicative exchanges between human agents in whatever contexts these occur, while allowing due weight to the differences those contexts import. Those rules are not specific to, and there is no reason to think that they vary fundamentally as between, particular natural languages.

Both our ancient civilizations provide illustrations of this, though the phenomenon is appreciably more prominent in ancient Greece than in China. To appreciate how both ancient civilizations brought to bear explicit concepts of logical categories and different modes of reasoning, we need to backtrack a little, to consider first the interest shown in the techniques of persuasion, second attitudes towards disputation more generally, and third the development of a vocabulary to identify and name logical mistakes.

Both ancient China and Greece were intensely interested in persuasion, though the nature of the interest shown differs in certain respects. The Chinese were not concerned with several of the chief types of context to which Greek rhetoric was applied. There was no Chinese parallel to the situation of the Greek law courts, where the dicasts, ordinary citizens chosen by lot, heard arguments from prosecution and defence and were then responsible for deciding issues of guilt and duly passing sentence—for acting as both jury and judge in those roles. Rather, the focus of Chinese attention was usually on persuading the ruler or his ministers or those in positions of power or influence—and to achieve this end, of winning people round, without being *seen* to be manipulative. In those contexts, the *shuonan* chapter of *Hanfeizi*, for instance, shows a subtlety and sophistication that surpasses anything we can find in classical Greek handbooks of rhetoric.[4]

Secondly, the Chinese were just as capable as the ancient Greeks of expressing disapproval of certain styles of argument. The term *bian*, for example, can be used pejoratively of disputatious reasoning in very much the same way as the Greek word *eristike*. However, with some exceptions, the focus of complaint, in Chinese texts, is not so much on the logical tricks that contentious reasoning involves, as on the way in which such behaviour is a lapse of good manners, indeed a sign of moral failings in the reasoners (cf. below n. 9 on Plato).

Similarly paradox is deplored in China rather because it is a waste of time, and a symptom of misplaced ingenuity. It does not so often become the occasion for the positive exploration of features of language use.

We do, however, find in Chinese texts clear recognition of the problem of inconsistency. I noted this was sometimes conveyed by means of the story of the all-penetrating lances and the impenetrable shields. But

[4] This is *Hanfeizi* 12, which I have discussed in Lloyd 1996a: ch. 4.

there was also an explicit vocabulary to express the idea. The term *bei* for example was used of claims that are self-refuting because contradictory.[5] One of the Mohist canons endeavours to show that to say that all saying is contradictory is itself self-contradictory.[6] Here then was an important conceptual tool for use in evaluating argument, which offers a beginning of a comparison with Greek interest in such. However, the armoury of Greek terms developed for that purpose is significantly greater.

To give some idea of the scale of that development: in the *Topics* Aristotle identifies four main kinds of fallacious argument[7] and five types of begging the question, and he follows that up in the treatise he devoted to *Sophistical Refutations* with a taxonomy of no fewer than six methods of apparent refutation by fallacies dependent on language and a further seven that are not.[8] The context of these moves, by Aristotle, is of course his attempt, in the wake of Plato, to draw up what amounts to a taxonomy of styles of reasoning and reasoner. Syllogisms may be demonstrative, dialectical, or eristic, that is contentious (*Topics* 100^{a}27–101^{a}4). Dialectical arguments are in turn distinguished from didactic, peirastic, and contentious at *Sophistical Refutations* 165^{a}38 ff., and dialecticians from rhetoricians and sophists, as well as dialectic from philosophy (*Metaphysics* 1004^{b}17–26).

In part these distinctions relate to the motives of those who engaged in discussions and arguments of different types (victory, reputation, making money, the search for the truth): in part they depend on the formal characteristics of the arguments themselves. In the process the roles of the questioner and the answerer—and indeed the audience— are defined, the ploys that are fair distinguished from those that are unfair (compared with cheating in athletic contests in the *Sophistical Refutations* 171^{b}22 ff.), where again Aristotle draws on a rich store of

[5] See Graham 1989: 187 ff., and cf. Harbsmeier 1998: 342 ff., who deals with this under the heading of paradoxes.

[6] Mohist Canon B 71 and B 79 on which see Graham 1989: 185 f., Harbsmeier 1998: 217.

[7] *Topics* 162^{b}3 ff. The four are: (1) when an argument only appears to be brought to a conclusion; (2) when it comes to a conclusion but not to the conclusion proposed; (3) when it comes to the proposed conclusion but not by the appropriate mode of enquiry, and (4) when the conclusion is reached from false premises.

[8] *Sophistical Refutations* 165^{b}23 ff., 166^{b}20 ff. The six that depend on language are equivocation, amphiboly, combination, division, accent, and form of expression: the seven that do not depend on language are accident, the use of words with or without qualification, ignoratio elenchi, petitio principii, consequent, false cause, and many questions. In several cases the term by which the fallacy is still known ultimately derives from Aristotle.

similar points in such dialogues of Plato as the *Protagoras*, *Gorgias*, *Euthydemus*, *Phaedrus*, and *Sophist* (cf. Lloyd 1979: 100 f.).[9]

But, we must now ask, what does it say about the two ancient societies we are dealing with that their interests in these subjects overlapped in some areas, but diverged in others? If the arguments in the preceding section are accepted, these differences do not tell us anything about radically incommensurable systems of thought. They will not lead to any conclusion to the effect that logic as such differs from one society to another or from one period to another. What does differ is the availability of principles or rules that can be invoked, in interpersonal exchange, to criticize reasoning of different types—whether that invocation may seem fair, in context, or sharp practice.

The differences we find are manifestations of different interests and concerns in the regulation of those interpersonal exchanges, and of course these can and do differ from one situation to another. We may remark that in Greece a considerable effort was put into the study of these issues from at least the mid-fifth century BCE onwards.

On the one hand, the elaboration of a rich terminology for describing and passing judgement on modes of argument and tricks used within them *reflects* the polemical and adversarial nature of so much Greek thought and life. On the other hand, the availability of all the distinctions involved, once they had been made explicit, *contributed* to that competitiveness. That extends far beyond merely logical points, to issues that are fundamental to all language use, to Aristotle's insistence, for instance, on the dichotomy between the literal and the metaphorical. Once he diagnoses non-literal use in his rivals' theories he can mount a challenge. Take Empedocles' idea that the sea is the sweat of the

---

[9] The *Sophistical Refutations* ends with a famous passage in which Aristotle claims to be an innovator. Whereas in rhetoric he acknowledges many predecessors, going back to Tisias, Thrasymachus, and Theodorus (183^b31 ff.), in the analysis of the materials covered by the *Topics* (at least) and maybe by the whole *Organon*, he says that before him the enquiry did not exist at all. Where syllogistic and the formal analysis of argument were concerned, that claim can be vindicated on the whole. But with regard to fallacious arguments, Aristotle himself cites the alternative analyses that others had offered (e.g. 177^b8 f., ^{b}27 ff., 178^b10–23, 179^b7 ff., ^{b}34 ff., 182^b26 f.) and he devotes ch. 10 of the work to a critical examination of the view he ascribes to (unnamed) persons to the effect that the key contrast is between arguments used against the word and those used against the thought (cf. Hecquet-Devienne 1993). Some of Aristotle's arguments come from Plato's *Euthydemus* (e.g. 179^a34 f. picks up *Euthydemus* 298c), and it would appear that that dialogue acted as a stimulus to the analysis of fallacious reasoning, even though in Plato himself the chief criticism that Socrates makes of Euthydemus and Dionysodorus is a moral one: their instruction is worthless since it does not teach virtue.

earth. Is the sea literally sweat? If yes, there will be problems. But if no, then Empedocles will be obliged to state what the metaphor is a metaphor *for*.[10]

Aristotle is a key figure, indeed, in the developments that take place in Greece, though, as noted, his was not the only formal logic that was put forward in Greek antiquity. But the crucial point for our own concerns is that Aristotle puts his logic to work in his theory of demonstration. Syllogistic was studied, to be sure, partly for its own sake. But the way the *Prior Analytics* provides the basis for the *Posterior* is even more important. The claim, in that theory, was to provide the wherewithal to yield conclusions that do not just meet the rules for valid argument, but that are true, indeed necessary and certain.

Thus although, throughout this discussion, I have emphasized the difference between formal logic and pragmatics, we can see that Aristotle insisted on the relevance of the former to the latter. But everything then depends on the terms used in informal reasoning meeting the criteria for univocity on which strict syllogistic validity depends, and when we get to the hard work of science or metaphysics, those criteria become increasingly difficult to meet—as indeed I would claim Aristotle himself shows signs of recognizing in both his metaphysical and his zoological treatises in particular (cf. Lloyd 1996b).

Yet his ultimate aim was not just to be persuasive—though, as he puts it, the truth is most persuasive of all. From one point of view, his analysis of arguments is brought to bear to win arguments and to silence the opposition. Of course formal logic offers, in principle, an entirely *im*personal set of rules by which to evaluate arguments, assessing their virtues and vices in abstraction from the question of who put them forward. So from another point of view the goal is to yield what everyone will have to agree is the indisputable truth. Yet those impersonal rules could be turned into effective polemical tools—and were indeed so used by Aristotle.

The final irony is that Aristotle is the very person who, in another context, that of morality, points most clearly to the relationship between reasoning and *character*. This is when he analyses what he calls practical reasoning. There he insists on the interdependence of the intellectual virtue, *phronesis* (practical wisdom), and the moral virtues. We can talk of skill in reasoning about ethical matters that is divorced

---

[10] I have explored the polemical origins and use of the dichotomies between the literal and the metaphorical, and between *logos* and *muthos*, in Lloyd 1990: ch. 1.

from goodness of character. But that is mere cleverness, he says. Conversely, goodness of character without the intellectual excellence of practical wisdom is mere *natural* excellence, not true moral excellence at all.[11]

Such a claim is, at first sight, surprising, especially coming from Aristotle who had insisted on the possibility of the purely abstract analysis of argument schemata in his formal logic. Yet that interdependence, on reflection, can be justified, and even reflects a profound truth. Is it not the case that the greedy person, for instance, *reasons* to the conclusion he or she reaches about what to do in the given circumstances of a situation of moral choice in ways that *reflect* his or her character? We recognize this often under the rubric of rationalization, but there is no reason to limit the phenomenon to blatant cases of such. Practical wisdom involves taking all the circumstances of the individual case into account. As Aristotle is never tired of saying, being courageous is a matter first of a settled disposition, but then also one that is reflected in having the right reactions to the fearful. Not only must one know just how dangerous the situation is, and the consequences of different courses of action if one takes them, but one must also be *self*-aware, conscious, for instance, that one is inclined to be cowardly, or foolhardy, and ready to aim off for that tendency. Moral excellence is a mean relative to us, and we have to be clear-headed about our own characters and dispositions.

All of that shows that Aristotle was acutely aware that personality may indeed be reflected in reasoning. The same Aristotle also thought that in certain modes of *theoretical* reasoning that did *not* apply. He imagines the case of mathematicians whose skill in their subject is independent of the kind of persons they are.[12] That point may be granted and yet the distinction between the two types of study may not be as clear-cut as Aristotle himself evidently wanted to suggest. At least, in the matter of what he would count as theoretical reasoning, we might insist that, when it comes to the major components of a world-view, a cosmology, it would be hard to accept that reasoning in such a context is *purely impersonal*, for this reason, that a world-view is bound to encompass ideas concerning the place of humans, and that inevitably

[11] Book 6 of the *Nicomachean Ethics* is the chief text where Aristotle elaborates these ideas, especially at 1144^a20-^b32.

[12] Hippocrates of Chios was an excellent geometer but foolish in practical matters (*Eudemian Ethics* 1247^a17 ff.). Even the young can be good at geometry, but they cannot possess *phronesis*, practical wisdom (*Nicomachean Ethics* 1142^a11 ff.).

leads back towards morality, to politics, to sociology, even, we might say, to ideology. Just what a world-view comprises, and how, or under what conditions, we can agree with the idea that there is just the *one* world for us to take a view of, are problems I shall take up in Chapter 7.

I may now summarize the main lines of argument of this chapter. The key to the question we started with—is there a common logic?—is to disambiguate what 'logic' may comprise. Both formal logic and pragmatics are specialist studies where different options are actively debated. In that sense, we can talk of alternatives within both domains, alternative formal logics, and alternative sets of rules by which to make sense of the pragmatics of communicative exchanges. Yet neither point entitles us to talk of different logics in different societies, or implicit in different natural languages. Those languages exhibit their distinctive syntaxes and have their own semantics, to be sure.[13] But there is nothing to suggest they diverge on issues that bear on those specialist debates.

The diagnosis that different logics are at work in different societies generally stems from confusion about the nature of the speech acts that appear to diverge from what formal logic lays down as the norm. But those deviations can and must be understood by bringing the resources of pragmatics to bear, to analyse the communication situations in which they arise. That does not resolve all the difficulties, to be sure: many puzzling statements or items of behaviour defeat explanation, and not just those where we may suspect deliberate mystification. But the difficulties that remain are not such as to ground any view to the effect that, if and when we proceed to the construction of a formal logical system, we must adjust that to cope with differences that reflect the differences between natural languages.

Where societies, ancient and modern, do differ, however, is in the degree of interest shown in studying argument forms, and analysing their strengths and weaknesses, as such. Some of those interests are in the purely intellectual issues we classify as those of formal logic. Yet in the case of ancient Greece, notably, distinctions made explicit in formal logic were brought to bear in dialectical and rhetorical contexts, to win arguments or discountenance opponents. The comparative lack of the

[13] I shall be returning to the question of the relevance of that to the thoughts expressible in those languages in Ch. 6.

deployment of logical and linguistic categories in debating situations in China does not reflect a different underlying or implicit formal logic: it does not even reflect a different informal logic or set of pragmatic principles. Rather it gives us an indication of certain canons of behaviour governing the ways in which interpersonal exchanges were, or should in principle have been, conducted in Chinese life and thought.

The differences we find between the two ancient societies we have discussed are certainly important in evaluating the natures and styles of enquiry they each cultivated. But evidently different such styles can be and were developed—as we shall see in greater detail in later chapters— both with and without a heightened interest, even a preoccupation, with the questions of logical form. In any effective reasoning, and of course in both philosophy and science, consistency is a virtue, and so too clarity and the avoidance of ambiguity. Yet we have to allow semantic stretch in all modes of communication. Univocity is an ideal or limiting case, and cannot be held up as a criterion for intelligibility. We should not therefore delude ourselves about how far formal logical considerations can take us if we seek to understand the nature of the investigations we, or the ancients, undertake. One residual point, however, may be retained from our analysis of the different degrees of elaboration of explicit logical distinctions in ancient Greece and China, and that relates to the weapons available in the cut and thrust of debate. We shall return to that issue in our further discussions of differing styles of enquiry.

5

Searching for Truth

Surely all societies are concerned, are they not, with the truth? But do they all have the same notion of that concept? And what do we think should be the correct analysis of that concept?

On the last question, correspondence theories of truth are still, today, locked in dispute with coherence ones and we seem to be faced with a fundamental dilemma. There is no *direct* access to a reality 'out there'—access that is not mediated through words that are themselves all more or less theory-laden. But if correspondence to reality is, thus, strictly impossible, a mere consistency theory of truth is evidently not enough. It is clearly no good allowing just any set of statements or beliefs that are internally coherent to be, by that token, true—since we are all familiar with plenty of such sets that are palpable nonsense. Nor will it do to allow what is accepted by some group, maybe even some group of experts such as scientists or philosophers, to count as true. The histories of science and philosophy provide multiple examples of theories that were agreed at one time, only to be dismissed a couple of generations later.

Moreover on the first of my original questions, some serious scholars have claimed that the classical Chinese had *no* concept of truth.[1] I shall be disagreeing with that view, but it clearly raises the issue of the relativity of notions of truth to different societies and of the possibility that such a concept is not of universal applicability. Even a slight acquaintance with ancient Greek thought confirms that *aletheia*, roughly translatable as truth, is a central concern of Greek epistemology from Parmenides onwards, and since that term and its cognates are closely associated with the family of terms used to express being, *einai*, *on*, *ontos*, *ousia*, it is also evident that it occupies a central role in Greek ontology and cosmology. But do those ancient Greek obsessions

---

[1] See, for example, Hansen 1983, 1985, and Hall and Ames 1987.

correspond with our own puzzlement over truth? And why would there appear to be, at first sight, such a sharp contrast between two ancient societies, one preoccupied with truth, the other apparently free from any such preoccupation?

In the first two sections of this chapter I shall outline briefly what I take to be the cardinal points first in Greek, then in Chinese, thought on the issues, before turning in the third and final section to suggest some possible implications for the modern debate. Reflection on historical materials serves to highlight the question—for us—of what we should expect of a theory of truth. Should this be the province of abstract philosophizing, of working out what must be the case? That would provide us with a vantage point from which we can judge actual performance, with regard both to competing views about truth, and to actual truth claims. Or should we take our cue from that actual performance, treating that as our explanandum and aiming in some sense to save the phenomena? History, on the first option, might merely provide some of the background to the positions between which we must adjudicate. On the second—which I shall favour—it serves rather to identify some of the phenomena we need to account for, and in that way can help towards the resolution, or at least the clarification, of some of the philosophical issues.

Comparative historical analysis here, as so often elsewhere, is not a matter of trying to pin down, and then contrast, *the* Greek concept of truth, *the* Chinese one, as if there were, in each case, just the one. In both cases we are dealing with a complex of concepts linked more or less tightly to practices, and we shall find the practices are as eloquent about attitudes towards truth as the explicit theories. But my anti-generalization point can be brought out immediately by turning directly to some of the Greek data.

Very broadly speaking, we can distinguish three main families of positions about truth in Greece, the disputes between which are more or less where our own modern debates started. These are the objectivist, the relativist, and the sceptical. Each comes in different forms. Parmenides, in the first camp, associates truth with necessity. 'It is and it cannot not be': that is what starts you on the Way of Truth (Fr. 2). But Plato unties the knot between truth and necessity. Truth is a necessary, but not a sufficient, condition of knowledge (or understanding), for opinions can be true or false. In the *Sophist* (263b) truth and falsehood are analysed as properties of statements: the first says of a subject things that are, the second other things. But that did not stop Plato or any other Greek from continuing to apply the predicates true and false (*alethes, pseudes*) directly to objects.

Aristotle, following Plato's lead, is even more emphatic, in the *Categories* (2ª4 ff.), that while every affirmation and denial must be either true or false (the axiom of excluded middle), of things said not in combination none is either true or false. Among the four examples he goes on to give, human, white/bright, runs, conquers, the last two are unguarded, in that in Greek it is perfectly possible for a subject to be understood with such verbs. Yet he too continues to use 'true' as synonymous with genuine (as in what is truly just as opposed to what merely seems so, *Rhetoric* 1375ᵇ3 f.). The contrast between true reality and mere appearance provides one of the key articulating devices in his whole philosophical project, just as it had in Plato's, even though the two of them disagreed fundamentally on the account to be given of that ultimate reality.

I shall have more to say about the appeals to truth, and the proof procedures, we find in Aristotle and others later, but let me now introduce the other main types of Greek position. Over and above the disagreements within the realist camp, there were others from outside it expressed by those who dissented from any claim that beyond the appearances there is objectivity to be had. Plato is one of our chief witnesses (and a hostile one) to the relativist position. In the *Theaetetus* (151e ff.) he represents Protagoras as claiming that a human being is the measure of all things, of what is that (or how) it is, and of what is not that (or how) it is not. What appears hot to me is hot to me, even though it may appear (and so is) cold to you. As Plato develops Protagoras' position, the same relativizing principle applies not just to predicates that denote sensibilia, but also to moral qualities, good, bad, just, unjust. Nor does it matter, for our purposes here, where Protagoras' own ideas end and Plato's interpretation of them takes over—since we are concerned here with what positions were canvassed, rather than with who canvassed them. Sextus, responding no doubt as much to Plato as to whatever other sources he had for Protagoras, summed up:[2] truth is something relative because everything that has appeared to, or been believed by, someone is at once real to that person.

The other main challenge to the objectivist view of truth came from

---

[2] Sextus Empiricus, *Against the Mathematicians* VII 60.

the side of scepticism, it too not a single thesis but a group of them.[3] Some denied the possibility of knowledge concerning hidden reality or unseen causes, though it was soon spotted that since such a denial had to be based on some criterion, it breached the very principle it sought to advocate and so was vulnerable to the charge of self-refutation. Against those who took that so-called negative dogmatist view, the Pyrrhonian sceptics adopted the safer course of withholding judgement on hidden reality. It may or may not be the case that the ultimate constituents of physical objects are atoms, or earth, water, air, or fire, or whatever. But there is no criterion on which to base a judgement. Perception is unreliable, but so too is reason and so judgement should be suspended. As we can see from Sextus, the Pyrrhonian sceptics of the Hellenistic period ably exploited the apparent impasses in physical theory, in cosmology, even in ethics, claiming that on issues that went beyond the appearances there was just as much to be said on one side of the debate as on the other (the principle of equipollency). But already in the fifth century BCE Gorgias had thrown down the gauntlet—to Parmenides and the Eleatics and to anyone who had any pretensions to pronounce on reality. In *On Not-Being* he put it first that nothing exists, secondly that if it did, it cannot be known, and thirdly that if it did and were known, it cannot be communicated to anyone else.

These radically opposed Greek points of view on being and truth are all well known. I recall them here first to emphasize that there is no one Greek concept of truth. It is not just that the Greeks disagreed on the answers to the questions: they disagreed on the questions themselves. Is truth a matter of correspondence to objective reality, or one merely of internal consistency, or again of how things appear to individuals or to groups? The main lines of our modern argument go back to those Greek disputes—even though there are of course important differences, first, for example, in the notion of reality invoked by some ancient transcendental realists, and then also in the radical nature of ancient scepticism where that was a matter of suspending judgement with regard to belief as well as knowledge. That left the ancient sceptics living by the appearances alone. As philosophy has become more academic, some modern sceptics (though of course not all) treat their scepticism more as an abstract solution to a theoretical problem than as a guide for life.

[3] For evaluations of ancient Greek scepticism and its later influence, see, for example, Burnyeat 1983, Annas and Barnes 1985, Long and Sedley 1987, Barnes 1990, Hankinson 1995.

But already in classical antiquity competing cosmological, ontological, ethical theories were locked in controversy, and the rivalry on substantive issues is a major factor contributing to the development of the second-order enquiries I discussed in the last chapter. In the Greek situation of often strident adversariality that I have described elsewhere (Lloyd 1996a), would-be Masters of Truth sought to make their reputations by outdoing all comers and most saw the need to back up their ideas on first-order issues with a well-thought-out repertoire of responses to second-order challenges concerning the very basis on which they claimed superior knowledge or understanding in the first place.

Yet not all Greeks were directly concerned with questions to do with fundamental reality. If we turn to examine how truth and the true are invoked in writers such as the historians or the orators, there the important issues relate not to some ultimate criterion, but to such matters as the honesty of witnesses, the accuracy of reports, the diagnosis of intentions, and the like. Thucydides, for instance, at the more theoretical end of this spectrum, says that the truest cause—as opposed to the alleged or apparent reasons—for the Peloponnesian war was the fear that Athenian ambition inspired in the Spartans (I 23).

Again the fifth- and fourth-century orators provide a wealth of evidence on the subject. Lysias' speech *On the Murder of Eratosthenes*, for instance, illustrates a number of standard moves. First (I 5) the speaker protests that he will omit nothing, speak the truth, and indeed go through everything that happened (cf. 'the whole truth and nothing but the truth'). In I 18 he claims that he questioned the slave-girl who is one of his key witnesses, threatening her with a beating to ensure (so he says) that she will tell the truth. As regards the prosecution, wrongdoers, he says (I 28) do not agree that their opponents are telling the truth, they lie and stir up anger in their audience against those who act justly. The trustworthiness of witnesses was, in fact, particularly contested when they were slaves. Some argued that the slave would only speak the truth under torture, while others countered that in that situation the slave would say anything to have the torture stop.[4]

In the natural philosophers and scientists themselves the actual procedures used to check or prove results are often more complex than

---

[4] Such themes appear prominently in, for example, Antiphon, *First Tetralogy* (II β 8, γ 4, δ 7) and in *The Murder of Herodes* (V 32, 35, 36, 42, 50).

the explicit theories on the subject allow. Aristotle sets out a theory of strict demonstration in the *Posterior Analytics* that proceeds from primary premisses via valid deductions to incontrovertible conclusions. In that schema, the ultimate primary premisses (axioms, definitions, hypotheses) are themselves indemonstrable (on pain of an infinite regress) but self-evident. Yet in practice, as I said, he rarely, if ever, adheres exactly to such a model in his physical works.

His proof of the sphericity of the earth in *On the Heavens* II ch. 14, for instance, is typical in drawing on both abstract arguments and empirical considerations. The former include the notion that heavy objects all travel towards the same point: they do not fall in parallel lines but in lines directed to the centre of the universe deemed to coincide with the centre of the earth. That might be thought to beg the question, but he also has empirical evidence that points to sphericity, namely (1) the shape of the earth's shadow in a lunar eclipse (but then you have to know that they are caused by the earth's intervention) and (2) the changes in the visibility of constellations above the horizon, and in those that never set, as the observer moves south (which suggests convexity at least on the north–south axis).

The obvious problem with the model of axiomatic-deductive demonstration in any context other than mathematics was the difficulty of securing self-evident axioms. Most Greek attempts outside mathematics were guilty of wishful thinking, and even in mathematics the debate that raged over Euclid's parallel postulate illustrates that its claim to be self-evident was contested. But in mathematics and elsewhere you could settle for less, for truth, rather than demonstrated certainty. Archimedes tells us that Democritus knew the relation between the volume of the cylinder and the inscribed cone, though it was not until Eudoxus that that result was proved.[5] How would Democritus have decided on the three to one ratio, if he had not demonstrated it? We do not know. But that just reminds us that he could have made the discovery in a variety of ways. Besides, it was a correct result.

In other more empirical contexts we find the author of the Hippocratic treatise *On the Heart*, for example, showing the function of the valves at the base of the aorta and of what we call the pulmonary artery by trying, and failing, to force water, and air, back through them.[6] Again Galen dramatically demonstrated the function of the recurrent

[5] Archimedes, *Method*, HS II 430. 2 ff.   [6] *On the Heart* ch. 10, L IX 86. 13 ff.

laryngeal nerve by severing it in a live pig, an operation that suddenly deprived it of its voice.[7] The drama, in that case, was undoubtedly part of the effect he aimed for. But in one such case after another, we ask such questions as whether the procedures were carried out correctly, and whether they warranted the conclusions, where 'correctly' covers in the first instance *their* protocols, though they in turn can and should be evaluated in the light of later standards. It is not as if we have to stay with the ancients' own criteria concerning what serves as a good empirical test, since sometimes, then as now, some practitioners were notably less critical in the evaluation of their own procedures than they were in assessing those of their rivals.

It seems worth emphasizing, then, that over and above the occasions when major epistemological positions were being propounded, the range of issues where truth is at stake in ancient Greece stretched from truth-telling and authenticity to the checking and demanding of accounts in a wide variety of contexts. But let us turn now to the Chinese and their supposed lack of the concept.

The style of Chinese philosophizing is in certain respects rather different, as we have already noted, from the aggressive adversariality cultivated by so many Greeks. Chinese intellectuals do not regularly undertake the total demolition of their rivals' views by way of undermining their epistemological and methodological assumptions. Contexts of communicative exchange are relevant here, too, just as they are in the Greek case. Where Greek polemic so often adopts models influenced by the law courts and political assemblies,[8] Chinese advisers often envisage a situation of persuading the person whose opinion really counted, namely the ruler (or his ministers), even when the advice they offered was not on affairs of state (as it so often was).

Yet so far from lacking a concept of truth, there are four prime contexts in which Chinese, already in the period before major Buddhist influence, make considerable play with related ideas.[9] We can begin first by remarking that classical Chinese has no difficulty whatsoever in assigning truth values to statements. The commonest way of doing so is by recording that things are so (*ran*) or not so (*bu ran*).

---

[7] Galen, *On Anatomical Procedures* XI chs. 3 ff.

[8] Those contexts also provided, as I explained in the last chapter, *negative* models, of styles of argument that some said should be avoided, as well as positive ones, of styles to be imitated.

[9] Cf. especially Graham 1989: app. 2, Harbsmeier 1989, 1998: 193 ff., Wardy 2000: 59 ff.

Again, the antonyms shi^i and *fei* are used to mark the contrast between, on the one hand, what is, and what is right, and, on the other, what is not, and what is wrong. Shi^i is further used as a demonstrative, this, and to register affirmation or assent: yes. Xunzi, in the third century BCE, remarks that 'calling shi^i shi^i, and calling *fei fei*, is called straight (zhi^i)', which Harbsmeier,[10] taking shi^i as what is, *fei* as what is not, compared with Aristotle's account of what it is to tell the truth, *aletheuein*, at *Metaphysics* 1051^b3 ff. However, Xunzi's dictum also covers calling right right and wrong wrong—when that happens, that is called straight in the sense of upright.

More remarkably, the *Zhuangzi*, in the *qiwulun* chapter,[11] takes a different view from Xunzi's on the very possibility of judgement, insisting that both affirmation and denial are relative to a viewpoint. What one person deems to be so, shi^i, another denies, *fei*, and that, in the *Zhuangzi* view, undermines the whole ambition to draw distinctions. In one respect this goes further even than Protagorean relativism, for that allows that something may be the case on the proviso that we relativize that to a subject: the wind *is* hot to the person who feels it so. Zhuangzi moves from the observation of the differences in what people deem to be so, and the shifts in the reference to which such claims relate, to conclude to the impossibility of deeming something to be so in the first place, though he concedes that you have, in some sense, to rely on it being so, where he uses the term *yin shi*, rather than *wei shi*, his expression for taking something to be the case. His chief concern, no doubt, in all of this is not with logic nor with philosophy of language as such, so much as with how we should live.

Thirdly, verifying that a claim is correct is a Chinese concern in a variety of contexts, as also is assessing whether appearances are quite what they seem (in the matter of human character, for example, not least with regard to questions of sincerity or truthfulness, often expressed by means of the terms *cheng* and *zhen*). Mencius (Mengzi) already questions the truth of historical statements (5A4, 5A7). The historian Sima Qian does not go out of his way to emphasize the historicity of his own account in *contrast* to a category of the legendary or the mythical—in the way that Thucydides claims his history to be no mere ephemeral entertainment, but a 'possession for always' (I 21–2). But without aggressively distancing himself from his predecessors,

[10] *Xunzi* 2: 12, Knoblock 1988–94: i. 153 and n. 35, Harbsmeier 1998: 194.
[11] *Zhuangzi* 2, cf. Graham 1989: 183 ff.

Sima Qian frequently expresses himself unable to pronounce on the veracity of legends that circulated concerning very early times: he corrects others' views on points of geography and chronology and in general presents himself as a scrupulous recorder of events who has been at pains to check the accuracy of his own account.[12]

Again, similarly, both Xunzi and Wang Chong query claims made about ghosts and the powers of spirits.[13] Although the concept of axiomatic-deductive demonstration is foreign to classical Chinese mathematics, we find plenty of examples in the mathematical texts where algorithms are validated and shown to be correct, as when Liu Hui remarks that the effect of the procedures is that the quantities remain the same—and so truth is preserved.[14]

Fourthly, there is a recurrent interest in the match or mismatch between names and things, in the topos of *zhengming*, the rectification of names, that goes back to Confucius (Kong Fuzi). From the *Lunyu*, through Xunzi and on,[15] that topos focuses not on semantics as such, but rather on conduct and morality. Unless names and things match, there will be disaster: social ranks, for instance, will be confused. But the remedy then proceeds in an unexpected direction, for it is not so much a matter of correcting names so that they correspond to things, but of correcting things to correspond to their true names (those that the sage kings laid down to establish proper social ranks and the like).

Even a rapid survey such as this is enough to show that there are important and in some cases distinctive Chinese reflections on matters to do with truth, knowledge, and objectivity. But what conclusions does this suggest for the major issues of the debates on truth I mentioned at the outset? On the one hand, we can use comparative history to indicate where the problems of truth come from. On the other, it may, I hope, serve not just to identify some of the issues, but also to contribute a little to their resolution.

The questions to do with truth we should not lose sight of include, as

---

[12] Sima Qian, *Shiji* 129: 3253. 5, 130: 3295. 9 ff., 3296. 1 ff., 3319. 6 ff. Cf. Lloyd 2002: ch. 1, with references to modern scholarship.

[13] *Xunzi* 21, Knoblock 1988–94: iii. 109, Wang Chong, *Lun Heng* ch. 65.

[14] Cf. above, Ch 3 p. 29 on Liu Hui's commentary on *Jiuzhang suanshu* I.

[15] The topic of *zhengming*, the rectification of names, goes back to the *Lunyu* 13 and is a concern of *Xunzi* 22. Among many discussions of the issue, see Gassmann 1988 and the articles collected in the number of *Extrême-Orient Extrême-Occident*, 15 (1993) by Djamouri, Lackner, Levi, and Vandermeersch.

a central core, truth-telling, authenticity, checking, and warranting. Williams (2002) has recently argued that sincerity and accuracy are the twin virtues of truthfulness and truth, but we should be careful. No one is in any position to confirm that these are universal human social concerns, and as to the values attached, we should be positively wary of assuming cross-cultural universals there. We have only to think of the way in which, in certain contexts at least, the ancient Greeks positively admired those (like Odysseus) who were good at lying and deceiving. They praised, under the rubric of *metis*, cunning intelligence, the skills that included the ability to win by fair means and by foul—provided you were not found out.[16] Again we shall be considering in the next chapter the case of the Baktaman, studied by Barth (1975), where it is accepted that individuals are deliberately misled and systematically lied to by their elders on their path to higher understanding.

The contexts in which the veracity of speakers, the reliability of witnesses, may be questioned, and the procedures that can be used to check them (when indeed that option is open), are all enormously varied. So too are the degrees of accuracy and of precision that are to be expected. The approximation that a builder can tolerate for the circle-circumference ratio differs from the goal a mathematician may set in determining its value.[17] The notion of the approximately true gets into bad odour with logicians, since it destroys the transitivity of entailment. But plenty of ordinary human calculations make do happily enough with just such approximations.

An awareness that there are problems to do with veracity and with warranting antedates anything that we could label philosophy, let alone science, in Greece, in China, or anywhere else. Our comparative historical excursus enables us to identify some of the broadly social factors at work in the developments of the topoi of truth and objectivity. Styles of reasoning in both Greece and China reflect the situations in which the investigators operated, including their 'career opportunities', how they made a living, and whom they were hoping to persuade. Heavy-duty epistemology in Greece, for instance, seems to have been stimulated by the need to support the counter-intuitive claims by which Masters

---

[16] See especially Detienne and Vernant 1978.

[17] Both Greek and Chinese mathematicians attacked the problem of evaluating π by using inscribed and/or circumscribed regular polygons to get closer and closer approximations. In the Chinese case that led, in the thirteenth century, to the calculation of the area of inscribed polygons of up to 2^{14} sides: see Volkov 1996–7, 1997.

of Truth hoped to make their reputations—and they hoped to make them with the heavy-duty epistemology as well.

Relativists might also take heart from the fact that history repeatedly shows that most of what was actually claimed to be objectively true, in physics and philosophy, by those who thought that possible, turned out to fail to carry conviction beyond the groups of the proponents. Yet the objectivists are surely right not to settle just for what is agreed by a given group, even of self-styled experts. The standards of the investigation into what actually happened, and why, in a court of law, are applicable—within limits and with reservations—in other contexts too. There are facts of the matter to be reconstructed, sequences of events to be determined, and intentions to be evaluated, however hard it may be to do that and even though no final verdict is ever in. As has often been said, in the enquiry into physical phenomena, the statements of what has been observed, and of the results of tests carried out, are never themselves value-free. But there are degrees of theoryladenness, and we would do well to make the most of that, even in the face of the demands of the principle of excluded middle. Truth tables and bivalence are fine for well-formed formulae: but I remarked that well-formed formulae are not the common coin on the vast majority of occasions when truth is called into question.

The lessons I would draw from this comparative analysis are pluralist ones. The protocols of warranting are, no doubt, relative to a problem situation. In today's scientific investigations verification takes forms undreamt of a hundred years ago, let alone in antiquity wherever in the world you were. With the increase in the range of what can be provisionally confirmed goes also a greater sense of what is beyond that range—and not just in the case of Heisenberg's uncertainty principle.

The variety of manifestations of the problems of truth calls for context- or at least domain-specific responses, rather than the invocation of a single universal principle.[18] Correspondence, in the sense of unmediated access to reality, is, in any case, I said, unattainable. We should be wary of consensus, while consistency is not adequate for the task in most fields. But that does not mean that the search for truth is hopeless and has to be renounced—let alone that we have to look in an altogether new direction, such as art or religion, to find *the* key. That is

---

[18] I would thus agree with Williams 2002: 63, when he resists the demand for a single definition of truth.

more likely to add to our difficulties than to put us out of our misery, if, as I argue, there is no *single* key.

Truth has, on the contrary, important roles (in the plural) to fulfil in law and history, as well as science and philosophy. The capacity of humans (philosophers especially) to doubt—which is where the challenge to validate a claim generally arises—is almost limitless, but that is not to say that it is always reasonable, even though we have no algorithm to tell us when that is the case. In the final analysis, Aristotelian *phronesis*, or practical reasoning, seems more relevant to the problems than his search for incontrovertibility, and on that score the Chinese, for whom that quest was entirely foreign, would undoubtedly have agreed.

6

The Questionability of Belief

How do beliefs get to be challenged, on what kinds of subject, and by whom? Obviously those questions raise key issues for our under-standing of the development of enquiry, not just about nature or the external world, but about other matters as well. Yet a prior question is: have we any right to treat belief as a cross-cultural category? Does that term pick out a cognitive attitude, faculty, or disposition that is exem-plified by humans everywhere? The ethnographic literature is full of reports of what the members of the societies studied are said to believe, but whether that term is appropriate is more problematic than is some-times acknowledged. This can be seen especially in the case of what has been discussed under the category of 'apparently irrational beliefs'. I have mentioned before the Dorze notion that the leopard is a Christian animal and the Nuer one that twins are birds—where the question of what commitment the Dorze or the Nuer have to those ideas (and how to interpret them) has been the subject of intense debate.

One consideration that may weigh with ethnographers in saying that the Dorze and Nuer *believe* rather than *know* those items may be the common Western assumption that you cannot know what is not the case. Sometimes it seems the beliefs are being evaluated from the standpoint of the ethnographer rather than of those whom he or she cross-questioned.

Yet the first problem with that is that even Westerners have often claimed to know what has later turned out to be false, such as the view that the earth is at the centre of the universe. We are accustomed to claim that we believe a certain item (a fact or a proposition) when we feel ourselves not to be in a position to make the stronger claim that we have knowledge—though it may be said that in Western religious discourse knowledge is often claimed even in circumstances where ordinary patterns of verification—by readily accepted criteria—are not available. I know that my Redeemer liveth. A pagan ethnographer, faced with some Christian statements and practices, might well report them as items of (just) belief. I shall be returning to this later.

But the second problem is more fundamental. This is that to use either the label 'knowledge' or the label 'belief' may be to force an issue. It gives an epistemic ranking to the item in question and diagnoses the cognitive attitude taken towards it. In every society traditions are handed on from one generation to the next in a great variety of ways. The child is corrected when he or she says or does something thought to be inappropriate or incorrect. The processes of full social incorporation may involve one or more marked rites of passage. In the case of the Baktaman, studied by F. Barth (1975), six or seven such rites follow one another in sequence as the individual grows older: they are not limited to the transitions from childhood to adolescence and then to maturity. At each stage the individual is taught that what was learned at the last or earlier stages is quite mistaken, morally unsound, indeed. They discover, for instance, that in an earlier rite of passage they broke an important taboo, not inadvertently, but because that was what the ritual enjoined. Only the very oldest members of the society can have any confidence there are no further surprises in store for them. One would think that the experience of being successively taught and then untaught fundamental lessons concerning the nature of things and the human condition might well instil a deep scepticism as to whether any lesson is final, though each one is represented as just that.[1]

What custom approves may or may not be the subject matter of explicit claims to know or to believe. Myths or sacred tales may be rehearsed on special, or even on ordinary, occasions, but as Veyne (1988)

---

[1] In many other contexts, too, the beliefs judged to be important within a society are the privileged possession of specialist groups. Bronkhorst's recent study (2002) of certain Indian debates is doubly interesting, in this regard, first for the light it throws on the exchanges in question and then for what it tells us about attitudes towards esoteric beliefs. The discussions held between brahmans or between them and kings (*ksatriyas*) may seem like the debates we are familiar with in modern societies (or from ancient Greece). However, the subjects discussed are not ones on which anyone other than the debaters themselves can pronounce—for example on what *atman* or what brahman is. The questions and answers are subject to certain rules: thus you should not ask a question to which you do not know the answer. But the winning of the debate is a matter which only the participants can adjudicate. This they do not on the basis of the way the argument goes (for argumentation as such is rare) but rather from who is left in the position of final speaker. The winner is the person whose claim to superior learning cannot be, or at least is not, challenged. Moreover the person or persons who are defeated (as is shown by their silence) are expected to submit to becoming the victor's disciples. They must offer their new master food, and the pupils themselves may be humiliated by being given only the left-over scraps to eat. These are contests of prestige, but about beliefs that are beyond the understanding of any but the contestants themselves.

already suggested for the ancient Greeks, the issue of whether the myths are *believed*, and the question of what *was* believed about the subjects they dealt with, are problematic. It is just as problematic, we might say, in our own society, if we ask whether or in what sense *we* believe that works of high literature (*Madame Bovary*, or *Don Quixote*, say) reveal the truth about the human condition.

At a much more mundane level, how to greet people, how marriage ceremonies should be conducted, how to bury the dead, and many other matters relating to action and behaviour need not be verbalized at all. Where they are, statements about them do not need to be preceded by 'I believe that', or 'we believe that'. 'I believe that *p*' may add nothing to the statement *p*, for that already implies a commitment of some kind to the truth of its content, even while the strength of that commitment may range over a wide spectrum.

Swayed by considerations such as those, and influenced by the doubts that Wittgenstein had expressed on the subject, Rodney Needham was led to infer that belief did not constitute a cross-cultural natural resemblance among mankind. That may strike many as an excessively sceptical conclusion. Yet since he wrote, in 1972, the questions have become, if anything, more disputed still. I have in mind in particular the controversies that divide commentators such as Putnam (1999), Searle (1983), Davidson (2001a: ch. 13, 2001b: ch. 10, ch. 14), Dennett (1991), Fodor (1983), Karmiloff-Smith (1992), on whether or not thinking involves mental representations, and whether or not it is, in some sense, modular. Those who reject the whole talk of mental representations tend to do so on the grounds that the mind does not need pictures to mediate between the subject matter about which it is thinking, and its thinking of it. The difficulties we may have in characterizing that relationship are not (on that view) in any way alleviated by supposing, for instance, that the apprehension of the data presented by sense-perception proceeds by way of mental images.

Against that, however, those who argue for the modularity (in some sense) of mind disagree not just about conclusions but more fundamentally about methodology. The issues (on that view) are not ones to be decided on purely conceptual or a priori grounds. Rather they are open to empirical, experimental research, the investigation of patients with brain lesions or other abnormalities, and more especially the study of cognitive growth in children. Developmental psychologists express confident views about the beliefs that children entertain about the external world at various stages in their early life. To be sure, the study of very young infants, who cannot *tell* the researcher what they think, depends upon tricky inferences from patterns in their behaviour. Their eye movements, for instance, are held to indicate not just what they are interested in, but also what they are surprised by. If presented with pictures that represent what in some sense they 'know' to be anomalous situations—such as heavy objects floating unsupported in space—they will attend longer than when offered boring old pictures of familiar states of affairs.

Those who investigate young children tend nowadays to agree about some at least of the broad stages through which cognitive development proceeds, though there is still considerable disagreement on the ages at which transitions normally take place, and indeed controversy on the precise nature of the core modules involved. I shall be returning to some of these issues in Chapter 8. For now I mention these ongoing controversies to underline the opacity of many of the problems surrounding belief. The ascription of belief is more problematic than is often supposed: the universality of belief has been called into question; the processes involved or the states it represents are disputed. Yet that does not mean that no progress is possible in the analysis of at least some of the phenomena, not that I intend to attempt to resolve, from the outside, either the ethnographic disputes, or those that divide the cognitive psychologists. Rather I wish to venture some remarks that I hope will shed some light on what I may call the sociology of belief and its historiography.

Let me begin at home with some remarks about English usage before I attempt some comparative comments on ancient Greece and ancient China. I note incidentally that there are some interesting divergences even within European languages in, for example, the relative preferences for verbs whose core meaning is thinking over those with a core meaning of believing. In English 'I think so' is used in many contexts where the natural Spanish expression is 'yo lo creo' and the French 'je le crois bien'. Again 'croyance' in French has a more restricted use than 'belief' in English. But I shall not pursue those divergences further here.

Roget's *Thesaurus* devotes three whole columns to its entry 'Belief', listing some 386 words or phrases as near synonyms, and that is before it cross-references twenty-five other entries. Many of the items in the main entry fall into one or other of two conflicting categories (though that is my observation, not Roget's), namely *either* hesitant assent (e.g.

'be under the impression', 'surmise', 'guess', 'have a point of view') *or* full-blooded conviction (where Roget includes 'take for gospel' and 'be orthodox' among the verbs, 'credal', 'dogmatic', 'canonical', 'doctrinaire', and 'authoritative' among the adjectives).

Thus a statement of a belief may be an indication of a lack of certainty or a limited ability to justify a claim. I believe it will rain—but I am not sure. If you challenge me, then I may be able to offer grounds—which themselves may vary all the way from folklore (the cows are lying down) to science (the barometer is falling). It is evidently not necessary to preface a hesitant view with a verb to express that hesitancy (I believe, I think, I surmise), for 'it may rain' serves to do that perfectly well. Indeed the statement 'it will rain', when expressed in a hesitant tone of voice may convey a warning or a likelihood, rather than a statement of future fact. The future tense will then have a different pragmatic function from the future tense in the statements that used to be made when you telephoned to find out the time and were answered by the so-called speaking clock: 'at the third stroke it will be ten o'clock precisely.'

But if, at one end of the spectrum, 'believe' in English may be strongly contrasted with 'know' and be a way of expressing a limited ability to justify or give warrant, at the other end of that spectrum the same verb is also used in statements of firm conviction. There is nothing hesitant about the Creed, about the statement made by the believer that: 'I believe in God the Father, God the Son and God the Holy Ghost.' There the understanding of what that means is more important than any warranting. Indeed the precise form of words of the Creed recited could be a matter of crucial significance, as the disputes on that question, between the Apostles' Creed, the Nicene, and the Athanasian, show. However, those controversies were not settled by warrant in the sense of empirical grounds, but rather by theological argument and by authority.

Though not now a believer myself, I was sent to a Church of England school where there was no option for someone from a nominally Church of England family but to attend chapel, and certainly then no option but to turn to the east at the proper time to recite the Creed in all solemnity every Sunday. That ritual served many functions at many levels and 'meant' different things to different participants. But at one level it was an expression of solidarity, of belonging to a group, although the extent of the belonging was carefully graded and controlled, since one did not fully participate in the activities of the Church until one had been confirmed at the end of a long-drawn-out process—the cate-chism—which served precisely to test understanding and belief in the sense of commitment.

At first sight it might seem extraordinary that the same verb in English should have *both* the function of expressing limited assent *and* that of expressing apparently unlimited assent. But what both ends of the spectrum have in common is as striking as where they differ, name-ly that the item believed is tacitly acknowledged to be beyond complete empirical justification. But while in the hesitant assent case, empirical grounds may be given for just that—for believing rather than know-ing—in the firm conviction case grounds of that type are not appropri-ate, since the issues are issues of faith. While the indeterminacy of the situation or the lack of full warrant, in the first case, leads to a down-grading of the claim (belief, not knowledge), in the second case the strength of the commitment is all the greater the further removed it is from straightforward empirical justification. *Credo quia absurdum*, as Tertullian said. It is because what is said about Christ is beyond belief that it has to be believed.

Most of the examples in Roget of what I called full-blooded convic-tion relate to religious belief, and not surprisingly—given the history of the English language and our cultural traditions—to Christian religion in particular. But the phenomena of adherence to articles of faith are exhibited differently in different religions, and are certainly not just confined to religious experience. Some religions do, others do not, have elaborate theologies, where the key items of belief are to be found. In some the emphasis is on doing, on participation in ceremonies and ritual, rather than on holding certain views. Some do, but again some do not, have well-established institutions to govern admission, control behaviour and belief, and impose sanctions on deviants. Nor is it only religious institutions, of course, that perform such functions. Once upon a time belief in the dictatorship of the proletariat could carry with it important consequences in the form of submission to party discipline, and indeed the converse is also true: membership of the Communist Party implied a commitment to that belief. While belonging to any group—political party, trade union, university, club—carries obliga-tions to obey the local rules, for some groups adherence to certain items of belief is the key and any backsliding on that score is construed as a threat.

Much more could be said about the kinds of items to which full-blooded assent may be expressed or demanded, but I now want to widen my horizons and move from the modern to the ancient world, to offer some tentative ideas advancing towards what I may call a taxonomy of challenges to belief—a taxonomy of the questionability of belief. My exploitation of Roget brought to light a spectrum stretching from hesitant assent to total commitment, and I suggested that what both ends of the spectrum have in common is a tacit acknowledgement that the item believed is beyond total empirical justification. The factor I wish to retain where religious belief is concerned is that positive commitment is not based on an epistemological argument securing knowledge, but is rather a matter of faith and trust in authority. Bearing in mind my own earlier, sceptical, comments about the difficulties and dangers of cross-cultural comparisons in this area, I may now ask how far the data from the two ancient societies I know most about—Greece and China—fit that picture or enable us to modify it.

Both ancient Greece and ancient China produced sophisticated literate elites and works of high literature in a variety of genres (though not always the same genres in both societies, if we allow ourselves the use of the term 'genre' cross-culturally in the first place). Criticism of common and traditional beliefs was evidently possible, and can be exemplified in different contexts from the earliest extant literature on. Yet the modes of expression of criticism were far from always identical, and this provides my opening for my tentative taxonomy. We may investigate who did the criticizing, who or what was criticized, and especially on what grounds. A first obvious common difference is that there was no institution at all comparable to the Christian Church in either ancient pagan Greece or ancient China to ensure adherence to certain beliefs about God.

Given that our chief evidence is literary texts, it is not surprising that we can say that whoever else may have cast themselves in the role of critics of received opinion, many extant writers did so, not just those whom we label (maybe unguardedly) philosophers, but also, for example, historians and medical writers. It is also the case in both ancient Greece and ancient China that it is not just the common mass of ordinary people whose ideas are criticized as stupid (though in many cases one may doubt whether they were actually as stupid as they were made out). Those who think they know better, about how to behave, about the world, about the gods, about the efficacy of rituals, criticize others, their colleagues or rivals, who for their part are just as keen to make the claim that *their* knowledge is not inferior, but superior. The personal attacks on earlier authorities (including Homer and Hesiod) in Xenophanes and Heraclitus are notorious, and that tradition continues, in more or less hard-hitting vein, throughout Greek philosophy. In China similarly, Confucius comes in for mockery in *Zhuangzi*, and in the third-century BCE philosopher Xunzi we have a chapter (6) explicitly attacking, by name, twelve of his most prominent predecessors, including not just Modi, founder of the Mohist lineage of philosophers, but Zisi and Mencius, both notable followers of Confucius, among whose *other* followers Xunzi himself is usually included.

But an examination of the grounds on which criticisms are mounted brings to light certain important differences between what we may call epistemological concerns and pragmatic or moral ones. Let me take the epistemological line of attack first. Though there are some exceptions, a contrast between reality and mere appearance is not strongly marked in China before the advent of Buddhism. Greek philosophers, by contrast, repeatedly employ that dichotomy to claim that their own picture of the way things are gives the truth, while others are deceived by the mere appearances. For Parmenides, ordinary mortals live in a world of seeming, *doxa*, with which his own account of the truth, involving the denial of both plurality and change, is fundamentally contrasted. For Plato, too, knowledge is a matter of being able to give an account of the eternal, unchanging Forms, while opinions, *doxai*, are hopelessly unreliable. But the point about such arguments was that they were in principle to be settled by ongoing, open debate.

That tactic of putting down opponents—to suggest that they are radically misguided on matters to do with the underlying reality—is not the preferred mode of attack in China, which more often proceeds by way of moral or pragmatic considerations—not that they are *absent* from Greek polemic, of course. It was after all primarily on moral grounds that Homer and Hesiod were attacked by Xenophanes and Heraclitus, and much later again by Plato, who further mounts a scathing attack on those among his contemporaries whom he considered to be irresponsible teachers, the sophists in other words.

But Xunzi—to revert to my previous example—repeatedly reprimands his opponents for their moral inadequacies, their failure to recognize basic social distinctions, the uselessness of their teaching for the concerns of government, and their ignorance of how to behave. Indeed he ends the chapter with a section contrasting the demeanour and style of the gentleman, *junzi*, with those of the individuals he attacks.[2] Equally elsewhere, when he criticizes popular beliefs, in demons and spirits and in ways of exorcizing them, by beating drums and sacrificing pigs, he points to the waste and to the wasted efforts—the folly in other words—as much as to the falsity of the conceptions in question.[3] Yet Xunzi at the end of chapter 6 makes plain his ideal: he describes 'the heart of him to whom the whole world would willingly submit', the sage king, in other words, who would govern justly and for the benefit of all. His personal ambition, like that of Confucius before him, was to find such a person and serve as his adviser.

The existence of both epistemological and pragmatic challenges in both China and Greece rules out any general conclusion associating each ancient society with just one mode. Yet it would seem possible to suggest certain correlations between the *preferred* modes of challenge that we find in our two ancient societies and in the Christian West with certain dominant social structures, institutions, and values in each case.

In the extravagantly anti-epistemological mode adopted by Tertullian, belief is an expression of solidarity with the faith and with the Church's authority. Challenge in that context was possible only at the risk of exclusion, of anathematization, eventually of excommunication. In the determinedly epistemological mode adopted by many Greek philosophers, opposing positions on reality battled it out in public debate, in competitions for prestige—and indeed for pupils—but with victory going to whoever could justify claims to knowledge rather than to mere belief. Of course who *had* given such a justification was subject to revision from one generation to the next. In the moral and pragmatic mode we find in prominent ancient Chinese thinkers, the focus was neither on the authority of a Church, nor on rational argument as such, but on what was useful, indeed what promoted the welfare of 'all under heaven'. The ambition of most Chinese cultivators of the Way was not only personal fulfilment, but to influence the way the world was governed, to gain the ear, indeed, of those who governed it, the

---

[2] 'Let me now discuss the conceited manner of your students. Their caps are bent low over their foreheads. Their cap strings are loose and slack. Their manner is insolent and rude. They seem smug and pretentious as they amble about, but their eyes dart nervously around. They may seem complacent, comfortable, and settled, but their gaze is confused and frightened. With that excited and flurried air, they betray an inner impurity and foulness through their wide-eyed stare' (*Xunzi* 6: 45, Knoblock 1988-94: i. 228-9).

[3] *Xunzi* 21, cf. above Ch. 5 n. 13.

rulers of the Warring States and eventually the emperor after the unification of China carried out by the Qin in 221 BCE.

While the first part of my discussion emphasized the difficulties of diagnosing belief and rehearsed some well-known problems in the psychological and philosophical analysis of belief, my brief survey of some of the historical and comparative data, in the second part, has aimed to bring to light certain disparities in the modes of questionability of belief and of its validation. There are, I argued, important differences in the ways in which challenges are mounted and in their implications. One principal factor that must act as a widespread deterrent to anyone who is inclined to deny what is commonly believed is that that may be seen as undermining group solidarity. The undesirability of rocking the boat is felt in every kind of social collectivity, not least in today's scientific communities, although the distinctive feature there is that if the iconoclasts get away with it, and persuade their peers, or at least the next generation of researchers, of the superiority of their own ideas, then their reputations get a very considerable boost. The stakes are still high, even though the sanctions on deviants who do not succeed are not as severe as was sometimes the case where religious heterodoxy was in question. Even so, deviant, or even highly innovative, ideas may always be said to be a risky business.

So why, we may ask, does any individual choose to risk it? Obviously the cost–benefit analysis will vary depending on just how authoritarian the group or society challenged is, and on the perceived urgency of correcting what is amiss. Three main kinds of consideration may well suggest such an urgency, that what is criticized is damaging to the state, that it is immoral, and that it is false.

The first line of argument turns the tables on those who would outlaw the critic as a dangerously disruptive element in society. On the contrary, those critics will reply, unless their own ideas are accepted, the government, the state, the world, is faced with disaster. Over and over again in classical Chinese thought critics fearlessly diagnose the confusion, *luan*, that is liable to stem from current policies. It is to restore order that they speak out, and indeed the record of Chinese thinkers admonishing rulers is truly remarkable, even while some paid for this dearly, not just with loss of favour, but with exile, castration, death—of themselves and their families.

To that pragmatic argument about policies may be added a more directly moral challenge, namely that the views criticized are positively evil, a potentially even more dangerous personal attack on those who put them forward. It is a relatively mild matter to challenge another for advocating plans that will bring no benefit to, or may even harm, the state. It is appreciably more serious where the criticism is of another adviser's immorality or corruption. You do not do that unless you are either very sure of your own ground, or desperate.[4]

But then the third line of attack, less common in China, though well developed in some quarters in Greece, is that the mistaken beliefs must be rooted out because they are false. The appeal is not to their being ineffective or immoral, but to their being objectively untrue. In principle, that argument may be directed at the belief, rather than the believer. Yet in practice the boundary between an impersonal and a personal criticism may be hard to maintain. The fate of the chief Greek exemplar of that line of argument, namely Socrates, shows this dramatically enough.

Repeatedly Plato has Socrates protest that he is not interested in discomfiting his opponents, nor in what any particular audience may think of what he says. He is only concerned with the truth—as if that were a totally impersonal and objective matter.[5] Yet whether or not that was a plea that the historical Socrates often actually used, we know that he was sufficiently unpopular with enough of his fellow Athenians that when the malicious prosecution was brought by Meletus and others, they voted to condemn him. When according to Athenian convention he then had to propose an alternative to the death sentence demanded by the prosecution, he first claimed that what he deserved was free meals in the Prytaneum, and although he retracted that and proposed a fine as his penalty, the majority against him for the sentence was greater than for the verdict—so we are told by Diogenes Laertius (II. 42).

---

[4] One instance of the latter kind is the attack that the prime minister of Qin, Li Si, mounted on Zhao Gao, the adviser who came to dominate the second emperor of Qin and who eventually had Li Si put to death. In an attempt to recover his influence, Li Si submitted a memorial to the emperor that included an all-out attack on Zhao Gao. 'Now Gao has a depraved and unbridled ambition, and his conduct is dangerous and subversive . . . He practises a combination of the seditious methods of Tian Chang and Zihan so as to oust the awe-inspiring good faith of Your Majesty . . . If Your Majesty does not take precautions, your servant fears that he will make a rebellion' (*Shiji* 87: 2559. 4 ff., 8 ff., trans. Dawson 1994). Li Si's plea was to no avail: indeed the next time he tried to get a message through to the emperor, Zhao Gao intercepted it. It was not long before Li Si was tried again and this time executed.

[5] See, for example, *Gorgias* 454c, 457e, *Protagoras* 360e, *Phaedo* 91ac, *Phaedrus* 259e–260a.

The moral of his fate may be that where the criticism of ideas is concerned, those who hold them are always implicated, even when the criticism claims to be totally impersonal. The only safe beliefs to object to are those that are no longer held—and who would want to do that? Meanwhile many criticisms of past figures, in China and in Greece, deceived no one: they were clearly understood to be covert reprimands of contemporaries.

The argument of my last chapter was that the search for a single theory of truth falls foul of the different modes of warranting that are appropriate in different contexts. Our survey here of the conditions of the possibility of challenge to beliefs serves to underline first the different values that may be at stake, solidarity, utility, morality, truth, and then, so far as that last criterion goes, the difficulty of achieving that total segregation of the impersonal and the interpersonal that the abstract analysis of truth, as a property of propositions whoever states them, demands. In so far as persons and audiences of particular kinds are imagined to be in mind, the discrediting of inaccurate ideas may all too easily be taken as grounds for offence. Merely not going along with commonly accepted beliefs may be construed as subverting solidarity, especially so, perhaps, when the beliefs are not such as to be capable of straightforward empirical warrant. The pressures to stay with what your peer group—however defined—accepts are accordingly all the greater, and the range and forthrightness of the criticisms that can be exemplified in both China and Greece all the more remarkable: nor should we underestimate the strength of such pressures even in today's pluralist world, and even in science and philosophy, where that abstract notion of objective truth is most precious and holds most sway.

7

Styles of Enquiry and the Question of a Common Ontology

The companion question to the one raised in Chapter 4—is there a common logic?—is: is there a common ontology? Is there just the one world to which all ontological theories are directed, at which they aim, and which they either succeed or fail to describe and explain? Or should we acknowledge a plurality of worlds, each an independently valid object of investigation?

The two contrasting answers to those questions correspond, very broadly, of course, to two well-known radically opposed types of position in the philosophy of science, the plural-world answer to philosophical relativism, the one-world one to one or other of a variety of brands of philosophical realism. Realism insists that there is just the one world for any scientific enquiry to investigate. So in that sense if we find Westerners and Chinese, for instance, differing, they must be thought to be just giving different accounts of the same world, the only one there is. But against that, the relativist insists that truth is relative to individuals or groups. So in that sense we could allow that Westerners and Chinese do inhabit different worlds and further that there is no single world by reference to which their accounts can be judged more, or less, adequate.

What light can be thrown on these questions if we focus on early Chinese and Greek cosmology? First I shall examine briefly the nature of some of the differences in the world-views we actually find in ancient Chinese and Greek writers. That will lead me to some reflections on the philosophical issues and how they relate to problems of historical interpretation. Building on some familiar, if still sometimes contested, ideas from the philosophy of science, namely that all observation statements are more or less theory-laden, and the underdetermination of theory by data, I want to make a claim for the multidimensionality and openendedness of the data—of what there is for a theory to be a theory of—and warn against assuming that we know in all cases what it should be of.

We need to distinguish between different types of explananda and between the different modes of understanding sought. It may be tempting to think that our modern science can pronounce both on what was there to be investigated and on how it should be explained. But it provides more of a guide in some cases, so I shall argue, than in others. In the next chapter I shall broach the problems of diverging animal and plant taxonomies. In this, my examples of possible explananda range from the shape of the earth, to the movement of the sun, to eclipses, to colours, to sounds, to the cosmos as a whole. With some items, if causal explanation or prediction is sought, relatively straightforward answers are possible, and the problem then is rather whether those were indeed the goals. But with others, different causal accounts can and must be given of different aspects of what comes under the rubric of the same, general, subject matter. Where cosmologies are concerned, the hermeneutic task is evidently much greater. Thus we should be careful not to prejudge the answer to the question of what types of account were originally aimed at and recognize that evaluating them may be far more complex than just comparing them with what we consider we now know.

All theories are perspectival and reflect styles of enquiry. I shall comment in due course on how my use of that term differs from those of Crombie or of Hacking.[1] I favour the widest possible application to cover not just the manner in which the problems are defined and the results presented, but also the implicit assumptions made about how they should be judged and so also the strategic interests and preoccupations of the investigators.

Evidently a world-view does not stand or fall with any single item it contains. But to say that we must judge cosmologies in relation to the styles of enquiry they exhibit does not mean that there are no bridgeheads between them to enable comparisons to be made. No cosmology is totally immune to challenge and the best account of specific phenomena is often the subject of some debate. Aristotle reports the arguments that his predecessors had brought on the size, shape, and position of the earth in *On the Heavens* II ch. 13, 293^{a}15 ff., and the *Hou Hanshu* (*zhi* 2: 3028–30, cf. Cullen 2000) records a discussion of whether the movements of the sun should be measured along the ecliptic or the equator.

---

[1] Crombie used the idea of styles of scientific thinking some time before the publication of his three-volume magnum opus in 1994. See Hacking 1992, who further explains how his own use of the term 'styles of reasoning' differs from Crombie's.

In both cases the participants disagreed about a set of determinate questions and adduced arguments and evidence in favour of rival views—where there was, for some of the participants at least—an eventual, if temporary, resolution. Different styles of enquiry do not constitute incommensurable systems of belief or paradigms, a notion against which I have mounted objections before. Rather the notion of differing styles serves to underline the importance of evaluating individual theories, concepts, and explanations in the light of the wider complexes of assumptions that their proponents made.

At a first stage of analysis it seems obvious that we must say *both* that ancient Chinese and Greeks had different world-views *and* that they inhabited the same one world. Let me tackle, first, the differences in the world-views and consider how far they support any suggestion that we should see their authors as inhabiting different worlds.

Take first what Aristotle, on the one hand, the *Huainanzi* on the other, for example, held by way of cosmological views.[2] For Aristotle, everything in the sublunary world is constituted (so far as their matter goes) by earth, water, air, and fire, while the region above the moon is made of a fifth element, aither, which has the distinctive properties of being neither hot nor cold, neither wet nor dry, and of moving naturally and eternally in circles. His earth is spherical and tiny in relation to the sphere of the fixed stars.

In the *Huainanzi* there is a flat earth, covered by a sky for the distance of which the text gives a determinate estimate, namely 510,000 *li*[l], a *li*[l] being about half a kilometre.[3] The book is concerned not so much with physical elements (substances that are unchanging in themselves, out of which everything else is made) as with the cycles of the five phases, *wuxing*. These are water, fire, wood, metal, earth, but we must be careful. The term we translate water, *shui*, picks out not so much the substance as the process. As the Great Plan puts it:[4] 'Water means soaking downwards. Fire means flaming upwards. Wood means bending and straightening. Metal means conforming and changing. Earth means accepting seed and giving crops.'

[2] *Huainanzi* is a compilation mainly put together under the auspices of Prince Liu An of Huainan before 122 BCE. See Major 1993.

[3] See Cullen's appendix in Major 1993, at p. 288, and contrast Major himself at p. 68, where he amends the figure in the text of *Huainanzi* 3: 4a from 510,000 to 150,000 *li*[l].

[4] The Great Plan (*Hong fan*) section of the *Documents* (*Shangshu* Ch. 32) is discussed by Graham 1989 at p. 326. Cf. Nylan 2001: 139–42.

Nor do the differences between Aristotle and the *Huainanzi* relate just to that fundamental contrast between elements and phases. Aristotle looks out on a world inhabited by animal kinds that are fixed and eternal. The *Huainanzi* gives an account of the origins of each of the main kinds of animals it deals with (humans included) and is, in general, more interested in their transformations and metamorphoses than in what Aristotle would have thought of as their essences. Such metamorphoses as Aristotle paid attention to proved something of a problem in his system.[5]

When we compare Aristotle's view of the shape of the earth with that of the compilers of *Huainanzi* we can say that that amounts to no more than a difference in the accounts given of the same explanandum, a difference in world-*views* in that sense. But when Aristotle focuses on substance and essence, and the *Huainanzi* on processes and phases, it looks as if we should say that they differ in what it is they seek to give an account of and that they are describing, in that sense, different worlds. But however we resolve that issue, we clearly cannot stop just there. We have to raise similar questions concerning the differences not just between Greeks and Chinese, but also between different Greeks, and again among different Chinese thinkers.

Take Aristotle and Democritus, for instance. Aristotle believes there is just a single cosmos, but Democritus held there to be an infinite number, separated from one another in space or time or both. Aristotle sees matter, space, and time as all continua, while for Democritus all three are constituted by indivisibles—atoms—and so one could go on. Nor is it the case that the Chinese all focus on the phenomena that the *Huainanzi* sought to explain. Mencius, Dong Zhongshu, and Wang Chong may all be said to diverge in their views of what there is to give an account of, and that is before we mention such a text as *Zhuangzi*, which famously problematizes the question of whether what we experience as reality is merely a dream.[6]

From one point of view it looks as if we may have a proliferation of worlds on our hands. Yet clearly from another perspective we cannot lose sight of the point that all the thinkers I have mentioned, and many

---

[5] See Lloyd 1996b: Ch. 5, and cf. below Ch. 8 on differences between Greek and Chinese notions of animal and plant classes.

[6] Graham 1989 provides a good introduction to the cosmological debates between different late Warring States and Han thinkers. *Zhuangzi* 2 ends by questioning whether the Zhuangzi who wakes having dreamt he was a butterfly is indeed who he seems—rather than a butterfly now dreaming he is Zhuangzi.

more, recognize, identify, and explain common features of one and the same world, the very one that we inhabit too. Aristotle and the *Huainanzi* were certainly both aware of the sun rising and setting, of the moon waxing and waning, even though they had different ideas about how they move above the earth and how far away they are. We are not in doubt as to the referents of the terms *helios* and *selene*, of *ri* and *yue*, even though the semantic stretches, the associations, and the symbolic load of those terms vary greatly as between Greek and Chinese, and (again) as between different Greek, and different Chinese, writers. The animal kingdom is cut up differently—for example what is included in the group of fish, *ichthus*, or *yu*, or in the main categories of (broadly) shellfish, insects, and the like. But the descriptions of most of the kinds of animals that figure in the accounts in Aristotle and the *Huainanzi* are determinate enough for us to be able to identify (within limits) what it is they are talking about.

Yet there is obviously a risk in carrying that line of argument too far. It would take a very naive realist to be satisfied with deciding our issue simply by asserting that reality is one and the same everywhere—and so all the diversity within cosmologies can be put down to differences in the accounts of the one same world. The fundamental objection that scuppers realism in its naive form is, as I noted before (Ch. 5), that there is no immediate access to that supposedly common reality, no theory-free vantage point from which it can be viewed and the truth about it delivered. Access is always mediated through some conceptual framework, expressed in some natural or even artificial language. We must recognize the implicit as well as the explicit assumptions in any such framework, in the very language within which perceptions of that reality are to be expressed.

There is, then, an inevitable input from the side of culture. Yet that does not mean that *everything* depends on cultural, or social, or linguistic, factors. Just as the naive realist cannot have the notion of an unmediated access to a pre-conceptual reality, so the extreme cultural relativist or social constructivist cannot (in my view) be allowed the claim that the *sole* criterion of what is to *count* as reality is the society, or the group within it that passes itself off as authoritative in the matter.

One version of cultural relativism that has been invoked in relation to China in particular is one that stems from the linguistic determinism of Sapir and Whorf, according to which language determines, or, in a weaker formulation, guides and constrains, the perception of reality. But such a view has by now been thoroughly discredited, both on philosophical grounds and on empirical ones, based on a re-examination of the original Hopi data that formed such an important part of the evidence cited by Sapir and Whorf. Whorf claimed that the Hopi language contains no reference to 'time' either explicit or implicit. Yet Malokti's exhaustive investigation of the issue made it abundantly clear that the Hopi had, and have, no difficulty whatsoever in drawing distinctions between past, present, and future.[7] Moreover so far as China itself goes, Robert Wardy's recent book (Wardy 2000) comprehensively demolished the positions of Sapir and Whorf in relation, in particular, to how the *Minglitan* translators got on with their rendering into Chinese of the Coimbra Latin version of Aristotle's *Categories*. They did not do at all badly, in short, and in many respects not appreciably worse than the original Coimbra translators themselves in *their* endeavours to render Aristotle's Greek into Latin.

Nor do other reductionist views fare any better. Everyone should acknowledge that scientists have always been influenced by what other scientists believe and think acceptable. But that is not to endorse the view that the truth is just what the scientists of the day happen to say it is. The so-called strong programme of the social study of knowledge[8] has much to its credit, not least the insistence that error is as much the historian's subject matter as what is accepted as success. But it is not as if all appeals to objectivity can or should be reduced to covert rhetorical appeals to a consensus. As I argued in Chapter 5, warranting takes different forms in different contexts and domains, and the scientists' claims for their work are subject to more, or less, rigorous methods of verification that go beyond passing the test of conformity to the prevailing view—including, it may be, passing tests that scientific orthodoxy had not previously imagined.

We are faced, then, with an apparent antinomy, the tensions between acknowledging, on the one hand, the commonality, and on the other, the differences, between the realities that Aristotle, the *Huainanzi*, and others confront. To advance towards a clarification and a reconciliation here, we need first to pay greater attention to the matter of degrees of

[7] Whorf 1967: 57–8, Malotki 1983: 625, discussed in Wardy 2000: 14 f.
[8] This is associated especially with the work of Barnes (e.g. 1974) and Bloor (1976), extensively debated, for example, in Hollis and Lukes 1982 and subsequently. Kusch 2002 takes some lines of argument from Barnes further in the thesis of 'communitarian epistemology'.

theoryladenness. It is generally accepted, nowadays, that no observation statement is totally theory-free—even though that acceptance does not prevent the point from being attacked, sometimes, as unhelpful. More importantly, the theoretical elements that observation statements incorporate vary, not just in that the theories are different, but in that the theoretical charge, or load, may be greater or less. Obviously at the lower end of the spectrum, where the charge is less, the possibilities for comparing theoretical frameworks are greater.

The statement that the moon has ceased to shine is less theory-laden than the statement that it is eclipsed, and that, in turn, from any statement that incorporates an explanation of the event (that might be not just in terms of the earth intervening between the moon and the sun, but in quite a number of other ways attested in Greece, in China, and in other societies ancient and modern).

We can talk, then, of a certain *common* interest in various astronomical events in both Greek and Chinese investigations, even though the *specific* concerns shown by different observers differ quite appreciably. Not all but many Greeks and a large number of Chinese considered eclipses to be ominous, for instance, and pondered what they might mean. The Babylonians, indeed, continued to believe them to be omens even after they had a clear grasp of the cycles of their periodicities.[9] But sometimes—as by some Greeks and Chinese—an understanding of those periodicities and an ability to predict the eclipses themselves led to a decline in the belief in their significance as omens, or even to a direct denial of that significance. That in turn brought about a shift in the focus of interest in those who undertook the observations or puzzled over the underlying causes.

In the astronomical case, *our* ability to retrodict planetary positions, or eclipses of the sun or moon, gives us a clear sense in which we can talk about what there was for ancient peoples to notice and interpret (*if* they chose to do so). Some ancient eclipse reports are quite fictitious, invented for political, religious, or symbolic reasons.[10] But others are well grounded. I am not denying, of course, that the interpretation of the records in question is always tricky. Is the text corrupt—and that is not just a question of the retrospective manipulation of what is represented as a prediction. How secure are the dates we can attach to the events

---

[9] Cf. above Ch. 2.
[10] This has been documented for example by Huang Yi-long 2001.

described? Can we, indeed, definitely identify the eclipse the text purports to refer to? But even though we never find (as I said) a pure observation statement, free of all theory (how could we?), we can match the descriptions we do find with what, using our own theories, of course, we can say, within certain limits of probability, was there to be described. But—to repeat my earlier point—that does not mean to say that we can assume that the ancients were solely, or even at all, interested in what we might be interested in, for example the greatest possible accuracy in their accounts. We have, in every case, the obligation to investigate *how* an interest in eclipses meshed with a wider picture.

The point about degrees of theoryladenness can help us to find a way of doing justice both to what is common and to what is specific in ancient accounts of different kinds of phenomena. But we have to recognize first that it gives us no hard and fast criterion, being always a matter of degree, and secondly that invoking the comparatively less theory-laden is appreciably easier in some fields (such as astronomy) than in others (for example in accounts of disease or illness).

But if I now take another example, from a different domain, that will serve to show that what there is for the theories to be theories of is, importantly, multidimensional. The perception of colour (which I mentioned in Chapter 1) has been the subject of many different kinds of study. One famous set, the work of Berlin and Kay and their followers,[11] purported to show that, despite the apparent vast variety in colour terminology to be found in natural languages across the world, the way that terminology was built up obeys certain general laws. Languages with three colour terms (only) always have black, white, and red, to which is then added blue-green, with other colours also following in a regular sequence, up to a total of eleven basic colour terms. This was then regularly held up as proof positive of certain cross-cultural universals, and many other studies, based on this model, have been undertaken to establish supposedly basic features of human cognitive development. In the wake of Piaget, but much fortified by the Berlin and Kay studies, investigators have claimed similar cross-cultural validity for the modular acquisition of concepts in basic physics, basic psychology, basic biology, even, according to Scott Atran (among others), basic zoological taxonomy.[12]

[11] Berlin and Kay 1969.
[12] See Atran 1990, 1994, 1995, cf. Berlin, Breedlove, and Raven 1973, Brown 1984, Berlin 1992, Ellen 1993, Carey and Spelke 1994. I shall be returning to this issue in Ch. 8.

Yet fundamental criticisms have been made of the original studies by Berlin and Kay that have quite undermined their claims, at least. Their investigations focused on hues. Indigenous peoples were asked to name or try to name the colours exhibited, under given conditions of lighting and so on, on colour charts or Munsell chips. But what was then reported as the results, with regard to the colour identifications present in different natural languages, was heavily influenced, if not determined, by the form of the questions put, the protocols of the enquiry. The investigators, or at least Berlin and Kay interpreting their work, got out what they had put in. That is most easily demonstrated by referring to languages where the basic discriminations, in colour terminology, do not relate to hues, but rather, for instance, to different intensities or the luminosity of colour, or even to such differences as those between living things and dead ones or between the wet and the dry. The terms may be related to certain hues and got to correspond to certain focal points on a colour chart: but that is not what they primarily connote. In such cases what they do connote may not show up on colour charts or Munsell chips at all, and that was downplayed, when it was noticed at all, in the Berlin and Kay reports.[13]

Lyons (1995) has followed up Conklin's classic study (1955) of Hanunoo colour terminology to make these points very clearly. The Hanunoo have no word for colour as such. But four important terms with a wide range of application that may be thought to correspond, roughly, to black, white, red, and green are *mabiru, malagti, marara,* and *malatuy*. Thus far, then, Hanunoo looks as if it exemplifies what Berlin and Kay called a stage 3 language, that is one with four basic colour terms, indeed those very four.

But what that interpretation fails to register is that, although those four words can, in some sense, be called colour terms, and could, no doubt, be elicited as such, with suitably framed questions, using standard colour chips, yet, according to Conklin, chromatic variation is *not* the basis of their differentiation. The two principal dimensions of variation are lightness versus darkness on the one hand, and wetness versus dryness, or freshness (succulence) versus desiccation, on the other. A

---

[13] Berlin and Kay (1969) note some non-colorimetric components as relevant semantic features of some colour terms, doing so in relation to Conklin's study of the Hanunoo (to be discussed below) in particular. However, that did not deter them from claiming universality for their analysis of colour terminology and its evolution across natural languages world-wide.

third dimension of variation, relating to indelibility versus paleness or fadedness, again serves to suggest the interdependence of Hanunoo colour vocabulary and Hanunoo culture, interests, and values.

The general methodological problem is clear. The investigation is bound to be distorted if the researcher uses questions that already presuppose the distinctions he or she is interested in. If you show the Hanunoo, or anyone else, colour chips, they will give you answers you can interpret in terms of chromaticity, even though that may be quite artificial for them, as further reflection on their own use of the terms can reveal. Nor is this some strange or exotic feature confined to such a language as Hanunoo. Ancient Greek (as Lyons 1995 also pointed out) exhibits similar features. *Leukos*, often translated 'white', is not a hue, so much as a brightness term, used of the sun and water, for instance—which it would be absurd to think of as sharing the same hue. Again the Greek word *chloros*, the term often translated 'green', connotes not that hue, so much as the quality of freshness, the living, the blooming. It is used of blood, for instance.

That already helps to show that there is no one target account to which all analyses of colour should be thought to be trying to approximate. But both China and Greece further illustrate how, once speculation enters in, colour taxonomies are developed to tally with quite other considerations in what I called the wider picture. One common classical Chinese classification identifies five principal colours (*bai, hei, chi, qing*[1], *huang*: roughly white, black, red, blue-green, yellow; that would correspond to stage 4 in the Berlin and Kay schema, though they made modern Mandarin a stage 5 one with a distinction between what they called blue and green). But that is in part for the sake of the correlations that can be suggested with other pentads, not least the five phases themselves. Aristotle correlates seven primary colour terms with his seven principal tastes. More strikingly, he analyses beautiful or attractive colours in terms of simple blends, where bright and dark are in proportions that can be expressed as ratios between small integers, 2 to 1, 3 to 2, and 4 to 3—on the analogy, evidently, of harmonious sounds.[14]

To conclude our discussion of colour: it is obvious that there are varieties in the perceptual apparatus as between different human beings and as between humans and animals. This is not just a question

---

[14] Aristotle, *On the Senses* 439^{b}25 ff., 31 ff.: cf. 442^{a}12–17, where he makes a similar suggestion concerning flavours.

of occurrences of colour blindness, but also, for instance, of the differences between dichromatic, trichromatic, and tetrachromatic vision.[15] But if colour discrimination is one thing, what colour terminology chooses to pick out as salient is another, where different natural languages exhibit considerable variation. But that is not a question of some being more accurate than others: rather the variety reflects the different interests and focus of attention expressed in the languages concerned.

The analogy with sound may serve to drive the point home. Descriptions of sounds may relate to one or more of a whole range of distinctions, in magnitude, pitch, rhythm, 'colour' (as that is applied in music, as in timbre), harmonies, and that is before we come to more symbolic associations. The fact that both ancient Greeks and Chinese happened to be particularly interested in the analysis of musical harmonies (which they carried out in rather different ways[16]) does not mean that they were the only worthwhile topic of investigation. Modern harmonic theory happens to prepare us to appreciate those ancient interests of theirs. Yet the potential acoustic analysanda are as complex as is the case with colour. The data are always multidimensional. To the point that no observation statement can be theory-free, we need to add the underdetermination of theory by data and the point that no theory can be total.

But now let me consider some of the implications of these philosophical points for our historical interpretations. One brand of positivist history of science pounces on the possibilities of comparison to construct a narrative that concentrates on scientific progress. All interpretation is evaluative, to be sure, but that type of history is preoccupied with the question of who got which bits of the answers right, judged from the point of view of later understanding. It was a large part of Joseph Needham's agenda, indeed, to answer the question of who got which bits of the answers right first—in China or the West. But that is to fall into the twin traps of anachronism and teleology that I criticized in Chapter 1. It is to assume, first, that earlier enquirers had our agenda (as if their analyses of matter and change, for instance, were just so many botched shots at chemistry) and secondly, that they should have known where they were headed (broadly speaking, in our direction). Yet clearly they could not have known what science was to become—

[15] These issues are discussed by Mollon 1995: 138–41 in relation to recent research.
[16] There is a brief analysis of where Greek and Chinese accounts converge and diverge in Lloyd 2002: Ch. 3.

any more than today's scientists can see exactly where their own subjects will be in thirty years' time, or even in three.

Our primary obligation, as historians, I said, is to try to reconstruct, as far as possible, how those earlier investigators themselves represented what they were doing, their definition of the problems, their ideas about how to go about resolving them, their criteria for evaluating results. That is where styles of enquiry are so important. That is a pretty vague expression, in all honesty, and a number of scholars have used it in different ways. Crombie, who at one point was attracted to the notion of 'mentalities', used 'styles of thinking' to contrast different stages in the development of early modern science, in terms of such factors as the use of postulates, the experimental method, measurement, hypotheses, statistics, an interest in genetic development, and so on. Some time before Crombie published his magnum opus, Hacking (1975) gave a very useful demonstration of the differences that the introduction of the modern notion of probability, from the seventeenth century on, made. Ancient probabilities were never more than a matter of what is true generally or, as Aristotle put it, 'for the most part'. When data are examined quantitatively, that affects the way the investigation is conducted, what it is an investigation of, and how the results are presented. A value can be assigned for the probability between 0 and 1—an idea that was simply not conceivable for ancient Greeks or Chinese.

We have already spoken of styles of enquiry in earlier chapters in relation to a number of formal presentational points, the concern, or lack of it, for demonstration, the interest in logical form and the use of second-order concepts of linguistic and logical categories, the contrast between an overt adversariality and a prizing of consensus and of more tacit ways of suggesting innovations. But now for the ontological questions at issue here we need to broaden the scope of what we may mean by a style of enquiry by reflecting on how substantive leading ideas, images, interests, and preoccupations help to create a perspective on the world (cf. Goodman 1985).

Let me illustrate by going back to the two cosmologists I started with, considering now not just the particular views they happen to have held, but their diverging leading preoccupations that influence, even constitute, their world perspectives. Aristotle's programme is indeed difficult to offer generalizations about, encompassing as it does so many different fields, from what he called physics to poetry. But in most fields he is looking for *aitiai*, causes or explanations, where he distinguished four types, material, formal, efficient, and final (applicable not just to physical objects, but also to events, and also to items such as political constitutions or poetic genres). Such an idea (the 'doctrine of the four causes') is not one that can be demonstrated, in the sense of deduced from higher principles: these are (among) the principles that any investigation presupposes and uses in *its* demonstrations, the ones he set so much store on giving (cf. above Ch. 5 p. 57 and further below, Ch. 9 pp. 133f.). True, he did think that he did better than any of his predecessors in identifying the different kinds of causes to be investigated. He did not think he could prove that there must be final causes: all that can be done (and he does it) is to recommend them by exhibiting them and by criticizing as incomplete any enquiry that tries to do without them.[17]

These ideas are so familiar that it is easy to underestimate the difference they make to the view of the world that Aristotle propounds. Since explanation has to be of what is general, and in terms of stable forms, it follows that the transient, changing, particular falls out of the frame—at least as the particular it is. Change itself is often (though certainly not always) evaluated in terms of the end result. Again, he sees the cosmos as an ordered whole, a hierarchy of beings with different levels of potentiality, different ways of attaining the good (their final causes), with humans sandwiched between the gods, on the one hand, and other living beings, animals and plants, and beneath them inanimate kinds, on the other. This is a view that does not just impinge on his physics and his zoology: it is central to his moral philosophy, since happiness, for humans, is a matter of living according to the highest capacity we possess, that is reason. In all of this, we have to adopt his perspective to see what he is advocating: though to adopt that perspective is not the same as agreeing with it, to be sure.

Similar points apply, *mutatis mutandis*, to the *Huainanzi*. That text is not concerned to give deductive causal explanations in the Aristotelian manner. There are plenty of occasions when the text says 'thus' or 'therefore' (*gu*) or 'for this reason' (*shi gu*), but (to generalize

---

[17] We may remark incidentally how Aristotle's schema allows for several explanations—of different types—of the same phenomenon, though that is evidently not the same as the multidimensionality I have been describing, where divergent perspectives are not limited to a matter of concentrating on, say, the material, rather than the formal, causes of the objects in question.

brazenly) these depend on following or spotting the associations of things. The opening of chapter 3 provides a rich haul of examples (1B1 ff., 2A2 ff., 2B7 ff., trans. Major 1993: 62 ff. modified): 'It is easy for that which is pure and subtle to converge, but difficult for the heavy and tur- bid to congeal. Thus (*gu*) heaven was completed first, and earth fixed afterwards.' Again, 'The Dao of heaven is called the circular: the Dao of Earth is called the square. The square governs the obscure; the circular governs the bright. The bright emits *qi*[i] and for this reason (*shi gu*) fire is the external brilliance of the sun.' Again, 'Fire flies upwards, water flows downwards. Thus (*gu*), the flight of birds is aloft, the movement of fishes is below. Things within the same class mutually move each other: root and twig mutually respond to each other. Thus (*gu*), when the burning-mirror sees the sun, it ignites tinder and produces fire.' We find a similar pattern in chapter 4 (7B8–9) (Major 1993: 167): 'All things are the same as their *qi*[i]; all things respond to their own class. Thus (*gu*) in the south there are plants that do not die; in the north there is ice that does not melt.'

The mode of understanding sought here is associative, not deductive. One of the leading ideas that guides the discussion and characterizes its style is that of the associations between things that govern the transformations they undergo. Here classes, or categories, *lei*, are not arranged in a hierarchical taxonomic structure, but used to plot the interconnections and relationships between things. The five phases, for instance, are each correlated with a wide range of items, not just (as noted) with colours, but also with cardinal points, with the sense- organs, with the main viscera in the body, with certain animals, with agricultural products, and much else besides including, for instance, cer- tain characteristics of the peoples who live in different regions of the earth. It turns out that the central region is best: the people there are clever and sage-like, and good at government.[18]

The focus throughout is on correlations, not on essences. The mes- sage is (repeatedly) one of the interdependence, of the five phases, of heaven and earth, and of *yin* and *yang*[i] in all their manifold manifesta- tions. The lesson becomes overtly political when the ruler's own con- duct is the subject of discussion, as it is in the so-called monthly ordinances, *yueling*, in Chapter 5. Just as the seasons, charted by the

---

[18] See Major 1993: 185 on *Huainanzi* 4: 10A–11A, and cf. p. 167 on 4: 7B–8A.

shifting positions of the constellations, follow the regular cycle of the increases and decreases of *yin* and *yang*[1], so the ruler has to observe rules for his behaviour, modifying his activities according to the seasons. There are months for more lenient punishments, others for severer ones, months for the enfeoffment of nobles or for the building of fortifications, and months in which those activities should be avoided. If the ruler deviates from these patterns, the consequences will be dire, natural disasters and social ones (not that the *Huainanzi* distinguishes between them in those terms).

At this point two objections might suggest themselves. Given the clear political repercussions of the world-views expressed in such different styles in both Aristotle and the *Huainanzi*, it might be thought that what we are dealing with, in both cases, is sheer mystification—that the accounts of the seasons, animals, and so on are mere ideology, passing moral and political evaluations off as if they were natural. Yet values, even if not overtly political ones (though sometimes these too), are inherent in all science. Besides, these writers engage in their investigations in part with an eye to the lessons they can yield not merely for understanding, but for how to live. The ideology, in the political messages, is there, but that does not mean that these cosmologies are not also serious attempts to understand experience, both the macrocosm in all its complexity and the human microcosm within it.

Then the second objection would follow the first and attack the very idea of adopting another's perspective to see what he or she is on about on the grounds that it is tantamount (in many cases) to abandoning all critical sense. In empathizing with alchemy, the point would be, you can hardly stop short of turning yourself into an alchemist, or, to cite a real life example from the anthropologist Tanya Luhrmann (1989), studying witchcraft meant becoming a witch. But first I emphasized the contrast between adopting a perspective and agreeing with it. Then while I maintain the possibility of understanding alien systems of thought, I concede, secondly, that the attempt to do so can only be justified by what we can learn from the close encounter with the likes of Aristotle and the *Huainanzi*, that is, very crudely speaking, a different vision of the world and of the place of humans in it.

Let me now recapitulate the main lines of my argument in this chapter. Is there, I asked, a common ontology, a common world at which all world-views may be said to aim? That question must be unpacked to be answered. Certainly the worlds described by different Chinese and Greek thinkers—not just Aristotle and Democritus, the *Huainanzi* and the *Zhuangzi*, but many others—differ widely. Nor are the differences such that we end up just with certain generic contrasts between West and East, for that would leave out of account many important differences within Greek and again within Chinese cosmology.

The differences we find in different world-views can in part be associated with differences in styles of enquiry, themselves constituted by different perspectives and different leading preoccupations, where there are undeniable influences from the side of culture, of values and of ideologies. Thus far relativism makes valid points. Yet that is only part of the answer. Using first the differences in degrees of theoryladenness, and then what I called the multidimensionality and openendedness of the data, we can uphold the claim that, despite the differences in their world-views, there is still a sense in which Aristotle and the writers of the *Huainanzi* inhabit one and the same world, ours in fact.

That world is certainly not one that was accessible to them, or is to us, in a theory-neutral language. It is not single in the sense that it can be defined independently of a perspective. Yet the differences in perspective do not rule out points of contact between what there is for the perspectives to be perspectives of. That is precisely where the multidimensionality of the explananda allows for different, but still related, explanations. It is not that all explanatory schemata, all perspectives, are equally justifiable, or seemed equally justified to the contemporaries of those who put them forward. Rather they were often the subject of considerable controversy. Sometimes, as we have seen, the arguments focused on technical questions, as in the astronomical and geophysical examples I cited from the *Hou Hanshu* and from Aristotle. But more often what was in dispute included more fundamental, strategic, issues, the question of the kind of account to be attempted, or a vision of the world with potential implications for an understanding of the place of humans in it, for human conduct and for ethics.

In the view of many scientists and others, today's science should concentrate on the former types of question, to the exclusion of the latter. Yet while it is perfectly possible to do science without engaging in ethics, it is not possible to do so, I have insisted, without some more or less theory-laden assumptions. Besides a moment's reflection serves to remind us that today too scientific and cosmological ideas are often believed to have significance for our self-understanding, even if quite *what* we should infer from Big Bang, or the anthropic principle, or Heisenberg's uncertainty principle, or Darwin's evolutionary theory— or even whether anything *can* legitimately be inferred from them—is as much a matter of controversy as any ancient cosmological disputes. These points will be relevant as I explore further the differences in different styles of enquiry in the next two chapters.

8

The Use and Abuse of Classification

What influence do systems of classification have on the construction of world-views? How far do such systems form the basic and unchallenged presuppositions of such world-views, or to what extent are they the subject of conscious reflection and criticism on the part of those who use them? Classificatory systems have been extensively studied by social anthropologists, cognitive scientists, philosophers, linguists, historians. What light can an examination of their debates throw on the fundamental philosophical issues we have been tackling throughout this set of studies, namely the conflict between realism and relativism, the commensurability of belief systems, and the relation between science and popular belief? The comparative data of classifications both of natural and of cultural phenomena can be used to provide further illustrations of the multidimensionality of reality and of the diversity of styles of enquiry. This will allow us to follow up and elaborate the arguments advanced in the last four chapters on the problems of a common logic, the search for truth, the challengeability of belief, and a common ontology.

We may start with a well-known controversy, one that stems from a dilemma, or at least from two conflicting intuitions. The first is that natural kinds are cross-cultural universals. What 'natural kinds' include may be disputed: but certainly the biological ones, animals and plants, may be taken as paradigmatic. So the cross-cultural universalist view would insist that lions and tigers, for instance, are lions and tigers in zoos the world over.

But the second intuition is that classifications of natural kinds spring from, or are the work of, culture. That was a prominent theme in Durkheim and Mauss (1901–2/1963), and more recently Tambiah (1969) put it, following Lévi-Strauss (1962/1969), that animals are good to think—that is, good to think with. This view insists, then, that the ways in which animal codes are used to think about other things are enormously diverse world-wide.

My tactics will be first to elaborate and clarify these two positions, evaluating some of the evidence and arguments used on either side. I shall then turn to the role of classification in the styles of enquiry developed in the two ancient civilizations on which I have been concentrating, namely Greece and China. The questions we must investigate there concern first the assumptions made about classes, categories, and domains of classification themselves. How, for instance, were classifications of natural and of social phenomena related? To what extent were any of those assumptions explicitly analysed or challenged? What room was there for what passed as new knowledge to be integrated into existing classifications, or how far did it suggest the need to modify them? Some of those who have argued that natural kinds are cross-cultural universals have postulated a convergence to a single system of classification as enquiries develop. To what extent does the evidence from Greece and China support such a view? But if it does not, or to the extent it does not, can we identify the factors that may account for continuing divergence, whether in the classes identified or in the very notion of classification itself? Classification is, no doubt, a pervasive implicit feature of all language use. But how far was it a necessary condition, for enquiry itself to develop, that existing, traditional systems of classification had to be overhauled and maybe even abandoned? Or how far could enquiry grow within the framework of such systems?

The first stage of our investigation takes as its starting point the blunt, simplistic question: are natural kinds cross-cultural universals or not? Both the assertion and the denial come in different forms: both theses come in a strong, and in a weaker, version. The strong version of the assertion holds that the perception of animal kinds (for instance) is innate—or corresponds to a cognitive module—in *all* humans: the weaker version allows that this is true mostly, of most animal kinds, in most humans, but does not commit itself to this being universally the case. As we shall see, sometimes the claim is that the *ranking* of animal and plant taxa is identical for all humans: but sometimes the claim is to do with the perceived species of animals and plants themselves.[1]

---

[1] Cf. below on Berlin, Breedlove, and Raven 1973 and Brown 1984. As an illustration of the varying strengths of the hypotheses expressed concerning actual perceived classifications of animals and plants, compare Atran 1995: 221: 'virtually all humans, at all times and in all places, categorize the animals and plants that they readily perceive in a very similar way', with Atran 1994: 322: 'to be sure, cultural factors can increase the psychological salience of secondary biological properties.'

The strong version of the denial has it that the classifications of animals and other natural kinds that we find in different cultures are purely cultural products (on a par with their classifications of social groupings): but the weaker version merely insists that culture is the dominant factor, not the only one at work.

Evidently the more dilute the thesis, on either side, the greater the chance of their reconciliation, though there may still be disagreements, however weak the thesis, on questions of emphasis, on which, precisely, is the more important factor at work, nature or culture. By the end of our study, however, we shall see the need to question certain assumptions that *both* sides in the debate generally appear to accept, namely concerning the viability, in biology, of the notion of species itself.

Further clarifications will be needed as we go into the different types of evidence and argument that have been adduced in relation to these themes: but three points should be made straight away. There is all the difference in the world between the claim that there is (or that there is not) an innate tendency to classify, and one that there is (or that there is not) one to classify in a particular way, with a particular set of genera and species. Is the claim that nature (or that culture) governs the finding of kinds (in general)—or the findings of the kinds there are? Some statements of the universalist position are compatible with the former, though usually they imply the latter. As to *which* those kinds are, on the universalist account we ought to know (ought we not?) by introspection which they are: my original example was lions and tigers. On the cultural relativist account, by contrast, it is the diversity of cultures that is cited to explain the assumed diversity in the actual classifications attested across the world. As to how far they *are* diverse, that is a key question, but not as straightforwardly resolvable by empirical enquiry as one might suppose.

Secondly, and relatedly, are we talking about the *explicit* classifications we actually find across cultures, or are the theses theses about what is *implicitly* recognized in those classifications or otherwise in the natural languages that express distinctions between kinds? Are the theses to do with reports of what people *say*, or with what they *assume*—where that can be investigated by asking the appropriate questions or looking at other features of their language. Thus in some cultures where there is no term for 'plant' as such, there may be grounds, nevertheless, for saying that the people in question recognize them as such. One could infer they have the concept, even if not the term, for example if they use a particular numeral classifier for all and only plants (as is reported for Tzeltal, for instance[2]). Thus some (but not all) versions of innatism allow that there is quite a diversity in the actual animal, vegetable, mineral taxonomies in the ethnographic literature, but argue for innate *universals* at the implicit level.

Thirdly, to follow up the last point, is the claim that the explicit or implicit universals pick out what is the case or not? What is the relation between the supposed universals and the findings of science? Some sociologists of science argue (as I have noted) that science itself has to be relativized to the community producing it. On a cultural relativist view, the expectation would be that what a society picks out as the classes or kinds of animals and plants will correspond to *its* science, but on that view that entitles no inference to science as a universal, non-culturally relative, phenomenon. However, not many of those who have led the debates in social anthropology and developmental psychology in question are sociologists of science of that ilk. They tend rather to adopt a naive realist view of science, though the question of whether the universals that the innatists postulate or find correspond to science on that view remains an open one. I shall come back to that in due course.

So much, then, by way of preliminary clarifications of the various ways in which the issues have been presented. The evidence that has been brought to bear is of three major types, first the work of developmental psychologists studying infants or young children in the manner of, though of course not necessarily in agreement with, Piaget. Second there is the analysis of actual classification systems from different societies. Third there is ethnographic fieldwork directed not so much at describing actual classifications, as at investigating what is implicitly recognized by the people who use them (that corresponds to the second distinction that I made just now). In each category, the potential field of research one might attempt to survey is vast. Within the scope of this discussion I must be drastically selective, despite the risks of bias I thereby run. I shall concentrate, in the main, on the work of Carey and Spelke in the first mode, on work such as Brown's done in the wake of the classic paper of Berlin, Breedlove, and Raven in the second, and on the research of Atran and his associates in the third.

In an influential study by Susan Carey (1985), followed up by work

---

[2] See Berlin, Breedlove, and Raven 1973: 219, cf. Hunn 1977.

with Elizabeth Spelke (Carey and Spelke 1994) and by subsequent revisions, the claim was made that young children do not initially have a core domain that corresponds to Living Kind. They do not, that is to say, initially have a naive innate *biology*. Rather, they have a domain of Animate Being, which includes both humans and animals, but is organized solely on the basis of a naive *psychology*. At first, animal behaviour is understood in purely psychological terms—in terms of wants and beliefs, for instance—and only later does the child come to see that biological processes may not be psychologically driven, that is, when the child has *acquired* a new cognitive module corresponding to a naive biology. In 1985 Carey put that transition at around the age of 10, but a decade later (1995: 299) she put it a bit earlier, namely between 6 and 7 years old, while still insisting that naive biology comes later than naive physics and naive psychology.

From the perspective that principally concerns us here, two points are fundamental. The first is that (as in Piaget himself) we are dealing with a *transition*, or maybe more than one, between *stages* in the child's development. So far as hard-wiring (innateness in that sense) goes, it is not as if the child is, on Carey's view, hard-wired for *biology* from the outset, though the innatists may still want to claim that the child is hard-wired to *acquire* the naive biology at a particular stage of development.

The transition opens the door—and this is my second point—to questioning the factors at work, and indeed the possible input from the side of culture in the process. Cognitive modules (some have suggested[3]) may not *require* innateness: but then how they are *acquired* is always going to be problematic. Just how much stimulus comes from the side of culture? Just what is the effect of the acquisition of the natural language of the society in which the child grows up? The study of Western children's development is controversial, as the debate on Carey's results testifies. But the cross-cultural study of non-Western children, by researchers paying due attention to the problems of possible cultural bias, may at present simply not be advanced enough to yield decisive evidence to discriminate between the contending theses. We may note, however, that some studies of the development of Japanese children by Inagaki and Hatano (1993) seem to suggest that they acquire *distinctive* vitalist conceptions, ones that seem to owe

---

[3] See Carey 1995: 271.

something to the Japanese concept of *ki* (cf Chinese *qi*[1]), that is breath/energy.[4]

Reference to the actual classification systems contained in various natural languages takes us to our second main type of evidence. Berlin, Breedlove, and Raven (1973) summarized a very considerable body of data on folk biological taxonomies, the result of extensive enquiries among, and by, ethnographers across the world. This work took as its model the study of colour terms by Berlin and Kay (which I discussed in Ch. 7), imitating its methodology and coming to similar results. The principal findings were that there were five or six general, if not universal, ethnobiological categories that underpin and are present in such taxonomies world-wide. In the five-category version, these are: unique beginner, life form, generic, specific, varietal. Brown (1984) was one who developed this to suggest a sequence in which the categories are acquired—though it should be noted that Berlin himself, in his more recent book (1992), has modified some of his own original positions.

I have rehearsed the general methodological difficulties in this area of research in the last chapter, principally those that stem from the researcher using protocols that already presuppose the distinctions he or she is interested in. The problem, in the work on colour terms, was that when subjects are presented with colour chips, their answers are then interpreted as distinguishing hues, although the basis of the original differentiation in the terms they use may be quite different. So, if the questions put presuppose existing animal or plant species or groups (as the researchers themselves identify them), a similar objection applies. The answers will be matched to the assumed natural kinds, even though they may not correspond to the original connotations of the terms used.

Some disarming remarks by my next witness, Atran (whom I shall be considering shortly), can be brought to bear on the methodological issues and the difficulties that some claims for cross-cultural ethnobiological universals face. Atran himself is interested, as we shall be seeing, not so much in actual explicit taxonomies in the groups he studies (principally the Itza-Maya of Peten in modern Guatemala), as in the implicit categories they recognize. But in a footnote to one of his papers

---

[4] Carey and Spelke 1994 cite Jeyifous 1986, whose studies of Yoruba children have been taken to suggest that there are differences between the naive biology they acquire and that of American subjects: but both the data and their interpretation have been contested (Atran 1995: 228).

(1994: 336 n. 4), and in some comments he made on the topic in an oral presentation to a Paris conference in 1993, he records some of the problems he encountered when he first arrived in the field. He had secured considerable funding to study the Itza-Maya, one of the last remaining groups of Maya in central America. His research team (almost as numerous as the subjects they were studying) were all keenness itself: and yet when they first started to question their informants, they got nowhere. Their, Itza-Maya, classifications were in terms of the distinctions between wild and domestic animals, between edible and non-edible kinds, between land, water, and air creatures, and that, from the point of view of Atran's programme (the quest for cross-cultural universals), was hopeless. It was only when he and his team started questioning the Itza-Maya about what kinds are 'companions' (*et'ok*) to others that they found they were able to elicit the recognition of the similarities and differences they were after.

I shall be reviewing Atran's own thesis in a moment. But for now the point in relation to some of the ethnobiological studies carried out on the model of the work on colour by Berlin and Kay is that the framing of the questions may elide the *original* interests. As Atran's own preliminary experience shows, the folk taxonomy the Itza-Maya (at least) presented him with was not concerned with zoological systematics, but with the contrasts that are crucial for *their* culture, such as domesticability, edibility, and habitat.

But what about Atran's own work, with its very different focus, not on the explicit taxonomies reported in answer to the question of the groups of animals recognized, but rather the implicit ones, elicited by asking which animals are 'companions' to which, that is which are similar to which, and how close their similarities are? His analysis of degrees of resemblance is sophisticated: but there are problems with other aspects of the methods used. His Itza-Maya studies were based on a tiny number of informants (ten in the 1994 paper, twelve in the 1995 one in a comparative study with the same number of Michigan students), and these informants had to be trained ('familiarized') to use the name-cards for different species that were presented to them. They had in some cases to be *taught* the correct names: they were then tested to see if they understood, and any who did not were not subsequently used in the study. Moreover they were questioned on how they ranked, for 'companionship', a variety of creatures (and other objects) that they had never seen. That included the 'robin', but to the objection that that term is ambiguous, as between the North American robin and the quite different European bird that passes by the same name, Atran's once again disarming defence was that it did not matter. Both birds are kinds of thrush, and robins are going to come out closer to peacocks than to mahogany trees either way.

But methodological issues aside, what about Atran's results? Although there was, he claimed, a high degree of correlation both between his Itza-Maya subjects and the group of Michigan students whom he also investigated, and between both and 'science', i.e. what evolutionary taxonomy would suggest, he ended his 1994 paper by challenging the idea that there is a normal conceptual convergence *towards* science, and elsewhere too he has contrasted the cross-cultural biological universals he discovers with the views of science. The ideas that there is such a convergence, and that increasing complexity of taxonomy goes with increasing accuracy, have been widespread in both philosophy and psychology since Piaget himself.

But the problem that arises, at least on a realist construal of science, can be stated in the form of a dilemma. If the cross-cultural universals coincide with science, we would seem to be all innate scientists. Science would then simply confirm what we know all along, thanks to our core cognitive equipment (a view that, as with other, Chomskyan, notions of deep structures, has obvious affinities with Platonic *anamnesis*, the idea that knowledge is 'recollection', in Plato's case of eternal intelligible Forms). But it seems highly implausible to represent the debate in evolutionary taxonomy over recent years as merely the result of more or less accurate introspection on the part of those involved. I shall be coming back to that debate shortly.

But if the results do not coincide with science, how does any scientist come to *dis*confirm what is known as part of his or her own cognitive equipment? It looks, on that story, as if someone has been playing games with that equipment.

A *via media*—our core module gives us some but not all of what science tells us, but there is still more work to be done—still leaves problematic the relationship between the two.

Atran mentions the problem of the 'rupture' (as he puts it) between science and what he calls 'common-sense', but claims that it is not one between what is 'true' and what is 'false'. 'Rather, it is between how the world (ideally) is in itself, independent of human observers, versus how it must appear to people, whatever science holds to be reality' (Atran

1995: 229). But this seems to discount the human input into science, in the sense that, to gain access to how the world is in itself, we as humans have no option but to call on human observers. Moreover the formulation leaves quite unresolved how it is that human scientists are supposed to come to deny how the world must appear to everyone, themselves included.[5]

Besides, what we now think we know, about animal and plant taxonomy, is highly complex and should be deeply worrying for some versions of the cross-cultural universality proposal. Science has not just rejected essentialism, but also radically subverted the notion of species in zoology and botany—so that there is now an immense literature on what Mayr (1957, cf. Mayr 1969, 1982, 1988, Hull 1965, 1991, Stanford 1995) has dubbed the species problem. True, there may be reasonable taxonomic evolutionary order in the higher animals, but that soon runs out with lower life forms. As Jardine (1969) and Jardine and Sibson (1971) demonstrated, to arrive at an orderly taxonomy, the similarities and differences invoked have to be *weighted*, and that obviously risks circularity: you get out what you put in.

Jardine and Sibson identified no fewer than six criteria to decide which groups of populations should be accorded species rank. They were (1) morphology, (2) differences in ecological range, (3) interfertility, (4) cytology—e.g. chromosome number—(5) serology, and (6) the extent of DNA hybridization. Although some of the results of using different criteria converge, that is far from true across the board. In particular morphology and interfertility do not. If just the gene flow argument is used, every *individual* in asexual organisms will have to be considered a *species*, for they do not export or import genes (Jardine 1969: 45), and Jardine further remarked (1969: 50) on the distortions that arise from the attempt to impose a hierarchic classification in such cases as the enterobacteriaceae and the sapotaceae. Nor are the problems

---

[5] When faced with examples, such as whales and bats, where the findings of 'science' appear to conflict with 'common sense', Atran's response is to insist on how rare such cases are, and on how much of 'common sense' remains in place in the face of science (e.g. 1990: 268). Yet quite why science should ever correct common sense, on his view, and quite why science is ever needed, if common sense delivers the way in which we—all of us—as humans perceive the world, are questions that Atran has, in my opinion, never satisfactorily resolved. Thus in his 1990: 2 f., he put it that 'speculation can . . . prevent common sense from exceeding its proper authority—for common sense remains valid only so long as it is restricted to the manifestly visible dimensions of the everyday world, that is, to *phenomenal* reality'. Yet he had just said that 'no speculation can possibly confute the grounds for this common-sense view of things because all speculation must start from it'.

confined to the question of species. The *orders* of plants, above the family level, remain deeply controversial, despite the very considerable efforts that have been made, including by international committees set up for the purpose (see, for example, Lanjouw et al., 1961), to impose standardization.

My rapid survey of some recent studies of cognitive modules can hardly claim to do full justice to the richness and complexity of that work. But it is enough to indicate both the variety of evidence attested, and the diversity of positions that have been maintained. But what about the cultural relativist side, it too with its hypotheses of varying strengths, and it too with its conceptual and empirical problems? The classic studies that date from the 1960s and 1970s, from Lévi-Strauss (1962/1966, 1962/1969), through Douglas (1966, 1970), Bulmer (1967), Tambiah (1969), and so on, showed how the animal code (or rather codes) were used in different ways, not just to make sense of animals, but to make sense of a variety of other things as well. Animal taxonomies often relate to, and can throw light on, kinship relations, marriage rules, ideas of pollution and taboo, religious, social, and moral values generally. But those are not the only ways in which animals are 'good to think with'. The perceived or assumed differences between animals are very commonly used to map both the differences between human characters and those imagined between human races.

But if those general tendencies are very widespread, the actual ways in which animals are so used vary enormously. Both the ancient Greeks and the Chinese, for instance, have animals that stand for cunning, deceit, gluttony, lechery, filth, bravery, cowardice, intelligence, stupidity, cruelty, industry, opulence, and so on: but it is not always the *same* animals in each case in both cultures.[6] Again, representations of other peoples as or as like animals is very common (it flourished in early modern Europe especially), but not only was there great variety on the question of which races were assimilated to which animals, but so too the underlying animal symbolisms fluctuate, even just within Europe.[7]

But as the problem for the cross-cultural universalist is to make any, or enough, allowance for the actual diversities in the animal codes

---

[6] Some such Chinese symbolic uses of animals are discussed in the special number of *Anthropozoologica* devoted to China, 1993. The pig, for instance, stands for wealth and prosperity, rather than filth, in some Chinese perceptions. Sterckx 2002 contains a wealth of material on different aspects of the cultural perception and significance of animals in China.

[7] See Lévi-Strauss 1962/1966: 115 ff. and cf. Goody 1977: 153 ff.

encountered across the world, so the problem for the cultural relativist is the converse. The cultural relativist's strength is in relating the actual ideas about animals (for example) found in different societies to the uses those ideas are put to, in the context of the cultural specificities of the society in question, its value system, marriage rules, social ordering, or whatever. But the converse weakness is that this sometimes makes it appear as if there were *no* constraints whatsoever on the ways in which animals can be so used, as if cultures could adopt any boundaries they liked—whereas what they actually do is, rather, to make the best use they can of the local fauna, from lions and tigers to pangolins and cassowaries. The units out of which cultural codes are constructed generally correspond to recognizable zoological groups even though those codes may also include 'ghosts' or 'spirits' or legendary creatures treated on a par with other animals.

Thus far my comments on the psychological and ethnographic debates have been from the sidelines, for I cannot claim expertise in the relevant domains. I have certainly not myself conducted experiments on 3-year-olds to probe their cognitive modules or lack of them, nor have I undertaken fieldwork on folk taxonomies in Meso-America or anywhere else. But first, positions taken in those debates certainly bear importantly on the strategic topics that I have raised in relation, especially, to ancient societies, particularly the analysis of the conditions under which enquiry develops and the constraints it may be under as it does; and secondly and conversely there are points that come from a study of the ancient world that may be thought to have a bearing on the more general issues at stake in those debates. We have some well-articulated explicit theories in both ancient Greece and ancient China: we do have ancient reflections on and criticisms of them, and we can study these matters diachronically and ponder the reasons why views changed—whether or not such changes were in a direction that might later be taken, either inside the society in question or outside it, to be towards a more accurate account.

Both ancient Greece and ancient China amassed a range of information on animal and plant kinds, including on such matters as the periods of gestation of different animals, their habitat and diet, their predator/prey relations, their methods of reproduction, and so on. On the Greek side, we have, most notably, the zoological and botanical treatises of Aristotle and Theophrastus. On the Chinese, even though there is nothing quite as systematic as that, there are discussions of nomenclature in such works as the *Erya*, there are specialist works on herbals and veterinary medicine, and in the *Huainanzi* especially some sustained reflections on such topics as the generation of animals, their patterns of behaviour, origins, and metamorphoses.

But although in both ancient societies we can trace the development of certain types of enquiries into animals and plants, how far they were motivated by the same interests and preoccupations, by the same programme of research in other words, is a very different matter. We can use our two ancient societies to test hypotheses concerning the changes that take place both in systems of classification and in the notion of classes itself.[8] How far did sustained enquiries lead to modifications to traditional assumptions: how far did they merely make explicit what had been implicit all along? Do the data for those ancient societies support either the hypotheses of the cross-cultural universalists or those of the cultural relativists or do they suggest that there are problems with both?

At first sight significant broad similarities can be suggested between the use of animal codes in China and in Greece. I have already remarked how animal species—though not always the same ones—are used in the stereotyping of human characters. The same applies also to representations of other peoples, where we may note as a distinctive feature of the Chinese language that the terms used for many of the foreign peoples they were familiar with incorporate the radicals for animals, the pig (*shi*[II]), sheep (*yang*[II]), 'insect' (*hui*), footless reptile (*zhi*[II]), and especially dog (*quan*). The last figures in the names of no fewer than nine quite well-known tribes (*di, yun, guo, yao, mu, liao, xun, xiao, luo*[I]) as well as many less known ones.

Then a second point of similarity concerns the assumption of a hierarchy or scale of beings. In general, in Greece, it has often been forcefully argued (Vernant 1972/1980, Detienne 1972/1977), humans are sandwiched between the gods on the one side, and the other animals on the other. They share with the other animals that they are mortal: but they are marked out from them, among other reasons, because they sacrifice to the gods. In China, too, humans, *ren*[I], are frequently contrasted with spirits, or the divine or demonic, *shen*, on the one hand, and with both domesticated and other animals on the other.

Moreover in both ancient societies, those ideas are codified and

---

[8] In what follows I draw on Lloyd 1997 and 1999.

become the subject of explicit elaboration. Aristotle thinks of a scale of vital faculties. Plants possess the nutritive and reproductive faculty alone. Animals, at least according to the usually stated view,[9] possess perception as well, and may have locomotion, desire, and imagination in addition. Humans add to those faculties that of reason, *nous*, but the fact that they share those other faculties establishes their common nature with other animals. Gods, of course, are different, in that they have the faculty of *nous* alone.

That classification of vital faculties is not identical with, but at least is broadly similar to, the stepped ranks of beings that are set out in *Xunzi* 9: 69 ff., for instance. There we read: 'water and fire have *qi*[I] but do not contain life (*sheng*). Grasses and trees contain life, but have no knowledge (*zhi*[III]). Birds and beasts have knowledge, but no righteousness (*yi*). Humans have *qi*[I], contain life, have knowledge and also have righteousness and so of all that is in the world they are the most noble' (cf. Graham 1989: 255). It is striking that where the Greek philosopher distinguishes humans via a cognitive faculty, the Chinese one does so via the moral sense.

Thus far Graeco-Chinese comparisons yield some strategic resemblances, both in the interest in animal and plant classifications, and in a variety of their uses. The classifications, on either side, are anything but value-neutral, and the animal codes, in particular, are deployed to express differences between human types that are steeped in moral evaluations and value judgements of all kinds.

Yet when we look further and deeper, fundamental contrasts begin to emerge. If we take the framework within which the *Huainanzi* develops its observations about the different kinds of animals, in chapter 4 especially, that is in certain crucial respects quite different from what we find in Aristotle. It is true that the extent of Aristotle's own interests in zoological classification as such is disputed.[10] Yet on all sides it is agreed, and it is obvious, that the zoological treatises engage in analyses of the *causes* of the zoological phenomena he describes. This is a branch, one of the most important, of *phusike*, the study of nature, and it is particularly valuable, as Aristotle himself tells us in *On the Parts of Animals* I ch. 5, 644[b]24 ff., in that we can, if we make the effort, learn a very great deal about every kind of animal, not just humans, the kind most

---

[9] Cf. however below for some reservations on this issue.

[10] Thus Pellegrin 1982 and 1986 denied taxonomy, though conceding some classificatory interests, in Aristotle.

familiar to us, but about every other kind as well, however lowly it may be. Yet our enquiry, he hastens to add, should be directed principally at the formal and final, rather than at the material, causes. It serves indeed to reveal the beautiful in nature.

Huainanzi 4, for its part, certainly sets out the main differences between the five main classes of animals it identifies. These are (1) the naked (here identified with humans[11]), (2) the feathered, (3) the hairy, (4) the scaly, and (5) the shelled (16A9 ff.) (cf. Major 1993: 208 ff.). I may note in passing that the *Huainanzi* does not here use an overarching term for 'animal' as such. The word often used for non-human animals in general, *shou*, is here used for the hairy ones: nor does it employ the term *dongwu*, literally 'moving things',[12] while the other generic term available, namely *chu*, generally signifies domestic animals. However, the *Huainanzi* certainly may be said to have the concept, one that corresponds to what these five classes are classes of. At 9B1 ff. (cf. Major 1993: 179 ff.) the text brings to bear a set of paired, contrasting, differentiae, including (1) egg-producers and foetus-producers, i.e. ovipara and vivipara, (2) swimmers and fliers, (3) animals that swallow without chewing and those that chew, that last opposition being correlated with (4) animals with eight bodily openings and those with nine. Further (5) horned is opposed to hornless, (6) 'fat' to 'non-fat', (7) those with 'front teeth' (incisors) and those without, and (8) those with 'back teeth' (molars) and those without. These pairs combine in a variety of ways to yield not a single dichotomous hierarchy, so much as a complex polythetic network (cf. Needham 1980: ch. 2).

But the text also deals with the *origins* of each of the five kinds, and in each of the last four cases (the naked excepted) the structure of the account follows a similar pattern. We begin with a mythical or fabulous creature, one that has, as part of its name, the name of the kind that will come from it. Thus the feathered kind descends from a creature called Feathered Excellence (16A11), and the shelled from one called Shelled Pool. Those first creatures then produce a distinct type of dragon (*long*) each, and passing through a number of other divine or fabulous

[11] *Ba* (for the text, see Major 1993: 312): elsewhere, however, other terms for 'naked', *luo*[II] or *luo*[III], are applied not to humans, but to smooth-skinned or relatively hairless creatures, exemplified in the commentators by such animals as tigers and leopards. See, for instance, *Guanzi* III 8. 1a and *Liji* 6 62, 44. 11 ff., and cf. Yates 1994: 91, 105, on Yinqueshan texts that speak of 'naked' 'insects', the most *yin* of which is said to be the frog or toad.

[12] As opposed to *zhiwu*, stationary things, sometimes used of plants.

creatures (they include the *feng* or phoenix, and the *qilin*) we come, in each case, to the ordinary or common (*shu*[II]) birds, beasts, fish, and turtles, from which are born the feathered, hairy, scaly, and shelled kinds as a whole. The origin story of the naked kind, and of ordinary people, is different. They do not come via dragons, but via Oceanman and sages. Yet by the end of the account, all five kinds are said to flourish in the outside world and to propagate according to type (16B9).

Two fundamental features, in this account, stand out, and will point the way to some radical divergences between the Chinese and the Greek ways of classifying, the interests at work in the processes of classification, and the concepts of classes and categories themselves.

(1) First there is no sense, in the account in this chapter of the *Huainanzi* or elsewhere in that work, of a radical *break* between divine or mythical creatures from past time, or creatures that have never been seen, and ordinary animals. On the contrary, the common or garden animals we know have origins that all go back to the mythical creatures named. This is, of course, no evolutionary theory, nor are what we might call the 'zoological' interests clearly marked off from the stories of origins. That is not to say, however, that there is no sense of the viability of the principal existing groups themselves. They are clearly characterized with definite features, and, as noted, propagate according to type. Yet the framework within which the account is set is one of the story of change and transformation. It is certainly not a story of the fixity of species for all time.

The contrast with Aristotle (at least) could hardly be more striking.[13] One of the main articulating concepts of his zoology—although it usually goes without saying—is the notion of nature itself, and it structures his investigation in certain fundamental ways. First he is constantly on his guard, in the zoology as elsewhere, against what savours of the mythical in a pejorative sense. He repeatedly criticizes 'what is generally believed', 'what is said', or 'what is reported', when that seems to him unlikely or absurd[14]—or he just suspends judgement and demands further investigation or verification. Particular writers, not just poets, but also prose writers such as Ctesias and Herodotus, are

[13] Yet if the comparison is with Empedocles, his ideas share far more of the features of those in the *Huainanzi*, notably in his interest in the origins of different types of animals, and in his readiness to invoke creatures that are not part of ordinary experience, such as ox-headed humans and human-headed oxen, which I shall be mentioning shortly.
[14] Yet Aristotle regularly *starts* his investigation with the common opinions or the beliefs of other, reputable, authorities.

rebuked for their gullibility. Hesiod may have delighted in giving an account of the generations of the gods that eventually leads to humans: but that is just 'theology'. Empedocles, who fantasized about ox-headed humans and human-headed oxen (Fr. 61), is no better.[15] What the enquiry into nature has to investigate is not such speculations, but what is true 'always or for the most part', regular natural processes in other words. What is contrary to nature, *para phusin*, is recognized, in the sense of the exceptions to the general rule, but not as what stands outside the realm of nature altogether.

(2) Then the second radical difference picks up the point about change and the transience of the categories themselves. To begin with Aristotle, this time, it is true that the question of the extent of his commitment to the eternity and fixity of species is, again, a disputed matter (Lennox 2001: ch. 6). There are some incidental references, in the zoology and elsewhere, that have led some scholars to the view that Aristotle did not entirely rule out the possibility of changes to species of animals, just as he certainly did not rule out, indeed he maintained, changes in the distribution of land and sea masses on earth, an idea connected with his view of the cyclical changes that affect the conditions, including the political conditions, of human life.[16] But again to cut through the controversy, it is agreed on all sides that the working assumption of the zoological treatises is that the species of animals he is talking about *are* permanent. Nature allows growth of individuals, without a doubt, but the natures of natural kinds are *not* subject to change as the natural kinds they are.

But if we turn back to the *Huainanzi*, change, transformation, metamorphosis, are not just ruled out: they are the topic of recurrent interested comment. First and foremost there are those original transformations, in the story of how the different kinds were produced by their respective originators. That already shows that the kinds in question are not imagined as unchanging, fixed for all time. To that we may add an interest in the metamorphoses that various species continue to undergo. To be sure, metamorphosis is a theme that, as Joseph Needham showed (1956: 420), came to be much developed in later Chinese thought, under the influence of Buddhism. But that influence is not responsible for its presence in the *Huainanzi*, since that was

---

[15] See for example *On the Parts of Animals* 606^{a}8, *On the Generation of Animals* 756^{b}5 ff., *Metaphysics* 1000^{a}9 ff., *Physics* 198^{b}31 ff., 199^{b}9 ff.

[16] *Meteorologica* 351^{a}26 ff., cf. *Politics* 1329^{b}25 ff., *Metaphysics* 1074^{b}10 ff.

composed well before the rise of Buddhism in China. Yet our text shows an interest not just in the transformations of insects, for instance, but in those of other creatures as well. Certain birds, for example, are said (9B3 ff.) to change into clams. Quite how such ideas are to be interpreted is the subject of some speculation. But the moral to be drawn concerning some Chinese classificatory systems—and what they classify—is clear. The focus of Chinese interest is generally certainly not on fixed, eternal, natures, but, precisely, on change and transformation.

The fact that Aristotle copes, better or worse, with the data known, or admitted, by him on the question of animal metamorphosis is testimony (I would argue) to his readiness (on occasion at least) to respond to the problems by some shifts in his basic positions.[17] But what Aristotle found moderately embarrassing was accepted without qualms by most Chinese observers for whom animal metamorphosis tallied well enough with their expectations of process and transformation.

We come, then, to the crucial question, of the Chinese concepts of classes and categories themselves. They did not operate with the dichotomies of nature and culture, and of *logos* (as rational account) versus *muthos* (in the downgrading sense of fiction). But they were nevertheless deeply concerned with the true characteristics of things (*jing*[I] used initially of refined rice and sometimes translated 'essence', though not in an Aristotelian sense) with their feelings (*qing*[II]), their characters (*xing*), with their patterns or immanent order (*li*[II], used of the grain of wood or the markings in jade), with, indeed, their kinds or categories, *lei*. That last is the term used in the *Huainanzi* of the five main kinds of animals, but it is also used of social groupings—the four 'classes' of *shi*[III] ('officials', 'gentleman retainers'), farmers, soldiers, merchants—and again of rulers and ministers, and more generally 'those above' and 'those below', the foundation of social order on which so much emphasis is put.[18] But further afield *lei* is also used in such other contexts as mathematics, in relation to geometrical figures, that is of the classes of such, though once again these are classes that are subject to transformations.[19]

---

[17] I deal with the evidence concerning Aristotle's views on metamorphosis in my 1996b: ch. 5 and give other examples, elsewhere in that book, of his flexibility in response to the difficulties he encounters in the data.

[18] Cf., for example, *Lüshi chunqiu* 25 2, 1642 (Knoblock and Riegel 2000: 627 ff.) for the general importance of categories, and 25 5, 1669 (Knoblock and Riegel 2000: 637 ff.) for that of ranks or positions, *wei*.

[19] For example Liu Hui on *The Nine Chapters* (Qian Baocong 1963: 168).

But a recurrent key point is this. It is not just that an individual item may figure now in one category, now in another. More fundamentally, the categories themselves are often not fixed entities, but relational, aspectual, interdependent. *Yin* and *yang*[l] exemplify this strikingly. They do not denote permanent essences, but aspects of a constantly shifting balance or interrelationship. What is *yin* in one regard may be *yang*[l] in another: typically either *yin* or *yang*[l] is on the increase, at the cost of the decline of the other.

Similarly we have noticed that Chinese accounts of change are in terms not of essences, but of phases, cycles of transformation, of mutual conquest, or of mutual production. In the conquest cycle, wood overcomes earth, which overcomes water, which overcomes fire, which overcomes metal, which overcomes wood, to start the cycle again. In the cycle of production, the sequence is wood, fire, earth, metal, water, wood. Yet each of these is thought of not as a substance, but, precisely, as a phase, not static, but dynamic and interactive.

Analogously, the classes or categories of living creatures are not fixed and eternal, nor the boundaries between them impermeable. They have a history and are subject to shifting cycles of transformations.

If we turn back to the Greeks, we find the terms *genos* and *eidos* (which do not, as many scholars have insisted, by any means coincide with 'genus' and 'species') used in a huge variety of contexts, either side of, and across, the boundary that many Greeks *did* want to emphasize, between nature and culture. They are applied not just to the kinds of animals and plants, and to colours and sounds, for example, but also to political constitutions, moral excellences, and the genres of literature and types of rhetoric.

There is often a Greek insistence on species boundaries even within what are (and were recognized to be) continua. Indeed some Greek thinkers theorized about such cases under the rubric of the investigation of the *limit* within the *unlimited*. The latter includes such continua as sound, colour, and what we think of as temperature, but the Greeks treat as the hot and the cold (or the hotter and the colder).[20] In some cases what is picked out as the limits, or species, within such continua, relates directly to distinctions made in ancient Greek, the natural

---

[20] One of the chief texts that develops such an analysis is Plato's *Philebus*. The extent to which he is there drawing on earlier Pythagorean beliefs is unclear, but according to Aristotle, *Metaphysics* 986ª22 ff., the notions of limit and the unlimited were at the head of the Pythagorean Table of Opposites.

language. Thus Aristotle's systematization of the kinds of colours stays close to ordinary usage. He focuses on *leukos* and *melas* (that is light and dark rather than white and black) and has five other main colours thought of as mixtures between them. But, I should insist, Aristotle was certainly in no way merely a prisoner of the natural language he spoke in the taxonomies he proposed.

This becomes clear when he finds he needs new terms to mark out the animal groups he recognizes. Thus none of the names for the four kinds of what he calls 'bloodless' animals is well entrenched, in Greek, in that usage before him. 'Bloodless' itself, too, is a new usage, though not a new coinage. Thus *entoma*, for insects, literally 'cut in pieces', had been used of victims sacrificed to the dead. *Malakostraka*, for the crustacea (mainly), literally 'soft-shelled', may have been a coinage of Speusippus, but the other two terms, *malakia*, 'softies', for the cephalopods, and *ostrakoderma*, 'potsherd-skinned', for the testacea, are very probably Aristotle's own inventions.

The classifications of animals and plants in Aristotle and Theophrastus bring out very clearly both their general expectations concerning species and genera, and the extent to which they were prepared to adapt those assumptions to what they perceived to be the data. Despite Aristotle's general confidence that he knows what an animal is, and what a plant, he explicitly raises as a problem where precisely the boundary comes, and where that between living things and the inanimate.[21] In that context, he even says at *History of Animals* 588^{b}4 ff., and at *On the Parts of Animals* 681^{a}9 ff., that nature moves in a *continuous* sequence between them. Faced with certain problematic creatures in the sea, he appeals, in fact, to several criteria, not just perception, to determine animalhood. Some creatures that he accepts as animals have, he says, no perception: yet they are animals nevertheless since they can live detached from the earth, even though he knows of other animals of which that is not true, which rank as animals, rather, by the perception criterion, not the detachability one.

His colleague and successor Theophrastus carries on the tradition of calling into question what was nevertheless a basic tenet of his metaphysics and science, namely the notion of species itself. His botanical treatises frequently problematize the question of where differences amount to a difference in species. He does this with regard, for example,

---

[21] The evidence is set out and discussed in my 1996*b*: ch. 3.

to the relations between the wild varieties of plants and the domestic, to the problems of degeneration, and to the effects of human intervention, in producing, by hybridization, new strains of fertile plants.

In the *History of Plants* (I 3) he first offers a fourfold classification of the most important kinds, into trees, shrubs, undershrubs, and herbs (corresponding roughly to what Brown might call a stage 3 language). But then he remarks that his definitions apply only generally, that there appears to be some overlapping, and that some plants, under cultivation, seem to change their nature, where what is shrub-like becomes tree-like, for instance (a notion that many Chinese thinkers would surely have found congenial). Theophrastus has, in other words, a keen sense of phenotypical differentiation. The upshot is that—as he says— we should not attempt to be too precise: the definitions must be understood as providing just rough and ready classifications of the general type.

So what can these rapid sorties into some of the ancient Greek and Chinese materials teach us about the general debate between the cross-cultural universalist and the cultural relativist with which we began, and about the underlying philosophical issues? We started with the simple-minded question: are natural kinds, principally the biological ones, cross-cultural universals or the products of culture? The one side argues that certain universals are innate, or otherwise correspond to core cognitive modules common to all humans, while the other claims that the differences observed in existing classifications are driven, in the main, or exclusively, by cultural needs and interests.

Both sides evidently take kinds or species as the focus of attention or in some sense the explanandum. But what that seems to leave out of account is that science long ago debunked the idea of essences and problematized that of species itself. There is no one 'correct' taxonomy of animals to which all classificatory endeavours must be thought to be directed. Reality, as I said before, is multidimensional, and that makes room for different programmes of enquiry. There is no unmediated access to reality. But where enquiries are directed, as classifications of animals are, to different aspects of the relations between them, there are no necessary grounds for supposing, rather every reason to deny, that the schemata on offer constitute totally incommensurable systems of belief, between which no mutual intelligibility is possible.

But the fact that different schemata may relate to different programmes does not mean that they cannot be judged objectively with
regard to whatever programme they pursue. You can clearly have more,
and less, accurate classifications of animals focusing on DNA, for
instance, or on morphology. Indeed we can make room also for correctness in symbolic systems, even though that has to be judged not so
much in terms of accuracy, as of appropriateness.

Moreover we can now see that you do not need modern science for a
challenge to be mounted to the notion of species itself. For the Chinese,
'classes' are often relational and aspectual, while some of the Greeks
explicitly raised difficulties about the boundaries between animals
and plants, and within plants, and clearly recognized the unbounded as
continua.

These ancient reflections may stimulate us to reflect more critically
ourselves on the sources of a certain zeal for classification, on its *varieties* and on its *exaggerations*. The taxonomic preoccupation has its
excesses. Of course, we can see that classifications are not just useful,
but inevitable. To acquire a natural language is to acquire a gamut of categories for use in classifying things, charting their boundaries—without which we could not manage our everyday existence. Firm social
boundaries no doubt have their contribution to make to the survival of
human groups, even though some societies seem to need them to be
much firmer than others, and some are quite intolerant of any relaxing
or erosion of those boundaries. It is not just the cognitive scientist who
may argue that there is an evolutionary advantage in being able
instantly to recognize lions and tigers—without stopping to ponder
whether the classes are relational or maybe even culturally induced.

Yet we should recognize, first, that classifications themselves come
in very different shapes and sizes: this is the point about variety. A
Linnaean-style taxonomy is *more* or *less* appropriate to different data.
Presupposing such a style in the interpretation of other people's categories is equally risky. Ellen (1993) in particular, has protested that pro-
cessing indigenous responses to questioning in terms of a taxonomic
model generally ignores the pragmatics of the communication situation
in which the responses are given—the urge to help the questioning
ethnographer and fulfil his or her expectations. That A is a kind of B, and
B a kind of C, may or may not go with any perceived notion of A as a
kind of C, and there are other failures of transitivity that defeat

taxonomy and point to underlying groupings that are non-taxonomic, non-hierarchical, polythetic, continuist.[22]

So variety must be given due weight: and secondly we should be wary of excesses. One of the most obvious examples is the use of animal kinds as a way of apprehending and reinforcing social boundaries, between roles, groups, races, character-traits. While the animal code emphasizes character-traits and makes them seem more fixed and permanent than would otherwise be the case, it does so at the price of stereotyping. Achilles must always be lion-like, even when he weeps over Patroclus. Again, language itself depends on marking differences, for sure, but there are differences in spectra as well as in discontinuous kinds. The gradational quality of many phenomena (like young and old, for instance) may be suppressed in the name of discrete quantum jumps.

The zeal to classify has an untold number of sources. But the constraints under which it operates are of different kinds, and while they sometimes reinforce one another, they can and do conflict, and sometimes that zeal runs up against what resists speciation in the first place. Some bits of nature are better behaved, in that respect, than others. We do not need to cope with clouds in the manner of Polonius,[23] because we can appeal to reasonable enough distinctions between cirrus, cumulus, cirro-cumulus, and so on. We do not need to cope with stones in the manner of Theophrastus, who identified them, often, merely by the locality, for example the particular mountain, they came from. At one, the better behaved, end of the spectrum, we have parts of chemistry. But at the other, there are continua where nature offers no marked boundaries, as with the wave length of light, or pitch, or temperature, or smells.

The rule of species (in other words) runs wide, but it runs out. That has been shown most dramatically by modern biology. But—as I have

---

[22] Besides, even among basically hierarchical classifications, I would insist on a difference between the Greek and the Chinese uses of such. The Greeks see the superior as itself *inde*pendent (so far as possible) from the inferior (as the master is to the slave—or so they imagined). For the Chinese the dominant idea is that of the *inter*dependence of high and low, differentiated though they are.

[23] *Hamlet*, 3. 2:

> 'HAMLET: do you see yonder cloud that's almost in shape of a camel?
> POLONIUS: By the mass, and 'tis like a camel indeed.
> HAM.: Methinks it is like a weasel.
> POL.: It is backed like a weasel.
> HAM.: Or like a whale?
> POL.: Very like a whale.'

argued—it did not need modern biology to bring that to light. Ancient reflections on species and essences already provide some of the wherewithal for different types of critique of common ideas of classification, the development of different ideas of classes, the challenge to the very notion of species itself. It is not that I would claim any continuity between the ancient Greek and Chinese authors I have cited and those who work with chromosomes and DNA. Not at all. Indeed many of those ancient ideas were, from the point of view of their impact, stillborn.[24] Yet those ancient authors began, at least, a process of enquiry where common assumptions came to be seen to be in need of revision. The question of how best, how most accurately, to represent the classes or groupings of things was then thrown wide open—as indeed it remains today.

While animal and plant kinds provide exceptionally rich materials for potential investigation, it is clear that when more systematic reflection began in Greece and China there was nothing inevitable, nothing preordained, about the way that developed. Rather, in each, different opportunities were taken to modify understanding both of animal and plant classifications, and of what a classification is. One route was the route that insisted on a nature/culture divide, and, in the domain of nature, sought, in principle, stable essences, genera, and species— though some recognized that in practice recalcitrant data defeated that ambition. The other route was one that from the outset allowed interdependence, interaction, process, resonance, transformation, while nevertheless seeking order through correlation.

Evidently it was not the case that there was a mass of obvious truths that somehow forced themselves on Aristotle and the authors of the *Huainanzi* as soon as they began to ponder the question of animal kinds and animal behaviour. But no more was it the case that all they did was to produce some theory that corresponded to preconceptions that were built into the social relations or values of the cultures in which they

---

[24] Much use was eventually to be made of the Aristotelian texts that speak of nature passing in continuous sequence between the inanimate and the animate, and between plants and animals (see above p. 111), in connection with the idea of the Great Chain of Being (Lovejoy 1936). But that idea was very different from Aristotle's in this respect, that it focused on the plenitude of creation, seen as evidence of the greatness of the Creator and as confirmation of the special place of humans in the order of things, while Aristotle's concern, in those passages, was rather with the problems of demarcation. The Aristotelian and Theophrastan worries over such concerns tended, indeed, to be generally ignored in pagan, as well as Christian, antiquity.

lived, let alone to ones that were already implicit in the language they spoke.

Let me elaborate those points briefly in conclusion, and first as to language. I have remarked on the coinages that Aristotle made in his ordering of animal kinds. In China, too, as knowledge of animals and plants expanded, so new names were needed and created, even though this was ultimately the responsibility of the emperor or of the imperial authorities. But in neither case should we say that observers in the field were the prisoners of their own natural language.

Then as to inevitability: I remarked on significant similarities between Greek and Chinese animal classifications, in that both make heavy use of animals to express differences between humans, and in both cultures the classifications are hierarchical or otherwise heavily value-laden. Nevertheless in other crucial features they differ. First there is a question of the manner in which debate and discussion proceed. Aristotle frequently explicitly rejects what other learned authors had proposed and what was commonly believed. In his bid to show his mastery of the field, he exhibits well-known Greek adversarial tendencies—though these are less marked in Theophrastus. By contrast, even though several aspects of the account in the *Huainanzi* are distinctive, they pass without being signalled as such in the text. A particular five-fold classification of animals is set out in *Huainanzi* 4 and these are correlated with the five phases in the next chapter. Yet neither text remarks on where its proposals differ from other views, although we know of other fivefold classifications from the *Erya*,[25] and I noted the variety of opinions on what the 'naked' animals comprise.

Then so far as the operative concepts of class and classification go, I suggested a broad contrast between a Greek insistence on stable essences and a Chinese focus on processes, transformations, interdependence. To some extent that contrast can be correlated with some of the salient values of these two societies. Certainly many Greeks expressed the importance of political stability—even though, or maybe in part because, instability was such a prominent feature of the political life at least of the city-states of the classical period. Again, Greek intellectuals, in their competition with their rivals, strove to secure certainty and eternal truths. Conversely interdependence is not just a key

[25] In *Erya* sections 15–19 the five main kinds of animals are 'insects' (*chong*), fish (*yu*), birds (*niao*), quadrupeds (*shou*), and domestic animals (*chu*).

motif in Chinese notions of categories in general, but also an expressed ideal for social relations in particular, for those between ruler and minister, father and son, husband and wife, older and younger and high and low in every context.

Yet it would be absurd to suggest that all that Aristotle and the writers of the *Huainanzi* were doing in their accounts of animals was to read off some conclusions from such assumptions, however deep-seated these may have been. That would fail to do justice, among other things, to the divergences within Chinese accounts that I have just remarked. Most notably, it would fail to explain how, faced with what they saw as problematic data, both Aristotle and Theophrastus raised questions concerning their own assumptions of hard and fast boundaries between and within animals and plants.

The ancient classificatory endeavours we have been discussing bear many marks from the cultures that produced them, from their value systems and ideologies. But they also exhibit a certain plasticity, a certain openendedness, which, in so far as it problematizes the notion of species itself, challenges a common assumption that underpins the debate between the cross-cultural universalist and the cultural relativist. Enquiry has always, to be sure, to be conducted with an explicit or a covert programme in view, and we have seen that the agenda of Greek and Chinese investigators differed in important respects. Yet the results obtained were not always predictable, nor always predicted by the ancient investigators themselves, thereby giving the lie to both extremist parties, both to those who postulate a universal common sense underlying all zoological classifications, and to those who assume they are all determined straightforwardly by cultural factors.

9

For Example and Against

The example of *example* provides us with a further opportunity to examine contrasting styles of reasoning and to probe the issues we raised in Chapter 4 concerning the cross-cultural applicability of the notion of a common logic. The modes of use of exemplification are as many and varied as those of classification. There is the example as an instance of a general rule, as an illustration of, or as support for, one; there is example as a model or pattern, as an ideal to follow or a counter-ideal to avoid—where we may compare the Kuhnian notion of a paradigm, as an exemplar that serves to guide a whole research programme; there are examples used in comparisons, where they may have the role of, or be incorporated in, analogies. We have examples used for the purposes of instruction, of edification, of heuristics, of proof, in grammar, logic, mathematics, the law, medicine, technology, architecture, military strategy, politics, morality, literary style—to name just some of the fields in which they may figure.

The aim of this study is to assess the strong and weak points of those varied uses and thereby throw light on the corresponding styles of enquiry that they help to constitute. One of the key questions, in that regard, relates to the degree of explicitness expected or demanded in sequences of argument. We can, through the study of example, trace the effects of the formulation of certain rules governing inference. This will turn out to be not a matter of a contrast between two supposedly alternative formal logics (the issue I discussed in Chapter 4) so much as one between more formal and more informal modes of reasoning. Once certain canons of validity have been set up, they can be appealed to in order to privilege certain modes of argument and downgrade others that do not meet their standards. But deductive rigour and explicitness have, as we shall see, their drawbacks as well as their strengths, in the varying contexts of argument that we have to consider.

In our analysis of informal techniques of persuasion, we shall need to pay attention not just to the availability of certain rules of argument, but also more generally to the pragmatics of communicative exchanges. That includes both what is left implicit in what is said and what can be assumed to be understood thanks to canons of relevance and cooperation (see above Ch. 4). It may also include such matters as the interpersonal relations and statuses of those between whom the communication takes place, and the more or less stylized, more or less routine, situations in which it happens. There indeed people and places may count, but it is not so much differences between whole cultures that may be significant, as those between, for example, the communicative acts that take place in a temple, a palace, a law court, a political assembly, or a market place.

The richness and variety of the use of examples in classical Chinese literature are such as to defeat any ambition to undertake a comprehensive survey. Nevertheless some attempt must be made to indicate some of the range of uses. We shall begin with some types that may seem familiar enough, before turning to some rather more surprising ones, and then proceeding to the first steps in a comparison between China and Greece.

First, in a whole range of practical contexts, examples are invoked in classical Chinese texts as precedents to help decide or influence courses of action in statesmanship, in warfare, in dealing with questions of right and wrong and of punishment in law, in medical diagnosis and treatment, and so on.[1] Discussion of policy regularly proceeds by way of the citation of cases presented or claimed as similar to the one in hand, with clear beneficial consequences to encourage or dire ones to deter. One of the functions of Annalistic writing, from the *Spring and Autumn Annals* (*Chunqiu*) and the commentary tradition on them, such as the *Zuo Zhuan*, onwards, may have been to act as repositories of useful historical precedents.[2]

---

[1] Thus we find individual case histories recorded in classical Chinese medicine in ways that are similar to, though to be sure not identical with, those in Greek or Egyptian medicine. The case histories of Chunyu Yi, set out in *Shiji* 105, have, in the first instance, an apologetic function: they support his claims as a reputable doctor. At the same time such histories provided information that could be of use in dealing with other patients. In Greece, in the classical period, the case histories in the *Epidemics* served as a database on which doctors could draw in arriving at diagnoses and prognoses, and as we shall see, the application of the lessons from one example to another became a key methodological principle in Hellenistic medicine. See further Hsu 2002.

[2] I have analysed this in Lloyd 2002: ch. 1.

To cite just one concrete instance, among many hundreds, of this type of argumentative use of examples, there is the account in Sima Qian's *Shiji* 87: 2541–2 of the response made by Li Si, when prime minister of Qin, to a proposal that foreigners should be removed from the state, a move that threatened Li Si himself since he was not a native of Qin. Li Si submitted a memorial to the throne which consists, in the first instance, of a sequence of cases where the rulers of Qin had gained enormously from the presence and advice of those brought in from outside the state. He details in particular the military successes and advantageous alliances made in the reigns of Duke Mu, Duke Xiao, King Hui, and King Zhaoxiang and concludes: 'yet supposing these four rulers had rejected aliens and not admitted them, kept such public servants at a distance and not given them employment, this would have meant that the state would be without the reality of wealth and profit and that Qin would lack the reputation for strength and greatness' (trans. Dawson).

In the sphere of the law, especially, the collection of precedents appears often to have been systematic—to the point where we find in the *Hanshu* a complaint expressed that their enormous number was defeating the purpose of clarifying the issues and leading to confusion. Corrupt officials were exploiting their very variety for their own private ends.[3] It was never the case, of course, that the applicability of a particular precedent to a particular further concrete problem was beyond all question, and the reputations of some notable jurists, such as Dong Zhongshu, were built up on their skills in interpretation in this regard (Bourgon 1997).

Sometimes, as often in philosophical discourse, a more general moral is drawn from a specific real or imagined instance. Mencius' general claim was that human nature is good. To show that, as he puts it, 'everyone has a heart that rejects what is intolerable', he asks at 2A6 (cf. A. Cheng 1997) what people do automatically if they see a child about to fall down a well. Their immediate reaction would be one of fear and empathy, unprompted by any thoughts of ingratiating themselves with the child's parents, or by any desire for being well thought of among their neighbours, or by any aversion for the child's screams.

Our own response to the citation of examples in such cases may be unproblematic. But it is important not to underestimate the extent to

---

[3] *Hanshu* 23 states that, in relation to the death penalty, there were 409 articles covering 1,882 cases, and that there were no fewer than 13,472 cases of judicial precedents for crimes deserving death. The chapter is analysed in detail by Hulsewé 1955.

which their openendedness could be and was exploited. This is the crucial characteristic of example when considered as a style of argument. In some cases the lesson to be drawn from them is anything but transparent, and while that may look like fudge or ambiguity, it may sometimes have the advantages not just of discretion but also of suggestiveness. The relevance of the example to the issue in hand can be developed in more than one direction.

Take the advice that Mencius offers to King Hui of Liang (1A3). The king complains that his careful policies are not leading to the increase in prosperity that he would expect, in particular not to the influx of population from other states that many of the sage kings of the past enjoyed. Mencius replies by taking an example from war, a subject dear to the king's heart. Take two groups of soldiers in battle, one of which flees 100 paces and then stops, the other of which flees only 50 paces and then does so. Would the latter be in any position to laugh at the former? The king duly says no, and Mencius concludes by saying that he should not long for a population greater than that of neighbouring states. Clearly the reference to fleeing soldiers, both groups of which are open to criticism, *could* be taken to suggest that King Hui too is far from perfect. Yet that is not spelt out: indeed it is an implication that could, if need be, be denied. Certainly the respect in which he may be falling short is not specified. The reference to fleeing soldiers is no more than obliquely suggestive and it leaves all the work of interpretation still to do.

Both the prizing of an ability to grasp meaning without having to have it spelt out, and the advantages of examples and analogies in general, are the subject of explicit comments, in certain contexts, in Chinese philosophical texts. In the *Lunyu* (*Analects*) (7.8), Confucius famously says that he will teach only those with a burning desire to learn. If he encounters a person who, when shown one corner, is unable to find the other three for himself, Confucius would not repeat the lesson. Then in a passage in the *Shuo yuan* (11.8, 87.22 ff.), when Hui Shi is criticized for not speaking directly, but using comparisons, he replies with a further comparison or example to illustrate his point of view. If someone does not know what the characteristics of a *dan* are, to give the answer 'like a *dan*' is totally uninformative. But if he is told that it is like a bow, but with a string made of bamboo, then he would understand. That is not to offer a formal analysis of example, of course, but, appropriately enough, to illustrate its usefulness with an example of example in action.

However, while in some cases relating to advice in practical situations a Western response might be to ask for greater explicitness in the point that the example is used to make, in some Chinese mathematics the working examples given are as concrete as can be: yet their relationship to the general rules they exemplify remains, at points, puzzling. The *Nine Chapters* itself consists very largely of questions and answers on specific problems. But quite how the answers (correct as they are) are obtained is generally not the subject of comment in the text itself—nor is the relationship between the different procedures to be used—though both points are certainly addressed in the commentators, beginning with Liu Hui. I shall come back later to the analysis of the style of mathematical reasoning that is here in play.

In one striking and recurrent respect the citation of examples from the past proceeds very differently in China from in classical Greece. This relates to the construction of the image of the distant past; in the Chinese case, the stories, accepted on all sides with few variations, that concerned the sequences of figures of rulers who were exemplary either for their wisdom (Yao, Shun, Yu) or for their cruelty (Jie, Zhou). The Greeks had no sage kings to look back to in the same way, for their Golden Age was one of a totally different cosmic dispensation. It was certainly not one ruled over by individuals whom ordinary mortals could use as models. Again, where the figures of exemplary, but historical, teachers are concerned, Confucius is an inspiration for many (though not of course for all) for his life. As for Socrates, however, it is for his death as well as for his life that he served as model, for Plato, for Xenophon, or later for the Stoics (cf. A. Cheng 1997). Moreover a third related difference concerns the status of the texts in which authoritative teaching is conveyed. The Greeks of the classical period had no writings with the canonical status of the *Spring and Autumn Annals* or the *Odes* (*Shi*[IV]).[4]

Those categorical denials need, to be sure, some qualifying. Homer's epics were certainly revered as works of literary genius, and the persons he portrayed provided many heroic models for character types, Nestor for the wise counsellor, Odysseus for cunning intelligence (*metis*), Ajax

---

[4] The situation changes, however, in this regard, in later periods. From Hellenistic times onwards, some of the great authors of the classical period, Hippocrates, Plato, Aristotle, as well as Homer himself, were treated with a reverence that borders on that accorded to the Chinese classics, even though none of those Greek authors became the basis of a core curriculum for a state academy.

and Achilles for two kinds of courage, one stubborn, the other impetuous. Even so as a source of inspiration and reflection, neither Homer nor Hesiod ever achieved the astonishing ascendancy that the Chinese classics did (Nylan 2001), and both were often the subject of criticism and even ridicule.

Of course there is no shortage of examples of the Greeks citing examples for argumentative purposes in many of the same ways as the Chinese did. These might be derived from fact, or fiction, from history, or mythology, or from what was—conveniently—not clearly categorized as either. Phoenix, trying to persuade Achilles to set aside his wrath, tells a long story about Meleager (*Il* 11 529 ff.), whose refusal to fight for the Aetolians, in what are represented as similar circumstances, led to dire consequences. Similarly the speeches of the classical Greek orators, and those we find in the *Histories* of Herodotus and, more especially, Thucydides, are full of what are offered as parallels to the situation in hand, with varying degrees of persuasive success.

There are certainly variations, as between one Greek author and another, just as there are within Chinese writers, in the frequency of recourse to examples, in the types preferred, and in the extent to which the general lessons to be extracted from them are made explicit. But the procedures of thought are, for sure, broadly the same.

In this regard, something of a high point is reached, in ancient Western military thought, in the first-century BCE Roman writer Frontinus, whose *Stratagems*, extant in four books, consists of nothing but a massive collection of examples culled from Greek and Latin literature and history. Book I chapter 1, for instance, starts off with thirteen cases of 'concealing one's military plans'. I 5 gives no fewer than twenty-eight examples of 'escaping from difficult situations', the majority of them Roman, but including six Greek and four Carthaginian. By contrast, the discussion of the art of war in the *Sunzi* seems appreciably more abstract in orientation and far readier than Frontinus to advance general theories: nor is this the only instance that might be cited to undermine common preconceptions as to the greater concentration on the particular in Chinese thought.[5]

There is no doubt that both Chinese and Greek reasoners appreciated very well that a number of moves can be made to counter an opponent's

---

[5] I shall be returning later to the general interests that underlie the citation of particulars in classical Chinese mathematics, for instance: see below pp. 136ff.

use of an example. Its relevance or applicability can be challenged: it can be reinterpreted to support your own, rather than your opponent's, case; it can be neutralized or overwhelmed by other counter-examples. Texts such as *Zhanguoce* are full of argumentative moves and counter-moves of these and other types, and much of the discussion in the *Yantielun*, the *Discourse on Salt and Iron*, proceeds by way of the citation of cases by the Grand Secretary and the Worthies against one another. Thus in one section of the debate the Grand Secretary opens with the argument that the fact that Yu and Tang had to contend with floods and droughts shows that heaven produces such misfortunes even in the time of good rulers (so, by implication, the present administration cannot be blamed for current calamities). To that the Worthies counter that when the Duke of Zhou cultivated himself (and was truly virtuous) there was Great Peace from heaven, no lean years, no violent rain or wind.[6]

Similar citations of examples and counter-examples are common enough also in Greece. But in some Greek writers a different type of challenge is mounted, not to the use of this or that example in this or that context, but to reasoning based on examples as a whole. Explicit analyses of various uses are undertaken that bring to light certain fundamental shortcomings when judged from the standpoint of strict validity. This is where formal logic begins to impinge on the issue. Aristotle is primarily responsible, in his analysis of what he calls the 'paradigm' (*paradeigma*) in the *Prior Analytics* and the *Rhetoric*.

First, however, we need to consider the background, both earlier analyses of reasoning by example in general, in Plato in particular, and doubts about particular uses. So far as the latter go, Greek suspicions of the citations of authoritative *exempla* may be said to be part of Greek suspicions of authority in general—though we must recognize that not all Greeks shared such a viewpoint.[7] The polyvalencies and inconsistencies of myth were, early on, appreciated as undermining its value as a source for models. The trouble about citing Zeus as the upholder of the authority of fathers and kings was that his own unfilial behaviour, in overthrowing his father Cronos, who had himself castrated his father

---

[6] *Yantielun* 6. 8, 48. 25 ff. How far this work, generally dated to the first century BCE, represents an actual, as opposed to a fictionalized, debate on the matters of state policy concerned is disputed.

[7] In particular, as already noted, there is a shift in attitudes towards authority, in the sense of authoritative texts, in the Hellenistic period.

Ouranos, ruined the point. Already in the sixth and fifth centuries BCE Xenophanes and Heraclitus might blame Homer and Hesiod for ascribing immoral behaviour to the gods (as in Xenophanes Fr. 11); but there was no way in which Greek mythology was going to be purged of all but its morally uplifting stories.

Plato had his share of criticisms to make of those who, in his view, made perverse use of the myths. But far more importantly, he also takes the first steps towards the more abstract analysis and evaluation of certain modes of argument as such. First, the dialogues contain, at different junctures, a variety of warnings against arguments based on images (*eikones*), the merely plausible or probable (*pithanologia*) or similarities (*homoiotetes*). In the *Sophist* (231a), for instance, the Eleatic Stranger is made to remark, about similarities in general, that they are a 'slippery tribe' and one should be on one's guard against them, and in both the *Phaedo* (92cd) and the *Theaetetus* (162e) a pointed contrast is drawn between merely probable arguments, based on an image or an analogy, and proper demonstrations (*apodeixeis*).

Yet as both Robinson (1941/1953) and Goldschmidt (1947), among others, showed a long time ago, Plato also has a positive role for examples, in the form of what he calls the paradigm, in two very different types of context especially. First, the Forms themselves are paradigms in the sense of the models which particulars resemble or imitate (e.g. *Republic* 592b), although quite how we are to understand that 'resemblance' or 'participation' is, of course, one of the central and most disputed issues in the interpretation of Plato. What is beyond dispute, however, and of cardinal importance with regard to the Chinese comparison, is that in this Greek writer, as in many others, the ideal is a *static*, not a dynamic one. Greek models, in general, indeed, tend to have to be *unchanging*, for fear of proving inimitable.

So on the one hand, an ontological and epistemological gap opens up, between the intelligible models and the perceptible particulars. On the other, that gap cannot afford to be, and is not, unbridgeable. It is not that Plato denies the possibility of *any* account of the physical world, for after all he presents one himself in the *Timaeus*. There the perceptible cosmos, described as 'greatest and best and fairest and most perfect' (of living things) (92c), is represented as the result of the work of the Demiurge or Craftsman, who imposes order on a pre-existing disorder.

But 'paradigms' also figure in a different role, with both didactic and heuristic functions, in the *Sophist* and *Politicus* especially. In the latter dialogue the Eleatic Stranger explains by offering a paradigm of para-digm itself.[8] He takes the case of children learning to read. When they have learned to distinguish each of the letters in the shortest and easiest syllables, but cannot yet identify them in other, more difficult, combi-nations, then the best way of teaching them is to 'lead them first to those syllables in which they judged the letters correctly, and then to set them in front of the syllables which they do not yet know; then putting them side by side, to point to the same likeness and nature existing in both combinations' (*Politicus* 278a f.).

This illustrates very nicely the didactic function, where the teacher in question evidently knows both the easy and the difficult cases and can guide the pupil from the former to the latter. Yet in both the *Sophist* and the *Politicus* the paradigms chosen (angling, weaving) not only provide practice in the method to be used in searching for a definition, but also turn out to be particularly relevant to the substantive enquiry on which they are engaged, namely tracking down the sophist, and the statesman, respectively. There are, for instance, important resemblances, so we are told, between the arts of weaving and of statesmanship (*Politicus* 308d ff.). In the latter case, it is a matter of being able to unify the diverse elements that go to make up the state. But if that ideal seems close enough to certain Chinese ideas, notably in the Confucian tradition, we should not underestimate the differences in the ways of achieving that unification. Plato cannot and does not just rely on the effect of the statesman's character, his virtue, to provide an ideal that ordinary citi-zens are to follow. As for the paradigm, however, the dialectician, it seems, can and does use them in a heuristic, not just a didactic, role, in situations where he does not know in advance the points of similarity in the particulars compared, as well as in situations where he does.

It was clearly not fortuitous that Aristotle too used the term 'para-digm' in his analyses of a mode of argumentation that he deems dis-tinctly inferior to strict demonstrative syllogistic. As for Plato's claim that the Forms are paradigms in the sense of models, Aristotle dis-misses that as nonsense and as mere poetic metaphor (e.g. *Metaphysics* 991^{a}20 ff.).

In his analysis of rhetorical argumentation, he distinguishes three types of argument based on paradigms (*Rhetoric* II 20, 1393^{a}22 ff.). First

---

[8] Compare Hui Shi, cited above p. 121, who also justified his use of comparison/example by employing one, though without explicitly remarking that that was what he did.

there is the citation of past events; then comparisons (*parabolai*, here illustrated with reference to what are called 'Socratic' arguments, where, for instance, politics is compared with such arts or skills as archery and navigation); and third, stories or fables (*logoi*, exemplified here by Aesop's animal fables). All three involve the appeal to a particular case that is either assumed or asserted to be like the case it illustrates. The paradigm, on this account, is the counterpart, in rhetoric, of induction, *epagoge*, just as the enthymeme, the other main type of rhetorical argument, is the counterpart of syllogism in the strict sense.[9] But one fundamental general difference between the rhetorical and the strictly demonstrative modes of argument consists in the fact that the former are based on probable, the latter on necessary, premisses.

Aristotle thereby strikes a double blow against some of the commonest types of argument that had figured in Greek thought and that can, indeed, be exemplified in any human reasoning in any language. First, the paradigm is classified as rhetoric and as such contrasted unfavourably with proper, philosophical reasoning. Secondly, both the paradigm and induction are subordinate to their corresponding deductive modes of argument, the enthymeme and the (strict) syllogism. When induction is investigated, at *Prior Analytics* II 23, 68^{b}15 ff., it is indeed *reduced* to the syllogism, in a surprising but very telling move. For an induction to be valid, Aristotle claims, *all* the particular instances that come under a general rule must be passed under review. This is what we call complete induction, often criticized first for the fatuity of merely accumulating examples (as if their number were somehow relevant), and secondly for the lack of any guarantee that any induction will ever *be* complete (the central problem of induction when viewed from the standpoint of deduction).

At this point it is worth comparing general analyses of argument from other traditions. The Greeks were not alone in attempting such in early times, for both the Indians and the Chinese also certainly did, even though the Chinese studies pose exceptional problems of interpretation. The fragments of Mohist logic, in particular, afford tantalizing glimpses of the discussion of the use of illustrations, parallels, and so on. In the reconstruction that Graham (1989: 154 f.) has offered, the steps in the account of how 'robbers are people' may be linked with 'killing

[9] On the background to Aristotle's theory of the enthymeme and his own use of it, see Burnyeat 1994a.

robbers is not killing people' involve the following explanations of terms: ' "Illustrating" is referring to another thing to make it clearer. "Parallelising" is putting sentences side by side and letting all proceed. "Adducing" is saying "if it is so in your case, why may it not be so in mine too?" "Inferring" is using something in which the one he rejects is the same as those he accepts to make him accept the former'.[10]

Such texts leave most of the hard work of interpretation for the reader still to do, but they are certainly suggestive of logical interests that are not otherwise well represented in extant classical Chinese writings. We see the beginnings of an explicit classification of argumentative moves, though how far that was combined with an analysis of the conditions of valid inference is unclear and disputed. So too is the answer to the further question as to why these Mohist studies appear not to have been followed up. It would be tempting to suggest that the mainstream of classical Chinese thought was more concerned with the content of arguments than with their form, but that would be a restatement of the problem, not an explanation. It would leave out of account that we certainly have powerful analyses of the psychology of persuasion (for example in *Hanfeizi*, cf. above Ch. 4 p. 45) and such a judgement may well just reflect our present state of knowledge and the bias and lacunae in our sources.

As for Indian logic, notably that from the Nyaya school,[11] here both the general similarities to, and the specific differences from, Aristotle are revealing. The first relate precisely to the analysis of arguments, while among the latter is the very different role assigned to example.

[10] This comes from the treatise that Graham reconstructed under the title *Ming shi* (*Names and Objects*), namely ch. 11, trans. Graham 1989: 155, corresponding to ch. 2 of the work that figures as *Xiaoqu* (*Choosing the Lesser*) in the *Mozi* canon. Johnston (2000 and forthcoming) offers rather different renderings of the four key terms, namely 'comparing' (for *pi*, Graham's 'illustrating'), 'equating' (*mou*, Graham's 'parallelising'), 'citing' or 'drawing an analogy' (*yuan*, Graham's 'adducing') and 'inducing' or 'inferring' (*tui*, Graham's 'inferring'). It is agreed on all sides, however, that examples also play a key role, in Mohist logic, in the relationship between the so-called Canons (or general principles) and the accompanying Explanations, in that the latter almost always proceed by way of examples. Some of these too are, nevertheless, extremely obscure, and we may presume would have been the subject of extensive glossing. Thus in A 77 the definition of *shi*[v] in the Canon reads, in Graham's translation: 'to tell, a reason'. The Explanation proceeds: 'To give orders is to "tell": the thing does not necessarily come about' (i.e. as Graham puts it, one can command without being obeyed). We then have, initially much more surprisingly: 'Dampness is a "reason": it necessarily depends on what is done coming about', where Graham glosses this as a reference to dampness as a cause of illness, one of the stock Mohist examples of a phenomenon with multiple causes, so that it does not operate as a cause unless it brings about illness.

[11] On the interpretation of the Nyaya analysis of the role of example, see especially Biardeau 1957, Matilal 1971, 1985, Zimmermann 1992, Mohanty 1992.

What has, quite misleadingly, been termed the Nyaya 'syllogism' proceeds in five stages. (1) First there is an assertion (in the standard example: 'there is fire on the hill'). (2) Second, the evidence ('there is smoke'). (3) Third, example ('that there is no smoke without fire can be seen, for example, in the kitchen'). (4) Fourth, the application (of that example to the fire on the hill), and (5) fifth, the conclusion ('so there is fire on the hill'). Everything depends, of course, on there being an *invariable* association of smoke with fire, for which the term is *vyapti*. But that is secured not by means of an induction, but by the citation of the example in step (3).

From the standpoint of his, quite different, interests, Aristotle's reaction to such an analysis would have been very negative. His interests, in the *Prior Analytics*, focused not on the component steps through which inferences may proceed, but, precisely, on the formal conditions of validity. In that context, at least, he insists that, for induction, *all* the particulars have to be passed under review. Even though elsewhere (for example *Posterior Analytics* 71^{a}6 ff., *Topics* 105^{a}11 ff., *Rhetoric* 1356^{b}12 ff.) he omits that condition when speaking more loosely of proceeding by induction from the particular to the universal, he stresses, in his formal analysis in *Prior Analytics* II 23, that for the validity of that step to be secure the induction must be complete.

Moreover in the very next chapter in the *Prior Analytics* he treats paradigm, that is example, from the same standpoint (II 24). It is said *not* to be based on all the particulars in question, 69^{a}16 ff., and yet that is precisely what it would have to be based on for the conditions of formal validity to be met. So it is said to be not an argument from part to whole (the move that induction aims to make), nor from whole to part (as in deduction), but from part to part, for it applies the general law recognized in one particular case to another particular case. But we should note that here too, as in induction, Aristotle's analysis proceeds with reference to the *general* law, and that is even less well established by the paradigm than by induction, at least when induction is complete.

This multiple downgrading, of induction with regard to deduction, of incomplete to complete induction, of probable premises to necessary ones, of rhetorical to demonstrative modes of argument, presents us with the foremost crux in our attempts to understand Greek responses to reasoning from examples. But before venturing some comments on that problem, we should add, first, that the texts in the *Analytics* and the *Rhetoric* that we have so far considered are far from giving us the whole of the picture of Aristotle's thought on this subject, and secondly, that there is—as usual—far more to Greek thought, in this area, than Aristotle.

So far as Aristotle himself goes, three aspects of his work serve to modify the mainly negative picture that has emerged thus far, first his own extensive use of examples, not least in his logic, second his account of practical reasoning, and third his recognition of a wider range of demonstration than some of his own analysis in the *Posterior Analytics* leads us to expect.

Thus first of all, as Ierodiakonou 2002 has recently insisted, Aristotle draws heavily on concrete examples throughout the *Organon*. One recurrent use in the *Prior Analytics* is to illustrate points to do with validity, that is to exhibit which combinations of premisses in which figures yield valid conclusions. Over and over again particular patterns of relationships are given concrete interpretations. There is nothing surprising in this, to be sure, and it might be said to tally well enough with the observation, in the *Topics* 157ª14 ff., that examples, especially familiar ones, serve to make points clear. Although the subject matter is very different, one might even compare the remark, in the *Rhetoric* 1394ª14 ff., that a single example cited after an enthymeme may be persuasive, while if put before the conclusion many are needed since they look more like an induction.

But apart from their usefulness in achieving clarity, it is important to see that Aristotle also employs examples actually to *establish* certain conclusions. This he does in three types of context especially. First negatively a single counter-example is, of course, enough to refute a generalization. Then, in the rather more complex case of his analysis of where no syllogism results from certain combinations of premisses in each figure, he frequently uses examples, often in pairs, to show that this is the case (see *Prior Analytics* 28ª30 ff., 37ª38 ff. and other examples cited by Ierodiakonou 2002: 145–8). Third, in *Prior Analytics* II 2–4 he again uses concrete examples extensively to show how true conclusions can be drawn from false premisses in each of the three figures. Thus while an example is never adequate to yield a necessary universal proposition, one may and often does serve (*a*) to refute a general statement and (*b*) to show a possibility.

Secondly, when Aristotle discusses what is called practical reasoning, the role of experience is duly recognized, and this is important since often, even though not exclusively, examples figure on the experience side of the experience/reason dichotomy. Indeed Aristotle makes clear that in certain circumstances practical experience, based on examples, may count for more than theoretical knowledge. He says, for instance, that someone who knows that light meats are wholesome, but does not know which meats are light, is less able to produce the desired results— namely health—than someone who knows that chicken is wholesome, but cannot give the theoretical explanation for this (*Nicomachean Ethics* 1141^{b}16 ff.).

Again, his analysis of lack of self-control, *akrasia*, centres on the problem of recognizing the particular as the particular it is, that is that it comes under a certain general rule (*Nicomachean Ethics* 1146^{b}24 ff., 1147^{a}5 ff., ^{b}9 ff.). Asking how people can, in a sense, go against their own better judgement, or be 'overcome' by desire, he suggests that what they may lack, or not consciously realize at the time, is the judgement that the particular comes under the general rule it does.

In general, we are reminded of the fundamental problem, broached but not satisfactorily resolved in the final chapter of the *Posterior Analytics*, II 19, 99^{b}22 ff., of how, starting from perception of the particular, knowledge of the universal is to be secured. That this happens, he asserts: on quite how it happens, he has no clear account to offer, even though that chapter identifies the issue. Aristotle shows, indeed, some concern with the problem. Yet from another point of view, we may observe that, when passing from the review of a series of diverse particulars to the universal, there is a gain, to be sure, in abstraction, but there may be a loss of information corresponding to that diversity. In that sense the particulars may be richer than the universal abstracted from them. But there can, of course, be no algorithm to determine when the loss of that richness is compensated for by the gain in abstraction.

Thirdly, in his own observations concerning demonstrations, and in his actual practice, Aristotle sometimes departs, and knowingly departs, from the strict models set up for the highest modes of philosophical reasoning in his *Analytics*. While those models require necessity, he explicitly allows, in a variety of contexts, both in his *Metaphysics* and in his physical treatises, modes of demonstration (*apodeixis*) that are looser (*malakoteron*), that may be more or less exact (*akribes*), even more or less necessary (*anankaion*).[12] Again, while validity in

---

[12] See, for example, *Metaphysics* 1025^{b}10 ff., *Meteorologica* 344^{a}5 ff., *On the Parts of Animals* 639^{b}30 ff., discussed in my 1996*b*: ch. 1.

argument demands strict univocity, he recognizes that with many of his most important theoretical concepts, including, for instance, actuality and potentiality, it is impossible to give a definition *per genus et differentiam*. They are to be apprehended, rather, by grasping the analogy that holds between different cases.[13]

While Aristotle was the first Greek to undertake the formal analysis of modes of argument, he was, of course, far from alone. Stoic logic cannot be said to have rescued reasoning by example from Aristotle's strictures. But by introducing an analysis of arguments that focuses on the relationships between propositions, rather than on those between terms, it makes room for individual terms in demonstrations.[14] Moreover in its theory of commemorative and indicative signs it allows for inferential schemata that are wider than those of the *Posterior Analytics*.[15]

More importantly, there were plenty of Hellenistic thinkers who restored the place of comparison as a key element in reasoning. Among the philosophers, the Epicureans advocated and practised a method based on similarity,[16] while among the medical theorists, the so-called Empiricists took their stand by the 'transition to the similar' (*metabasis tou homoiou*). Thus in the account of Empiricist methodology in Celsus' *De Medicina* (Proem 27 ff.), we are told that they rejected the enquiry into hidden causes of diseases and proposed that a doctor should base his treatment on the recognition of similarities between the case he had to deal with and others in his past experience.[17]

With these reminders that in logic and in scientific method, as elsewhere, the Greeks achieved no orthodoxy, nor even a moderately stable consensus on the principal issues, we may now turn back to the crux of

[13] See, for example, *Metaphysics* 1048ª35 ff. and other texts discussed in my 1996*b*: ch. 7 ('the unity of analogy').

[14] Thus individual terms (e.g. 'Plato', 'Dion') are standardly used as examples in accounts of the Stoic analysis of arguments, including the five indemonstrables, see, for example, Diogenes Laertius VII 76 ff., 79 ff.

[15] For the Stoic theory of signs, see Burnyeat 1982, Sedley 1982, and the texts assembled in section 42 of Long and Sedley 1987. According to Sextus Empiricus, *Outlines of Pyrrhonism* II 104, the Stoics defined a sign as a leading proposition in a sound conditional, revelatory of the consequent.

[16] On the Epicurean 'similarity method', see, for example, Philodemus, *On Signs* 34. 29 ff., section 18G in Long and Sedley 1987. It may be noted that this is one of several texts discussing signs in Greek and Latin authors where the same example, of the relationship between smoke and fire, is given as in Nyaya logic. Cf. Sextus Empiricus, *Against the Mathematicians* VIII 152 on commemorative signs.

[17] Cf. also Galen, *On Sects for Beginners*, ch. 2 (*Scr. Min.* III 2. 12 ff.) and his *Outlines of Empiricism* ch. 4, Frede 1985: 4 f., 27.

the Aristotelian downgrading of the paradigm. From one point of view, there may seem nothing at all surprising in this move, which might be represented as the inevitable logical consequence of his analysis of the conditions of strict deduction. The transference of a conclusion from one example to another is only legitimate if both are instances of the same general rule.

Formal validity is, of course, a virtue in reasoning. Yet the programme of the *Analytics* is aimed not just at ensuring validity, but at securing truth, indeed certainty, incontrovertibility no less, and if we investigate what drives *that* ambition, the answer needs, I believe,[18] to include more than just the laudable desire for intellectual rigour. What first Plato and then Aristotle sought to do was to establish the superiority of their high styles of philosophizing over what was on offer from rhetoricians, sophists, politicians, poets, and other would-be Masters of Truth, and the route they both took was to insist on the contrast between the merely persuasive (which was all that the opposition could manage to deliver) and the strictly demonstrative.[19] On the view I would favour, part of the solution to the problem of the distinctive Greek quest for certainty lies in the competitiveness of Greek intellectual life. The analysis of what would yield incontrovertibility was, in part, stimulated by the recognition that it provided something of a trump card in the argument with rivals. If you could achieve that, then indeed the opposition had to acknowledge defeat and your victory was ensured.

Yet the price paid was a high one, and the question we must now press is whether it was *too* high. Should the Aristotelian ambition to secure incontrovertibility be seen as aberrant—and even a highly damaging influence on subsequent Western thought—or at least, if not aberrant, a piece of irrelevant intellectual formalism? Or was it (as some have argued) an essential element in the construction of the ideal for philosophy and science? If the former, should the Chinese be congratulated on avoiding, or being spared, such lamentable lapses? If the latter, should we commiserate with them for settling for styles of argument that lacked the necessary rigour?

To make any progress here, we have to ask in what circumstances the conditions that Aristotle and others put on strict demonstration

---

[18] This is one of the major themes of my 1996a and cf. Ch. 3 above.

[19] Yet many of those criticized by Plato and Aristotle as producing merely persuasive arguments themselves used the language of 'demonstration' (*apodeixis*) of them, cf. Lloyd 1996a: ch. 3, especially pp. 56 ff., and cf. Mendell 1998b.

can conceivably be met, conditions that include not just validity and univocity, but also the securing of self-evident indemonstrable primary premises. Aristotle himself cites zoological and botanical examples, along with mathematical ones, in the *Posterior Analytics*, although his actual zoological treatises are notably lacking in any signs of attempting to present conclusions as reached by axiomatic-deductive modes of inference. Plausible candidates for axiomatic status in zoology are notoriously hard to come by: even in the case of definitions, fully-fledged examples of definitions of animal species are not, in practice, given. The nerve of Aristotle's zoological reasoning lies, rather, in his exploration of the manifold applications of such concepts as *pepsis*, concoction[20]—a matter of the recognition of analogies, rather than of anything that resembles, or might even prepare for, either the complete induction proposed in the *Prior Analytics* or the axiomatization of the *Posterior*.

Mathematics provides, of course, a far more promising field for axiomatic-deductive reasoning. To be sure, Euclidean mathematical argument is not syllogistic in form. However, it conforms to the Aristotelian model not just by being deductive, but often also by making its primary starting points, definitions, postulates, and common opinions explicit. This is true not just, most famously, in Euclid's own *Elements*, but also in some of Archimedes' works, even though his terminology and to some extent also his concept of postulates differ, at points, from Euclid's. Moreover, given that he can take some of those in Euclid for granted, he has no need to aim for the comprehensiveness that may have been Euclid's original ambition.

In that the likes of Euclid and Archimedes produced some notable results, that might seem to vindicate the Aristotelian axiomatic-deductive style. But we must be clear what those results owed to that style and where they were independent of it. Evidently a high degree of explicitness with regard to the postulates employed was achieved, even though, as Suppes (1981) among others has pointed out, Greek mathematical axiomatizations were, by modern standards, still quite incomplete (cf. Mueller 1981, Knorr 1981). Yet both mathematicians succeeded in making explicit a number of crucial foundational postulates and primary principles. Among the most important are (1) Euclid's parallel postulate, and (2) the definition of proportion on which the

---

[20] Cf. Lloyd 1996*b*: ch. 4 ('the master cook').

method of exhaustion depends, then (3) Archimedes' continuity axiom, and (4) the postulate used in his proof of the law of the lever.[21]

The implicit claim, in such cases, was to the self-evidence of the principles stated—the ultimate aim of the exercise was, we said, incontrovertibility. Yet the actual effect, of the parallel postulate at least, was eventually to focus attention on the question of the status of the assumption itself (see above, Ch. 3 p. 30 and n. 5). Already in antiquity some, such as Proclus, were of the opinion that it ought to be, not a postulate, but a theorem to be proved, and in the eighteenth and nineteenth centuries, as I noted, it was a similar view that led to the exploration of non-Euclidean geometries and the effective demonstration of the limitations of the claim that the postulate was undeniable. To make the indemonstrables explicit may have been a move in the construction of a would-be incontrovertible whole. Yet paradoxically it sometimes had the effect of drawing attention to the points at which a challenge could be mounted. We can see, however, that to make the foundations or first principles explicit was an all-important move not just for those who claimed that they were incontestable, but also for those who sought to contest them.

Presentationally, therefore, the adoption of the axiomatic-deductive model led to greater explicitness in the matter of the foundational assumptions made and greater clarity as to which were, precisely, the essential foundations. But the real work in the mathematical reasoning was often done elsewhere—not in the statement of what the method of exhaustion depended on, for instance, but in the application of that method itself.

Indeed more basically still, as Netz (1999) has recently suggested, persuasively in my view, the deductive structure of the argument depends crucially on the use of the lettered diagram, to the point where (as the range of the Greek term *diagramma* suggests) the construction of the diagram is the kernel of the construction of the proof. The diagrams are, moreover, of course, particulars: 'let ABC be a triangle', 'let ABCD be a circle', 'let ABC be a segment of a parabola bounded by the straight line AC and the parabola ABC', and so on.[22] Yet they are

---

[21] Euclid, *Elements* I Postulate 5, V Definition 5, Archimedes, *On the Sphere and Cylinder* I, Postulates 1–3, *On the Equilibrium of Planes* I Postulate 1. The last example illustrates, of course, that such foundational principles are not confined to pure mathematics.

[22] The constraints on the positions of the points so lettered vary, as Netz points out, though the sequences in which the points needed are named exhibit certain marked regularities.

investigated, to be sure, not for the sake of their particular features, but rather for that of the generalizable properties they exhibit.[23] The point is of cardinal importance, and yet it may be problematic. In principle, at least, though sometimes questionably in practice, the proofs do not lose in generality, even though constructed on the basis of a particular.

The comparison and the contrast with Chinese mathematics are eloquent on these issues, where I may pick up and develop the argument already sketched in Chapter 3. What roles do examples have in classical Chinese mathematical reasoning? Where one might think that the *Nine Chapters on Mathematical Procedures* is exclusively concerned with purely practical problems such as measuring the area of a field or calculating the labour needed to build an earthwork, recent studies by Chemla (1994, 1997, and forthcoming) argue convincingly that the interest is often, rather, quite general. The concreteness of the problem situation—the numbers that give it specific interpretation (such as 'a field $\frac{4}{7}$ *bu* in width and $\frac{3}{5}$ *bu* in length' in I 19)—should not mislead, though truth to tell many have been misled in the past. Yet the evident impracticability of such a reference as that to $3\frac{1}{3}$ persons (in I 18) should already have deterred anyone from treating this purely as a handbook for technicians in the field. Again, giving $7\frac{427}{3064}$ labourers as the answer to a problem in V 5 about digging a trench shows that the interest there is in the exact solution to the equation, rather than in the materialities of the situation. This is not, of course, to deny that practical interests are indeed in play in the *Nine Chapters*, only to insist that those are not the exclusive interests of the work.

However, the structure of the discussion is, in certain respects, rather puzzling. Whereas in some Western mathematical textbooks the problems are described in general terms, illustrated, for sure, by concrete examples and accompanied, sometimes, by further examples for the students to work through on their own (maybe checking their answers by looking them up in a separate section at the back of the book), what we have in the *Nine Chapters* is structured rather differently. We are given a series of concrete problems in the form of questions, with the answers introduced by the expression *shu yue* ('the method—or the working—states'), but often with little or no discussion in the clas-

---

[23] Aristotle already insisted, at *Prior Analytics* 76^{b}39 ff., that no falsehood is introduced into the mathematical reasoning when the geometer takes the line drawn as a foot long, and straight, when it is neither.

sic itself (as opposed to the commentators) on how the answers are arrived at.

The procedure, and the choice of examples, may seem quite arbitrary—until we see that what is being investigated is the general relationships of which the cases cited are *exemplary*. They are not there for their own sake, for sure, but for that of the general relations they instantiate, even though these are sometimes left implicit and have to be extracted from a comparison between the concrete situations.

In line with this reading of the *Nine Chapters*, Liu Hui's commentary may be seen as extending and making more explicit the interest in the generalizability of the problems and of the procedures used to solve them, and in the interrelationships that unify the discussion.[24] He repeatedly draws attention to the similarity in the algorithms used in different contexts, including those between different sections of the classic. His frequent cross-referencing, between different problems and more especially between different procedures, suggests that he sees the *same* general relations being explored throughout the text. So there are two levels of generalization here, the first in relation to the problem situations presented in concrete particular terms in the various sections of the *Nine Chapters* itself, and the second with regard to the relationships between those sections.

The two questions that then arise are first how far this pattern, in the use of examples, is a recurrent one in early Chinese mathematics, and secondly what are the consequences for our understanding of its style of reasoning? Two brief comments may be made on the first of these, before I put forward a tentative comparative suggestion on the second.

First, the main support for the thesis that Chemla has proposed comes, of course, from the commentary tradition to the *Nine Chapters*. She acknowledges that the classic itself does not offer much by way of direct statements to confirm that it shared the interests in the generalizability of problems and the cross-referencing of procedures that feature in Liu Hui. It normally stays resolutely at the level of the particular problems and the solutions to them that it sets out—leaving the reader to work out the connections between them. Yet that does not seem a

---

[24] Indeed in her latest study (Chemla forthcoming) she examines one case, in VI 18, where she interprets Liu Hui as pointing out that the procedure used in the *Nine Chapters* fails in generality and needs supplementing precisely in order to deal with the general class of problems in question as Liu Hui sees it. However I would doubt that we should see this as an objection to the classic, since Liu Hui's supplement proceeds, as he points out, by drawing on (he says 'imitating', *fang*, 196. 9) the procedure used in the very next problem, VI 19.

major objection, for it appears that we have no *better* way to understand the *Nine Chapters*, in this regard, than to follow the lead offered us by Liu Hui. Otherwise we are largely at a loss, as I remarked, to interpret the bare sequences of concrete problems and solutions presented in the *Nine Chapters*. Why choose *these* cases and not others, unless the interest is indeed general and they are taken to exemplify that? Moreover to the further claim, that we should not take the classic as exclusively practical in orientation, Liu Hui again offers at least indirect support. He certainly confirms his own realization that he goes beyond the merely practical, when he comments on the lack of direct usefulness of the study of the *bienao* and *yangma* in V 15.[25] Here too, however, a balance must be struck, for the very fact that Liu Hui mentions the point may suggest a certain diffidence on his part—as if he had to apologize for his interest—just as he sometimes shows some reluctance to engage in what he terms 'abstract', *kongyan*, reasoning.[26]

Yet secondly, we must recognize that some of the concrete numbers employed in the *Nine Chapters* can hardly be thought of as exemplary in one sense, namely that they are not exact. The prime example of this is the standard assumption of the value 3 for the circle-circumference ratio (or π), where Liu Hui devotes an extended discussion, not just to insist that that is incorrect (for 3 gives the *lü* of the hexagon, that is *its* circumference–diameter ratio, and therefore cannot do so also for the circumscribed circle), but also to offer a better approximation to the value. Here evidently we are dealing with a number taken not as an exemplification, but as an approximation—as indeed would be the case with any finite number chosen. But while here the *Nine Chapters* starts from a formula that is correct—namely that the area of the circle is equal to half the circumference times half the diameter[27]—the concretization of the problem inevitably involves an approximation and in that sense leads to a loss of accuracy.

My tentative comparative suggestion focuses, precisely, on the issue that this raises, of the generalizability of the results obtained on the basis of reasoning from examples. If we bear in mind the point made earlier, that in Euclid or Archimedes, for instance, much of the actual

---

[25] V 15, 168. 3–4, cf. Wagner 1979: 182. A *bienao* is a pyramid with right triangular base and one lateral edge perpendicular to the base. A *yangma* is a pyramid with a rectangular base and one lateral edge perpendicular to the base.

[26] This point is discussed in relation to comments on I 32, VIII 1 and 18, by Chemla 1997.

[27] I 32, 103. 9 ff.

mathematical work is done on, and with, diagrams that are themselves particular (and whose status is thus analogous to that of the examples we have been considering from the *Nine Chapters*), in that respect we may say that the styles of reasoning in Greek and Chinese mathematics are appreciably *closer* than is often admitted.

Yet where they continue to differ is in the preferred route taken for the justification or validation of the results obtained and in particular of their generalizability. The Greeks in the Euclidean tradition (at least) proceeded via axiomatization. Though some of that is mere window-dressing—designed merely to impress—its persuasive role depended on the point that it conformed to a model of reasoning that was recognized as securing incontrovertibility.

But what Liu Hui, for his part, does is to explore the links first between the various parts of the mathematical reasoning in the *Nine Chapters*, and then between them and other texts, including even the *Yijing* and its commentaries. This is the message of his preface (91. 1 ff.), with its references to the single principle (*duan*) from which the different parts of mathematics stem, or to the trunk of which they are the branches (91. 7 f.), and it is reinforced, in his commentary itself, by the concern we have mentioned before, namely to make explicit the 'guiding principles' (*gangji*) at work, e.g. I 9, 96. 4. Nor is this just the ambition of Liu Hui. Already the *Zhoubi suanjing* seeks methods that are 'concisely worded but of broad application' (24. 12 ff.). One needs to study 'similar methods in comparison with one another' and what makes the difference between stupid and intelligent scholars is, precisely, the 'ability to distinguish categories in order to unite categories' (25. 5).[28]

But in both these Chinese texts the movement of thought is essentially analogical or synthetic (cf. Volkov 1992), disengaging the same basic principles exhibited in different particular cases and showing that their range of applicability is not limited to just those cases. Indeed the openendedness of the principles—the possibility of extrapolating and extending their range—is remarked on as one of their virtues (as in Liu Hui's preface, 91. 9), thereby showing a fine disregard for any idea of the need for completeness of induction in order to ensure validity. Just as complete induction is far from the minds of these Chinese

---

[28] One of the chief contrasts between the *Nine Chapters* and the even earlier mathematical text the *suan shu shu* (discovered in 1983 in a tomb that was sealed in 186 BCE) lies in the degree of systematicity that the *Nine Chapters* exhibits: see Cullen forthcoming.

mathematicians, so too is any sense of the need to set out axioms which would somehow guarantee the incontrovertibility of the whole. Whereas some of the Greeks could not settle for less than self-evident axioms from which the whole of mathematics can, in principle, be deduced, the Chinese sought what is 'simple but precise', and that which allows communication between the different areas of the mathematical art (Liu Hui, 91. 8). That, one may say, makes the examples work harder. For it is not that their validity can be deduced from universal principles otherwise secured: but rather that they provide the wherewithal to apprehend the common principles.

For us to attempt to establish general rules, governing the legitimacy or otherwise of the uses of examples in philosophy and science, would be as misguided as it was for some of the Greeks to do so. The moments for the examination of assumptions, for the move to the general or the exploration of the particular, for the construction of models or their application and confirmation, for induction and deduction, for heuristics and proof, no less, cannot be laid down *in general* and *in advance* of the determination of the state of the field and the specific problem situations that make up the various types of enquiry we may be interested in. The ambition to lay down such rules marks, indeed, a characteristically hubristic streak in some Greek thought. By contrast, the very essence of the use of examples often lies, we argued, in their suggestiveness and openendedness.[29]

Three final remarks may be offered to conclude this study. First we can begin to understand why some Greeks downgraded example in the name of the strictest axiomatic-deductive demonstration, for in the competitive debates that marked Greek intellectual life, what was needed for victory was not suggestiveness, but certainty. If that was secured, then victory was well and truly won. A style of argument that exploited the elliptical implications of example might be persuasive, but it could not demonstrate its conclusions.

Secondly, we have observed that not all Greeks chose that route, for there were some articulate proponents of a methodology that is resolutely based on experience, and even some of the advocates of the axiomatic-deductive model drew heavily on examples in their practice.

[29] This is true especially, but by no means exclusively, in the fields of medicine and the law (cf. above nn. 1 and 3). For a general analysis of reasoning from cases, see Forrester 1996.

Third, we can say that there was some good sense in that search for axioms, at least in that it identified and made explicit the foundations on which the deductive structure was based. That had its uses, indeed, even where the foundations that were represented as beyond challenge were thereupon subjected to just that. In practice, many Greeks were as fluent in the citation of examples as were the Chinese. The fact that one Greek tradition of demonstration, and of its analysis, rather turned its back on them testifies to how far some were prepared to go, to win in the competitive situation within which they worked.

10

Universities: Their Histories and Responsibilities

Institutions of higher education have always had a major part to play in the development of enquiry and their role has never been greater than it is today. Yet they developed in rather different ways in the West and in China and in the process some of their original goals have tended to be downplayed, if not forgotten. My aim in this chapter and the next two is to use history not just to try to understand certain intellectual or philosophical issues that we continue to face, but also to see what we can learn from our analysis of the past that may be relevant to how we should tackle some of the problems, educational, ethical, political, of our modern situation.

Where higher education is concerned, some of the lessons take the form of warnings—of what happens when universities are insufficiently self-critical, or when they do not stand up for themselves and resist pressures from outside, including from government. But at least some of the morals are positive ones, from which we can draw strength. One of the Chinese lessons is to value the past, though that should not be to the neglect of the present and the future. One of the Greek ones is to value education in and for itself—as opposed to valuing it for the qualifications for a career that it may provide. Meanwhile, thirdly, we may reflect that whatever may have been the case in the past, we are now all in it together. No country, however powerful, exists in isolation, as September 11, 2001 brought home to the USA in the most tragic way. In the current situation of increasing globalization, the universities provide one of the very best opportunities for international cooperation.

In the West I would endorse the conventional view (cf. Rashdall 1936) that traces the origins of our universities to the great late medieval schools of Paris, Bologna, Oxford, and so on. In some cases they go back to the eleventh century CE. What was distinctive about those universities was that they awarded degrees. Bachelors of Arts and Masters of Arts thereby acquired legally recognized qualifications. More importantly, the higher degrees awarded in law, medicine, theology, were key qualifications for those aspiring to top careers in those fields—which thereby became, for the first time, fully *professional* in the modern sense.

One function of the medieval universities was, then, to secure and control the future membership of those professions. But another was to provide a basic education in the so-called liberal arts, the trivium (grammar, rhetoric, logic) and the quadrivium (arithmetic, geometry, astronomy, music). Scholars might be no more than 12 or 13 years old when they entered, and if not themselves the sons of the wealthy, they needed to have rich patrons. The founding of colleges where students lived and received additional tuition was a secondary and later—though not much later—development. Some of the Parisian colleges go back to the twelfth century (Schwinges 1992: 214).

Those medieval universities owed a fair amount both to earlier, less formally organized, patterns of education, and to much earlier schools, especially the great philosophical schools at Athens. The best known are Plato's Academy, Aristotle's Lyceum, the Stoa founded by Zeno of Citium, and Epicurus' Garden, all four established in the fourth or early third centuries BCE, although there were many other minor schools as well. If we are to understand the origins of higher education in the West, we have to go back to those Greek institutions, and we must be aware that they were, in certain respects, very different from medieval universities, let alone from the universities we are familiar with today.

The first fundamental point is that those ancient Western philosophical schools awarded no degrees. Those who attended them did so not in order, eventually, to obtain some legally recognized qualification that would give access to a profession. They did so because they *prized* what they were taught. I do not want to deny that there were elements of careerism, and even of snobbery, in this. In Cicero's day, in the first century BCE, it was the done thing for young Romans of good family to go to Athens for their education and he duly did. Moreover you could, in the process, learn not just about philosophy, but also about rhetoric, and that could be very useful in a career in politics and in law. So it was not all learning for learning's sake, then—even though it was very largely that, certainly to a degree that would have surprised medieval students, let alone modern ones.

But there were no degrees, there were no examinations, and no set curricula either. There were no formal ways, in other words, in which

young students could impress their teachers or their own contemporaries, other than by their *understanding* of what they were taught and
by their participation in the joint exploration of the subjects under
investigation. That understanding and participation were usually
mediated through the *spoken* word. Ancient Greek students did not
write essays to be corrected by their teachers: and there was no equiva-
lent, in Graeco-Roman antiquity, to the written examinations that came
to be fundamental to the recruitment to official positions in ancient
China. With no set curricula, ancient Greek students stayed as long as
they liked—that is, as long as they continued to prize the experience.
Thus Aristotle, who arrived in Plato's Academy as a 17-year-old, stayed
for twenty years.

To an extent that would have amazed the Chinese, Greek philosophical schools were locked in debate with one another, and indeed, with
the exception of the Epicureans, there was plenty of debate *within* the
schools, as rival teachers competed in their interpretation of what the
school should stand for—and what the founder himself did. Scholars
sometimes talk of heretical members of such a school as the Stoics, but
it is important to emphasize that, in a pagan context, what heresy meant
was very different from what it came to mean once Christian faiths
were in competition with one another. *Hairesis* originally meant 'sect',
or more literally still 'choice' (von Staden 1982). There was no enforce-
ment of an orthodox interpretation of Platonism, Aristotelianism,
Stoicism, and the rest. There was no orthodoxy in the first place.

Those ancient Western institutions were, then, very different from
their later counterparts in several fundamental ways. They were private, not state, foundations, receiving little or no state support, not at
least until, under the Roman empire, the headships of the main philosophical schools at Athens came to be endowed.[1]

This comparative independence from the state carried both advantages and disadvantages. Among the former, one stands out, namely the
freedom to decide what to investigate and how to investigate it. True,
some of the fruits of that freedom of thought may strike us as fanciful
or extravagant. Some Greek philosophers were prepared to deny that

---

[1] The main example of official state support in the Graeco-Roman world, though not for
philosophy, so much as for 'scientific' research, for literature, and for philology, was the
Museum at Alexandria, during the reign of the first three Ptolemies. Yet by Chinese standards, as we shall see, that did not amount to very much: nor did that support last for very
long.

change occurs. Others developed positions of extreme scepticism, not just that nothing can be known, but that there are no reliable grounds even for true belief. At the same time they could and did challenge contemporary religious beliefs—for instance in gods in human form. They questioned the rights and wrongs of different political constitutions. Not many social and moral conventions or customs escaped their scrutiny, and all this radical questioning only occasionally got them into trouble, as it did Socrates—and even then there was no Church to prosecute him: it was left to private individuals to do so, in part out of motivations of personal malice of course.

Some of the theoretical extravagance we notice may be associated with the *competitiveness* that existed between individuals and groups. To make a name, as a philosopher, or even as a doctor, you had to draw attention to yourself, often developing outlandish hypotheses or paradoxical arguments. At the same time, your contemporaries were your judge. It was their impression of you that counted. As a teacher, the education you offered had to justify itself in its own terms, as worthwhile for its own sake. If it did not do so, your pupils would vote with their feet and disappear. They were not even kept in the classroom on the basis of the argument that they would get no degree if they left. So everything depended on acceptance of learning and research as *valuable in themselves*. We even find philosophers, perhaps not surprisingly, claiming that they—learning and research, especially in philosophy— were essential to happiness, that you could not be fulfilled if you neglected philosophy. That claim aside, the fundamental point remains: the education on offer had to be seen, by teachers and pupils alike, to be valuable in itself, for if not, there was no incentive to engage in it at all.

It is time now to introduce some of the main features of Chinese higher education. First a note of caution is needed. In many of the standard textbooks you will read about the so-called Ji Xia 'Academy', set up in the third century BCE by the dukes of Qi. But the term 'Academy' is a misnomer here.[2] The model we should use to understand this institution is rather that of the other courts of the Warring States period, where ambitious and powerful rulers and ministers collected 'guests', *ke*, around them, often in large numbers. They were often a very mixed bag, among them entertainers and even hired assassins. The Ji Xia group included a fair number of intellectuals (such as the philosopher Xunzi)

---

[2] The evidence has recently been re-evaluated by Sivin 1995*b*: ch. 4.

but they were there primarily to redound to the glory of the dukes of Qi and to advise them—not to give lectures. The analogy would be not to Plato's Academy but to his ill-fated visit to the court of Dionysius II, tyrant of Sicily, in the hope of persuading him to become a philosopher-king.

Several other Chinese institutions are, however, of cardinal importance. What operated much more like Greek schools, even if certainly not in all, were the Chinese lineages, *jia*. This was a term that underwent considerable shifts in both sense and reference from the Warring States period on (see Csikszentmihalyi and Nylan forthcoming). It could simply mean 'family', and in a distinctive but influential text in the *Shiji* 130, Sima Tan used it of philosophical tendencies, for example of the doctrine that focused on law as the key to government (*fa jia*). But from late Han times it was used of certain groups of scholars, one of whose main functions was to preserve and hand on the teaching of a master or a canonical text, *jing*[II].

We should note, first, that this is text-based learning: the pupils memorized the text and were only expected to start interpreting it once they had it by heart. Moreover, the premium was on transmission and preservation, not on criticism. True, there had always been divergent interpretations, both of Mohist teachings and of the classical Confucian ones, within their respective traditions, but those debates were not a fundamental part of the *raison d'être* of the groups doing the transmitting. However, the Chinese *jia* did share one important feature with Greek schools, namely the value attached to learning, indeed the value attached to the canons in and for themselves.[3]

But the next kinds of institution I must mention are a very different phenomenon. First there was the rise in China, from the late second century BCE, of institutions of higher education sponsored by the state and serving the purpose of training personnel to run the increasingly important state civil service. That was responsible for overseeing every aspect of government, even, one might say, of life itself. Then I have mentioned before that most remarkable of institutions, the state Astronomical Bureau, charged with regulating the calendar and with

---

[3] Some scholars nowadays think that the cherishing of the past may have been in part a reaction to such anti-intellectual moves made by the first Qin emperor as the infamous episode of the burning of the books, ordered by his minister Li Si in 213 BCE. No doubt both that destruction and the persecution of intellectuals by autocratic emperors throughout the early days of the Han dynasty served to make scholars more conscious of the need to safeguard themselves and their traditions.

observing and interpreting celestial phenomena of all kinds—an institution that lasted for some 2,000 years all the way down to the last imperial dynasty, the Qing.

But from the outset there are five characteristics of the Chinese state institutions of learning that are crucial to our understanding of their role. (1) These were official, state, foundations—and in that very different from the Greek philosophical schools, though it is true not unlike the Alexandrian Museum. (2) The principal Chinese Academy taught a carefully selected group of texts. From 136 BCE the five classics became the core curriculum.[4] (3) One of the main functions was, as noted, to produce suitably qualified graduates for civil service appointment: in that sense the Academy was oriented towards jobs and the expectation of the graduates was that they would take up official positions. Indeed already in the *Lunyu* the orientation of learning towards an official career is marked. (4) Entry came to be controlled. Students certainly always had to meet certain informal requirements, to be of good character and family to start with, and from 600 CE they entered by way of what became an increasingly rigorous written examination system. This allowed some upward social mobility. Sons of not so well-to-do families got into the academies, often graduating from provincial ones to the imperial Academy in the capital. But the point should not be exaggerated. There was no way in which children from the very lowest echelons of society could compete for entry. Finally (5) graduates passed out on completion of further examinations. The examination system we are nowadays so used to was a Chinese invention.

The success of the principal imperial Academy can be judged from its exponential growth. There were, it is estimated, some 100 graduates in 124 BCE, but 250 years later our sources talk of some 30,000. While the main focus of the instruction it offered was on the mastery of the classics, technical questions on, for example, mathematical and astronomical topics also came to be included in the examinations set.[5] Nevertheless there remained a considerable emphasis on producing 'gentlemen', *junzi*, who knew how to behave, who were learned in the classics, and who appreciated the interdependence of those two attainments. We should not be too surprised at that. In European

---

[4] The five classics were the *Odes* (*Shi*[IV]), the *Documents* (*Shu*[I]), the *Rites* (*Li*[III]), the *Changes* (*Yijing*), and the *Spring and Autumn Annals* (*Chunqiu*). Nylan 2001 is an exemplary study of the diverse ways those texts were used and interpreted throughout Chinese history down to modern times.

[5] The classic study of this issue is Elman 2000.

universities too, those presented for degrees still have formally to be vouched for as being of good character as well as for having passed their examinations.

So the history of higher education in China and the West underlines certain obvious but fundamental points. The involvement of state authorities is, I said, a mixed blessing. Without sustained state support, the Greek philosophical schools were extremely vulnerable, and many went through periods of decline before they all finally disappeared. Yet they had much more room for intellectual manœuvre than their Chinese counterparts, and also than their medieval Western successors when they were controlled by guilds. The Chinese state institutions provided reliable support but this was at the price of setting the agenda. That certainly had adverse results, for instance on the work done within the Astronomical Bureau, where, despite the excellence of the record in observational astronomy, the theoretical agenda stagnated over long periods.

The obvious problem that remains with us today is that, if you enjoy state subsidies, you are likely to have to forfeit some of your freedom to determine your own curriculum and research programme, to innovate, indeed to criticize the state authorities themselves. When it is they that provide the finance, it takes an enlightened government to see that it is in their own long-term interests to foster critical institutions of higher education, in both the humanities and the sciences. Yet politicians who have themselves been the beneficiaries of higher education (and even those who have not) *should* see the point of supporting such institutions. If the universities are to provide leadership in research in all departments of learning, then they must be critical of what passes as received wisdom across the board. It is true, however, that universities both in China and in the West have sometimes placed much more emphasis on conservation and preservation than on innovation.

The recurrent structural weakness is that those who have mastered the curriculum, passed the relevant examinations with flying colours, and secured a professorial position on that basis may be disinclined to acknowledge that old ideas have been superseded and that change is needed, even if they themselves take prime responsibility for how their subject will grow. In China, Confucianism and neo-Confucianism had, at times, a stranglehold on education, though there were periods when it was rather Buddhism that was the dominant ideology. In the West too the problem has been an intermittent one, at least ever since the

Christian Roman Emperor Justinian banned the teaching of pagan philosophy in the sixth century. The rediscovery of Aristotle in the twelfth and thirteenth centuries was accompanied by a wave of innovation, but the reaction to that on the part of the Church was one of panic, with repeated proscriptions of Aristotle's ideas during the thirteenth century, even though by the end of it his writings came to constitute a large part of the Arts curriculum at the University of Paris.

If that is testimony to the independence and open-mindedness of some medieval Western universities, those are not the only tendencies that began to be developed. Aristotle himself in turn came to have, not just an honoured place, but an iron grip, on university curricula—so that by three or four centuries later, the chief efforts of the innovators had to be to criticize the very Aristotelianism that had been hailed as such a mine of wisdom in the thirteenth century.

We can find similar conservative tendencies at work in the control of curricula not just in the Arts course and philosophy, but even in medicine. Here too the rediscovery, in the West, of Hippocrates and Galen was eventually followed by their coming to attain the status of supreme authorities. Moreover even after Galen, especially, had been challenged successfully by the work of such anatomists as Vesalius in the sixteenth century, his treatises continued to be used as the main vehicle of instruction in the medical schools. In order to gain their degrees, Doctors of Medicine at the University of Oxford were required to expound passages from Galen throughout the seventeenth and eighteenth centuries. Even when the so-called New Statutes were introduced there in 1833 the degree of Bachelor of Medicine still entailed a compulsory examination in two out of four ancient authors (Hippocrates, Aretaeus, Galen, and Celsus). Those in charge of the medical curricula were evidently insistent that their successors should be as learned in the ancient texts as they were themselves, even when the strictly scientific content of those writings had long ago been superseded at least in such areas as anatomy and physiology. That surely is eloquent testimony to an ongoing problem, namely that teachers may be far keener to turn out pupils like themselves than to encourage those pupils to branch out and innovate.

Much more could be said about the varying fortunes and influence of the European universities from the late Middle Ages and on through the Renaissance and the so-called scientific revolution. But now let me jump right down to the present day. From many points of view, the post-scientific, post-industrial revolution world we now all inhabit is totally different from anything our predecessors faced—wherever in the world they lived. The explosions of scientific knowledge and of technology have been amazing, the one fuelled by the ambition to apply it, in the other, to increasing material welfare. It has often been said that there are more scientists alive today than in the whole of past history put together. As for those employed in the technological industries directed to applying their work, they outnumber the scientists in turn by far, not that the distinction between pure research and applied is a hard and fast one.

The adaptation of ancient universities to provide the higher education appropriate to this new world has been at best piecemeal and defensive. Some of the problems relate to the failures of the universities themselves to reflect critically on their place in modern society, but some stem from pressures from forces in society itself. Let me say something about how I see each, concentrating on Western universities in the first instance.[6]

Internally, many universities have been slow to meet the particular challenges of the explosion of knowledge, both in the sciences and outside them. It is true that the courses on offer have increased very considerably. It used to be the case, in Cambridge for instance, until the mid-nineteenth century, that the only subjects you could take the BA degree in were mathematics and classics—and indeed every graduate was expected to be competent in both (Searby 1997: 205). Now the choice is very great, and that is all to the good. Yet negative factors are also at work. First the newer courses tend overwhelmingly to be vocational. Secondly they tend to be increasingly specialized. No one can deny that the degree of complexity of many, even most, disciplines requires specialization. Yet that can and often does mean the increasing isolation of faculties and departments from one another, and sometimes the loss of a vision of the broader perspective of what higher education is for.

---

[6] China had to open up new subjects for study very rapidly at the start of the twentieth century (in several cases under the influence of developments that had taken place earlier in Japan), and ever since there has been an obvious concentration on what is seen to contribute to state interests. Even so, a sense of the need to preserve and recover elements of the Chinese past continues to drive a good deal of educational policy and research, both in the PRC and in Taiwan. This is so to a far greater degree than generally exists in Britain, let alone in the USA, even if, in the process, mythopoeic tendencies—in the construction of an image of Chinese continuity—are sometimes much in evidence.

Faculties run the risk of becoming increasingly closed in on themselves, inordinately conscious of the competition that other faculties and departments pose. Each one tends to demand higher and higher specialized skills and technical knowledge—of their pupils and of the staff that they recruit to teach them. That is fine in itself, except that there is usually no countervailing central force to resist internal departmental pressures. Such central authorities as there are are more concerned with the university's image vis-à-vis government. I shall be coming back to that.

But it is pretty clear that some drastic restructuring in the shape of university courses is needed, to cope on the one hand with that ever-increasing specialization of each discipline, and on the other with the general decline in the preparation for university work that can be provided at secondary school level. Faced with a similar situation in their secondary education, the American universities went over, some time ago, to a very broad and, by British standards, superficial first degree course with a wide choice of subjects combinable in a great variety of ways. But that often leads to a sense of fragmentation: it is left to the students themselves to provide the connecting links between what they are taught—for the university teachers themselves do not make them. Worse still, the universities sometimes offer the worst of both worlds, failing to provide the connections that should form the core of universal education, and abandoning much of the rigour of those more specialized disciplines.

What is needed is for the specialists themselves to be prepared to be more generalist in their own teaching at undergraduate level. This is unpopular because it comes to be labelled amateur—though to be a good generalist does not imply being superficial, rather being good at making connections. Unfortunately generalists do not get much credit for being that from appointments committees. Yet our predecessors *were generalists*, and if there was simply less to know, across the board from the arts to the sciences, that is no excuse for us not to try. The first lesson that history suggests is that the universities should once again take more seriously the ideal that they are places for the exploration and handing-on of *universal* knowledge, not fragments of it in specialist disciplines.

For that difficult goal to be attained, we do not need more vocational courses which have their *raisons d'être* to meet certain needs but can never make more than a marginal contribution to the broader picture to which students should have access. That should be constituted by the four core disciplines of mathematics, the sciences, the social sciences, and the humanities, where, in the last case, a genuinely ecumenical study of literature, of world history, and of the diversity of cultures should take pride of place, even though we have to recognize that language barriers make it exceptionally difficult to achieve. Ideally students should be introduced to some aspect of work at the frontier of knowledge, and to how that frontier was arrived at, in each of those four fields. For that to be done properly, the teaching would need to be rather different from present-day introductory courses, in this sense, that the emphasis would be not on how to lead the student to the next stage in specialization, but rather on getting them to understand how each discipline is constituted, the relations between them, and how each contributes to universal knowledge.

But the Western universities' own failures at self-examination pale in significance when compared with the problems posed by pressures from outside. This is, no doubt, an endemic problem, but again that is no excuse for us to ignore it or to be craven in our response. The chief difficulty stems from the insistence, in certain quarters, on treating higher education as if it were a commodity, and the universities themselves as education factories. But how can you tell what it is worth for a student to learn about biochemistry, say, or astronomy, or even ancient philosophy—I mean for the students themselves, not from the point of view of the wages they may be able to earn thanks to their degrees? How much value has been added to them—and again I mean in themselves—by the time they leave the factory gates? Such questions are daft: but they are extremely widespread.

Financial accountability is, to be sure, essential. Certainly cutting out waste and extravagance is both difficult and important, for vested interests treat what can be extravagant provision as the norm. History shows that the desire of university professors to clone themselves is very great, and that is generally not in the interests of the development of their subject. Yet the universities have not resisted vigorously enough the model of cost–benefit analysis that is currently imposed upon us.

Education is not a commodity. Rather it is a basic human value. The notion that primary and secondary education should be compulsory is accepted world-wide. But there is a recurrent fear—at least in Europe—of *too much* education, that higher education is a luxury and has to be rationed. We ought to insist, on the contrary, that while you can have *bad* education, mindless education, and *any* of that is already too much, true education is something you cannot have too much of, for it gives you the ability to fulfil yourself and is an ongoing process through life. What universities can do is to provide the most intense experience of that process of learning that can be used as a model by those who have undergone it even after they have left university. That kind of higher education should be accessible to all, that is to anyone who has the desire, the motivation, and the stamina to undertake it. As proper health care should be available to all, and second only to health care.

This will no doubt be criticized as excessively idealistic. How could universal higher education of that kind conceivably be afforded? Yet to that the counter-question is: how can any country conceivably *not* afford to make the very best use of the potential of its young men and women? In that regard many countries in the developing world seem more alert to the issue than Western ones. And what about the not so young? We may be emboldened, in our idealism, here, by new styles of higher education introduced, despite the initial chorus of gloom and doom, specifically for those wishing to re-enter education part-time at an older age. One example is the National Extension College, and another the Open University or University of the Air as it used to be called, both of which have been a huge success in Britain—and indeed in many other countries that have established similar institutions.

One final feature that should also give strength to the idealist relates to the internationalism of higher education. The scientists have—consciously or not—shown the way, for scientific knowledge is already truly international. But in some arts subjects as well there are signs of a similar breaking down of national barriers, even if this is slower and appreciably more difficult to achieve in some subjects (such as literature) than in others. But it is not just that what is there to be studied knows no national frontiers: those who do the studying have everything to gain from the widest possible international framework for their studies.

Neither the ancient philosophical schools at Athens nor the philosophical lineages of China envisaged their missions in the international terms we need today: I shall be returning to the political implications in the final chapter. But they certainly set down markers for the fundamentals of what a university education is for. That is, to learn about the world we live in, both the natural world studied nowadays from cosmology to microbiology, and the world of human culture and society, about the diversities of our literatures, our philosophies, our art, our music, about our histories and where we have come from, and where, and who, we are today, and finally to practise self-criticism and to be a source of criticism of society, even though we depend on society to support us. That has always been the dilemma of institutions of higher education, and the need for the universities to state and defend their role, not as guardians nor just as transmitters of received knowledge, but as critics and as innovators, has never been greater.

Human Nature and Human Rights

On what basis, if any, can claims to objective moral judgements be made? On what principles should personal and social relations be regulated? Do the claims customarily made, about good and evil, right and wrong, merely reflect the subjective feelings, intuitions, assumptions, or upbringing of those making them—let alone their prejudices and their naked self-interest? Two concepts that currently play a central role in this debate are those of human nature and of human rights. Yet both, as I shall argue in the first part of this study, are problematic. That should not, however, force us to adopt a relativistic position on these questions—as I shall argue in the second part of the chapter. Rather, for the discourse on human nature, we should substitute that of justice and equity, and we need to replace the discourse on rights with one that focuses rather on responsibilities, ties, and obligations. My aim in this chapter is, once again, to explore what a study of earlier thought can tell us about ongoing, twenty-first-century, problems.

The major difficulty that we face throughout this enquiry should be confronted at the outset. In the discussion of classification in Chapter 8, I already noted the immense diversity of cultures, a diversity that encompasses especially differences in views on how to behave, in particular customs, practices, legal and political arrangements. It was precisely that diversity that has been used to suggest difficulties for objectivity in any field of classification, including those of natural kinds such as animals and plants, where cultural relativism serves as a model, one might say, for relativism in science more generally. That other people's views on correct behaviour should be reported but not censured, and that the Western observer should not tell them what to do, were key assumptions from the start of ethnographic fieldwork, and ones that marked out the ethnographer from, for example, the missionary. However, the agenda of the ethnographer's own fellow-countrymen—including those most keen to engage in such research—only slowly came to be appreciated. The question of the ethnographer's role and responsibilities has been the subject of much soul searching ever since.[1]

Not just ethnography, but also history, serve to raise problems for any one who would claim that the concepts of human rights and of human nature constitute cross-cultural universals. Let me tackle briefly first human rights before turning to the more fundamental question of human nature itself.

True, since the Universal Declaration of Human Rights in 1948, the application of that notion has been widely accepted. Yet there is still plenty of scope for disagreement and confusion, evidently, on what basic rights should cover. For some they include the right to bear arms. But that leaves wide open the questions of the circumstances in which that can be allowed, and what controls must be in place, for surely some are needed. There is greater agreement on the right to freedom of speech. Yet again that cannot include the right to incite violence, to advocate intolerant political, religious, racist, views—and so the issue becomes one of defining where the tolerable ends and the intolerant—and intolerable—starts (cf. especially Dworkin 1978).

Although the discourse of human rights is now very common, it only goes back to the seventeenth century and its origin is decidedly Western. Is this not just a typical Western export? Some non-Westerners have certainly expressed that view and rejected its general applicability on those grounds, even while others from the Third World have contributed very considerably to the debate on what constitutes basic human rights (Bauer and Bell 1999, Angle 2002). As I have said before, it is not necessary to have a term to have a concept. But the question is how far back the concept itself goes. Did the ancient Chinese and Greeks address the problems that we tend to identify as involving human rights—and if so, how did they proceed?

In both ancient civilizations, as in our own today, some people were definitely more equal than others. In China, the locus of responsibility was the family rather than the individual person. The wrongdoing of a single individual often implicated his or her family as a whole. Social status defined what you could and could not do. The sense of the humanity of all humans is an important value in the Confucian ideal. But that carried obligations—to behave correctly and in accordance with your defined social role—rather than privileges.

---

[1] Descola 2002 provides an interesting discussion of the ontological, epistemological, and moral problems that face ethnographic research in the twenty-first century.

In Greece, the legal status of different individuals differed. Women, for instance, were under the control of the male heads of households, as also, of course, were the slaves who were their property. There were laws governing the inheritance of property when a man died leaving no sons, or indeed no children. Although in some states (such as Gortyn) daughters could inherit, that was not the general rule. In Athens the widow became an 'heiress' (*epikleros*), but that meant that a male relative could marry her and take over the property. Again there were laws concerning assaults against the person, and manslaughter, though where slaves were the victims, the offence was generally against the master, not the slaves themselves. Most slaves in the Greek world were chattels, treated not as persons but as possessions like furniture or cattle. Women were at best proxy citizens, in virtue of being the daughters of citizen fathers and equally proxy citizen mothers. The key point is that they could not exercise any political functions whatsoever.

There is no question, in either civilization, of an operational notion of human rights that stretched to cover all human beings (cf. Burnyeat 1994*b* on the Greeks). The issues which were discussed related to the law and to justice. True, Aristotle reports a debate on whether slavery is or is not natural: but that had no practical effect at all, for there was no move to abolish the institution. The Stoics promoted the ideal of all being citizens of the world, and the Mohists one of universal love,[2] but both remained just that, namely ideals. Both ancient civilizations point to an important conclusion, that while questions to do with legality and with justice were often discussed—as were also those that concerned the difference between those two—there is little or no expression of any idea that humans *as such* have certain inalienable privileges. That does not mean, of course, that the notion of rights is flawed or invalid: but it does mean that it is a recent, not an ancient, preoccupation.

So I turn now to the more basic question of human nature, and this is immediately complicated by the fact that, as mentioned already, we cannot assume the idea of nature itself to be a cross-cultural universal. Rather, our concept stems from the Greek term *phusis*, which was introduced in the sense of nature, as I have argued, in a distinctly polemical context. It picked out the area over which the so-called *phusikoi* or natural philosophers claimed special expertise, and they used it to refute

---

[2] The Mohists advocated a principle of 'concern for everyone' (*jian ai*) and the purpose of government was seen to be to unify morality, or uprightness (*yi*), throughout the world. See Graham 1989: 41 ff., 45 ff.

the views of traditionalists who had assumed divine intervention in such phenomena as earthquakes and diseases. That was a category mistake, so the naturalists argued, since all such phenomena have a nature and a natural cause.

By contrast the ancient Chinese, for instance, had no single concept that corresponds to nature as such. They talk about *tiandi*, heaven and earth—that is the universe—they capture the diversity of things with the expression *wanwu*, the 'ten thousand things', and they discuss what happens spontaneously, *zi ran*, that is naturally in the sense of without human intervention. But they do not, in ancient times, have an explicit category of nature nor do they identify that as an area of study that deals with a determinate subject matter. They do, however, speak (as I noted before, Ch. 8 p. 109) of the inherent or innate characteristics of things, *jing^I*, and they have a further term for character, *xing*, that can be used of humans, *ren^I*.

We have, accordingly, to reformulate this part of our historical enquiry. The most important issues relate first to views on the differences between humans and other animals (where we may pick up some of the points already made on the perceived differences between males and females), and then to how the differences between different groups of humans are represented. How did ancient Greeks or ancient Chinese think of themselves in relation to outsiders, members of other races, 'barbarians'?

We may make a start on the first topic by returning first to some of the points that emerged from our study of classification. *Huainanzi*, I remarked, identified five main categories of living things, of which one, the 'naked', corresponds to human beings. Although the text does not announce that it is giving a classification of *animals*, humans are here clearly included with other creatures, even though they are exceptional creatures in that their origin is different from that of the other four kinds. They come not from dragons but from Oceanman.[3] Again, the distinctiveness of humans is emphasized, as we saw, by *Xunzi*, when he says that while humans share *qi^I*, life, and knowledge with other things (all three with beasts and birds), what marks humans out is *yi*, the moral sense.[4] Here too then there is clear evidence of a category of human being, distinct from other animals but having certain properties in common with them. Moreover, *ren^{II}* in the sense of what makes a human

---

[3] Cf. above Ch. 8 on *Huainanzi*.   [4] Cf. above Ch. 8 on the *scala naturae* in *Xunzi*.

truly human, that is humaneness, is one of the central 'Confucian' virtues.

But whether humans can be said to be innately good or not was the subject of a famous debate that stretched over several generations,[5] with Mencius claiming that they are, Gaozi asserting that they are neither good nor bad in themselves, while Xunzi argued that they are inherently bad—before culture produces its civilizing effect. So the *yi* that, as I have just said, was the distinctive mark of humans, in Xunzi's view, is only, as it were, a potentiality for morality, and for its realization it needs culture.

The arguments on the question proceed by way of analogies. Gaozi is reported (by Mencius himself, to be sure) to have compared human nature to water that has as little tendency to flow eastwards as westwards—an analogy that Mencius turned against him with the observation that water certainly does have a tendency to flow downwards. In a famous passage I cited in Chapter 9, Mencius (2 A6) invoked what any human would do if he or she saw a child about to fall down a well and claimed that we all possess an instinct to help fellow-humans. Xunzi, for his part, took over a further comparison that Mencius had employed, with wood that possesses certain qualities that allow it to be put to good use, but insisted that for that to happen the wood has to be worked, even transformed, by craftsmen. Human nature has, in fact, to be straightened like crooked wood to be used. So the conclusion that the analogy should suggest was Xunzi's own, that humans are not innately good, but rather evil. To *become* good, humans have to be taught, trained, acculturated, civilized, in short.

The Chinese term *ren*[1], like Greek *anthropos*, covers humans in general, both males and females. But in certain respects the Chinese view of gender difference is very different from the ancient Greek (Farquhar 1994, Raphals 1998, Furth 1999). There are, to be sure, plenty of Chinese texts that emphasize the social distance and differences between males and females, and plenty that reflect the views that their male authors held on the superiority of males and the importance of male children to carry on the (male) line. But there is this important difference, that, if *yin* is often associated, as it is, with female, and *yang*[1] with male, the *interdependence* of those two is strongly stressed.

---

[5] The contrasting positions of Mencius, Gaozi, and Xunzi are discussed by Graham 1989: 117 ff., and Lloyd 1996a: 27 ff., 77.

160 | Human Nature and Human Rights

Nothing is ever one to the total exclusion of the other. An old man may be *yang*[I] in respect of social status with regard to a young man, but *yin* with regard to the same young man in respect of physical stamina. In the cycles of constant change, at the point of maximum *yang*[I], *yin* begins to reassert itself, and vice versa. Where many Greeks thought of their polarities in terms of an ideal of the *independence* of the superior from the inferior (the master from the slave for instance), the Chinese always stressed, on the contrary, their *interdependence*.

So far as Greek views on gender difference go, I have remarked that Greek women, the daughters or wives of citizens, had a definite, limited, legal status as such. Yet, notoriously, there were some prominent Greeks who treated females as a kind on their own. In Hesiod, Pandora, the first woman, is sent as a punishment to men after Prometheus had stolen fire and given it to them. Before Pandora men lived free of toil and disease.[6] Loraux's classic article, entitled 'Sur la race des femmes et quelques-unes de ses tribus', analysed Semonides' use of animal paradigms (for instance) to characterize different types of women. The sow, the bitch, the vixen, are all painted in very negative terms: not even the bee is all good by any means, for immediately after describing her, Semonides repeats the general moral, that women are a bane for men.[7]

Plato has yet another fantasy to tell about the origin of women. At the end of the cosmology in the *Timaeus* women are said to originate, by transmigration, from cowardly males. Although, in the *Republic*, there are female as well as male guardians, Plato repeatedly says that women are weaker. The *Timaeus* even explains women's inherently unstable nature in physiological terms. Their problem is that their wombs are like an independent living animal, moving around inside the body as an expression of uncontrolled desire.[8] No wonder, readers of the *Timaeus* might be left to conclude, they needed to be controlled by their menfolk.

One might think that Aristotle's extensive zoological researches would have led him to less obviously narrow-minded views, and it is true that his zoological treatises are full of detailed descriptions of ani-

[6] Hesiod, *Theogony* 585 ff., *Works and Days* 60 ff.
[7] Semonides Fr. 7, cf. Loraux 1978/1993.
[8] Plato, *Timaeus* 90e ff. sets out a story of the various metempsychoses of the souls of male humans. The inequalities of male and female guardians are stressed in the *Republic* 451c ff., 454b ff. The idea of the womb as an independent animal inside the female body is alluded to at *Timaeus* 91c (it was a notion that Soranus was at pains to refute, in his *Gynaecia* I 8, 7. 18 ff., III 29, 112. 10 ff., 113. 3 ff., IV 36, 149. 21 ff., see Lloyd 1983: 172).

mal behaviour including some that recognize that in certain species of animals—the bear, the leopard—females are generally stronger and more courageous than males. Yet he repeatedly states that females suffer from the inability to concoct semen (in the way that males do) and their chief contribution to reproduction is the matter they supply—while the male provides both the form and the efficient cause.[9]

Some Hippocratic doctors adopt the position that there is female, just as much as there is male, seed, but even they think of the former as weaker. Some are exercised over the question of whether there are quite distinct women's diseases and about whether they can believe what women themselves tell them about their own bodies.[10] But throughout our overwhelmingly male-authored Greek texts the inequalities of males and females are a recurrent theme, in many fantastic as well as rationalizing variations.

Even while both Chinese *ren*[1] and Greek *anthropos* provided categories to talk of humans as such, the tendency to differentiate already between males and females is strong—especially so in ancient Greece. But what about attitudes towards non-Chinese, non-Greeks? Both Greeks and Chinese have a marked sense of the contrast between themselves and other nations. For the Greeks, they cannot speak Greek and so just 'bar-bar' away. In China, as I noted, many of the other peoples with whom they were in contact went by names that incorporate animal radicals, pig, sheep, 'insect', and especially dog.[11] Dikötter's study (1992) has shown how deeply entrenched and persistent racist ideas have been. That certainly does not mean that the Chinese thought of non-Chinese as dogs (for instance). But in Chinese cosmography (just as in Herodotus) beyond the frontiers of the civilized world there are some very strange creatures, not just the 'hairy' people, for example, but creatures with one leg, or their heads on their chests, or no anus.

---

[9] Aristotle repeatedly states this doctrine in his zoological treatises and elsewhere. However, the recent study by Sophia Elliott Connell (forthcoming) underlines the importance of the qualifications that need to be borne in mind, not least those passages in which Aristotle recognizes a parity in the contributions that both the male and female parent make to their offspring. He does so, for instance, in his account of heredity and the resemblances that offspring may have to their forebears, where he talks of the movements that come from both male and female parents (*On the Generation of Animals* IV ch. 3, 767ª36 ff., 768ª11 ff.).

[10] See for example *On the Seed* ch. 4, L VII 474. 16 ff., ch. 6, 478. 5 ff. and ch. 7, 478. 16 ff., and *On Regimen* especially chs. 28 f., CMG I 2. 4, 144. 15 ff., 146. 6 ff., with discussion in Lloyd 1983: 89–94, *On the Eighth Month Child* ch. 7, CMG I 2. 1, 92. 15 ff., Lloyd 1983: 77.

[11] See above ch. 8 p. 104.

However, we must come back to one feature of Greek society that is far less prominent in ancient China, namely the institution of slavery. Although the Chinese economy depended heavily on various forms of unfree labour, it did not make anything like the use of slaves that we find in classical and Hellenistic Greece. The Chinese did not use them on a massive scale for such constructions as the Great Wall, which was built, rather, by conscript labour: nor did they have public slaves acting as the police force, as Scythians did in ancient Athens. The punishments that the Chinese meted out on criminals and their families, indeed often whole populations, make gruesome reading. But though there are exceptions, in the very early, Shang, period especially, the Chinese did not as a matter of course adopt a systematic policy of enslaving other people (let alone other Chinese) whom they defeated in war. Quite a number of Greeks readily assumed that some people—but especially barbarians—were natural slaves, though there was then the problem of telling them apart. Aristotle would have us believe that nature would have liked to distinguish natural slaves, but he had to concede that those with the body of a free man did not necessarily have a free man's soul (*Politics* 1254^{b}27 ff.).

Despite what I have just been saying, both Greeks and Chinese generally appreciated that there are certain biological characteristics that are shared by all human beings, and that humans are also linked by a shared moral potential. But neither of those ideas by themselves yields detailed recommendations as to how to live or how to treat others. Thoughts on those two issues necessarily draw on other sources— whether explicit theories or implicit assumptions—as well.

Aristotle claimed that humans are by nature political animals, more strictly city-state dwelling ones, though like so many of his definitions this has a strong normative ring. He was well aware that the vast majority of humans do not live in city-states, though that is their misfortune. Aristotle's ideas on happiness and true fulfilment depend crucially on the life that the free person can live, as a philosopher and as a citizen, in small-scale, face-to-face, political communities. It took the Stoic Zeno, in the Hellenistic period, to develop Anaxagoras' insight, that the philosopher is a citizen of the world. Yet it was still in terms of *citizenship* that the ideal was construed.

Yet while 'citizen of the world' has a fine ring to it, we must ask what kind of *state* that meant belonging to (cf. Schofield 1999). The Stoics held that, being the rational creatures we are, we participate in the rationality that is the principal factor that governs the universe itself. That is all very well, but in the real world there were no trans-national state structures to give substance to the image of our all behaving like citizens, participating in assemblies, councils, legal institutions, and the like. The actual political situation that Zeno himself faced was one where political power had shifted from the classical city-states to the Hellenistic kingdoms ruled by the successors of Alexander and vying with one another for control of the territories he had conquered. Later Stoics did have direct experience of the unified rule of most of the world known to them under the Roman empire (ruled at one stage, indeed, by the Stoic philosopher Marcus Aurelius). But that left little room for manœuvre for the exercise of the kind of political self-determination that had been the central prerogative of the citizens of the classical city-states.

Even when the notion of citizenship was taken over and adapted, again to suggest a universal ideal, by Christianity, in Augustine's picture of the City of God, the question of what citizenship meant remained problematic. As to the universal application of the idea to cover *all* human beings—often represented as a key breakthrough, separating Christianity from paganism (Baldry 1965)—we have to register that it was subject to two reservations especially. If we all have an immortal soul, some get to be saved and others not—their citizenship is forfeit. Secondly there was the further complicating, if not embarrassing, factor that some were born before, some after, the historic event of Christ's coming.

Utopian ideas of different types were developed in the Graeco-Roman world, and so too was the sense that utopianism was futile speculation. Along with a strong sense of the objectivity of *phusis*, nature, went different views of what was often its antonym, where the term *nomos* covered laws, customs, conventions. The very diversity of human *nomoi* was felt by some to undermine any claim that there could be objectivity in matters of right and wrong. For some 'laws' were invented by the weak to rein in the strong, while for others there was one supreme principle, the very principle that might is right.[12] Plato, who is one of our chief sources for the fifth- and fourth-century debates, took a third view. He held that human laws and lawgivers

[12] The variety of positions taken in the debate between *nomos* and *phusis* has been the subject of extended discussion, for instance, in Heinimann 1945, Guthrie 1969, Kerferd 1981.

should indeed be subservient to, and imitate, the cosmic, natural, dispensation, the true expression of order and rationality in the universe.

The recognition that human cultures differ profoundly did not bring tolerance in its wake, for it could and regularly did go with a distinct view of Greek superiority. How others were treated owed more to the realities of political power than to any deep-seated appreciation of the desirability to live and let live. When the world the Greeks were familiar with came under the effective control of the Romans, the Romans had to be allowed to be rather exceptional 'barbarians'. But tolerance of their ways did not just spring from a Greek recognition of their shared humanity, but also from a sense that they had no option.

The Chinese, by contrast, were never culturally in awe of foreign powers, not even when they were conquered by Mongols or by Manchu, for they Sinified their conquerors far more effectively than the Greeks ever 'captured' the Romans. Such tolerance as the Chinese showed to other groups came primarily from an effortless sense of their own superiority. They certainly never thought for one minute that anyone else's political arrangements (for instance) had anything to recommend them. There was, I said, never any question, in pre-modern China, of any other ideal than that of the benevolent rule of a wise monarch. But one idea associated with that picks up the theme I mentioned earlier. Just as *yin* and *yang*[1] are interdependent, so, throughout all the social hierarchies important for civilized Chinese life, *inter*dependence is the rule, of emperor and minister, old and young, male and female (though that did not extend, to be sure, to Han and non-Han). There is an interdependence throughout the processes at work in the transformation of things, where Chinese microcosm–macrocosm *resonances* contrast, rather, with some Greek ideas of the *gulf* between *phusis* and *nomos*.

Although the problems we face today seem, at first sight, so different from those of the ancient world, we can use our historical analysis to gain a useful perspective on them. One obvious lesson we can learn is that what was presented as an ideal for human kind often reflects just the interests of the group advocating it. Even when such ideas do not express the narrow interests of a given part of society, they often mirror political experience more generally. The ideal of the welfare of all under heaven, to which all should contribute, but especially the ruler himself, echoes Chinese experience just as surely as Greek ideas centring round the role of the citizen reflect theirs.

If so, one warning that our historical investigations serve to underline relates to our own preferred discourse, of human nature and of human and civil rights, in the modern world. What is thereby being exported to other societies looks to be certain Western, or at least insufficiently dewesternized, values. There can, to be sure, be no question of trying to put the clock back to recover either Greek or Chinese ideals as such. Yet reflection on their ideas can serve to broaden the framework within which we discuss the problems.

The ancient Greeks and Chinese belonged, and we still belong, to vulnerable, if not fragile, communities. Even though they both thought a person's place in them differs, depending on who he or she is, nevertheless they believed that we all owe it to our fellows to play our part, as members of households, villages, cities, empires. Aggressive individualism can, of course, be exemplified in the ancient world, where it attracted expected, if sometimes futile, condemnation. But much modern talk of rights might have seemed to the ancients to be aggressive individualism. Focusing on fairness, equity, responsibility provides a wider basis for approaching the problems than does the discourse of rights.

If the dangers of applying Western values uncritically are obvious, where, we must finally ask, does that leave us? In the face of the immense diversity of customs and of notions of right and wrong, we might be tempted to take the easy way out and to deny there can be any objectivity in morality. Yet that certainly will not do. First it is incoherent to say that infanticide, for example, or slavery, or torture, or female circumcision, are all right in one part of the world but not in another. The fact that such practices are sometimes condoned does not mean that we must or should condone them, though, to be sure, we have to investigate and try to understand *why* they are practised when they are. Yet to understand is not to agree, let alone to approve.

On issues such as those I have mentioned, we have to take a stand. But what stand is that? Three insights that come from Aristotle are worth bearing in mind. First the denial of absolute moral principles does not mean the denial of principles that can and should be applied as general, not as universal, rules. Second, while we need principles as criteria, action is always particular. To decide what to do, we have to examine with great care all the relevant circumstances of the particular case—

not that there is any rule that determines that relevance in advance of our exercising our best judgement in the matter.

Thirdly, to return to a theme from Chapter 4, we should be aware that the *way* we reason reflects the kind of person we are. Against the assumption that reasoning and character are independent of one another, Aristotle argued persuasively, in my view, that they are interdependent. When determining how much to give to some cause, does not a mean-minded person tend to use arguments that exhibit the lack of generosity that is part of his or her character? When assessing the risks of courageous action, does not the coward tend to exaggerate these? Although it was a Greek philosopher who theorized about that interconnection, the idea of the interdependence of character and understanding can be exemplified in Chinese philosophy too. Despite their disagreements on the goodness of human nature, both Mencius and Xunzi held a view of the indissociability of uprightness (*yi*) and knowledge (*zhi*III).[13] Sagehood is unthinkable without both.

The only way to secure the general principles we need is to start from such ideas as fairness and equity, the basis of justice.[14] As a starting point we can take, for instance, the belief that killing others is wrong: killing children is no exception, no more is executing criminals in the view I share, though not in others' opinion. But killing in self-defence may be justifiable, even if that is often (as we know) used as an excuse, in circumstances where there was mutual aggression. There are other occasions, too, when killing the aggressor is an excessive reaction. In such a case as that of euthanasia, when the terminally ill ask to die, the difficult questions are located elsewhere: is that really what he or she wants? Is he or she in a position to decide? But if they do not make the decision, who is competent to do so? However, no one can be in any doubt that taking your own life is qualitatively different from taking someone else's.

---

[13] See Graham 1989: 113, 126 (Mencius), 246, 252 (Xunzi). The interdependence of humaneness (*ren*II) and knowledge (*zhi*III) appears already in the *Lunyu*, 17. 8.

[14] This has, of course, been the subject of much recent moral philosophical debate, in the wake of Rawls 1971 especially, whether or not the contributors have adopted his idea of a 'veil of ignorance' as a test for the justice of social arrangements. My own proposals here have a more modest aim. Agreement to such general principles as that it is wrong to take life or inflict pain or deny food or shelter will indeed be criticized as minimalist. But my concern is simply with what are, or are among, the essential starting points from which moral judgements proceed, even though, as I noted, the application of those principles will involve also the evaluation of the particularities of the case in question.

A similar analysis applies also to pain, recognized in general terms as something bad, even though the evaluation of the (im)morality of inflicting pain varies with context and intentionality. The doctor's attempts to treat the patient may involve necessary pain, justified for the sake of the intended cure. The torturer's use of pain, both physical and mental, to secure information, to dominate, or out of pure sadism, will everywhere be acknowledged to be evil. In between there are many mixed cases: they include self-inflicted mutilations in the bid to conform to a culture's preconceptions of the beautiful, and mutilations inflicted on others—as in female circumcision—again in the name of some cultural norm.

In none of the important issues is there any simple formula to settle the matter. But that does not mean that there are no right, even if there are no perfect, no exact, answers. It does not mean, that is to say, that there is no way to discriminate between better answers and worse, answers that correspond more or less closely to what seems fair. The difficulties of deciding that must *always* give us pause. But that should not be allowed to lead to a total suspension of judgement, let alone to complete inaction. Evaluation is, in any event, inevitable, in this domain (especially) as also in others. We carry, accordingly, a particular responsibility to be both self-aware and self-critical, where again there are plenty of Chinese and Greek examples that serve to underline the point. One way in which we can help ourselves, in that task, is, precisely, to study how other people in other cultures and at other times have dealt with the problems.

What we can recover from ancient Greece is the cardinal importance of the principle of equality, even though that idea has to be applied far more broadly than it ever was in Greece, in its restricted application to citizens. What we can learn from ancient China is the sense of the importance of interdependent roles and of the mutual obligations they create. As a counter to the prevailing modern, hyper-individualist, language of the rights to which we can lay claim, we should rather start from the obligations that our global commitments entail and cultivate more actively the basic values of responsibility.[15] By studying the experience of ancient China (among many other societies) we can appreciate the enormous advantages of unity and consensus if they can be

---

[15] The transposition from the language of rights to put greater emphasis on duties and responsibilities is a major theme in O'Neill 2002, and cf. already O'Neill 1989: 225 ff.

achieved, even while we are repeatedly reminded by the ancient Greeks of just how difficult they have always been to secure. Meanwhile from both ancient societies we should recognize that what has been presented as an ideal for human kind has often just reflected the interests of those doing the presenting.

This has already taken us from morality to politics. For fairness in interpersonal relations fairness in the political dispensation is a necessary, even though not a sufficient, condition. My next study will accordingly focus on modern democratic institutions, their strengths but also their weaknesses and shortcomings, at the national and more especially the international level.

12

A Critique of Democracy

Most human societies do not actively question whether the relationships of power and authority they are used to are the best way of organizing political arrangements. But some, notably ancient Greece, allowed those questions to be raised and came up, indeed, with very different answers about the strengths and weaknesses of different political constitutions as well as many utopian dreams of the ideal. In modern times political debate has been stalled. Everyone agrees that 'democracy' is a good thing, but what that should mean in practice at national level is disputed. How, on an international level, the relations between nation-states should be regulated, and even whether regulation is desirable, are even more controversial.

One issue that clearly remains with us today can provide a way into the problems. Our investigations of ancient Greek and Chinese views about the world have already brought to light certain connections between the philosophy and science done in those civilizations, and the social and political institutions they developed and that formed the framework for those enquiries. Thus the political world of the classical Greek city-state was an intensely pluralist one. It is true that all classical city-states shared certain institutions, foremost among them slavery, though there are important differences between the enslaved Helot population of Laconia and the individuals and groups, from outside Greece as well as within it, who were enslaved as a consequence of capture or defeat in war. However, the variety of political constitutions imagined in theory and exemplified in practice was very great. They ranged from democracies of more or less moderate or extreme types, through oligarchies, to constitutional monarchies and tyrannies. To those actual constitutions philosophers added others they described in more or less utopian terms, from Plato's republic governed by philosopher-kings, to Stoic adumbrations of the notion of citizens of the world. In practice, the histories of such states as Athens and Corcyra are ones of recurrent constitutional change, as democrats and their opponents battled for control.

The impact of that complex political situation on the activities of intellectuals of different types in the classical world was itself complex—and so too were the influences in the reverse direction, the ways in which the ideas of the intellectuals helped to create that situation, not least by way of the political theories that I have just mentioned. But the political realities of classical Greece meant, in the first place, that those who taught philosophy, or practised medicine or architecture, for instance, were not confined to a single state. The professional teachers whom Plato called sophists moved freely from one state to another, collecting pupils as they went. If a teacher got into trouble with one state on the basis of what he taught or for any other reason, he could always move to another. That was an option open even to Socrates, although he refused to take it up because it would have meant betraying his mission to teach the Athenians, or, as they would have seen it, to be their gadfly.

Secondly, since radical reform of any given political constitution was possible, that contributed to opening up the analogous possibility of the fundamental questioning of common or traditional beliefs in other fields, including religious concepts and practices, moral beliefs, customs, and conventions, all the way to cosmological theories and assumptions. Again, the reverse influence should also be taken into account, namely the way in which the philosophers' challenging of customs could and did contribute to political speculation and change.

Thirdly and connectedly, that radical questioning was associated with a demand for justifications, for criteria, for foundations, for validity and legitimacy. It was no longer enough to invoke tradition to defend a belief or a practice. Here too there is a two-way process of interaction between different fields. There were differences, to be sure, in the types of account demanded to justify a political policy, or a position in a court of law, on the one hand, and those sought in philosophy or in medicine—to justify medical theories or practices—or even in mathematics. Yet they all share the feature that they offer support for a view that has been subjected to challenge.

Fourthly democracy, in particular, provided a powerful model for the belief that everyone should be able to express their opinion on matters of consequence, including how the state itself should be governed. To be sure, only male citizens enjoyed that privilege. Women, children, aliens, and slaves were all excluded. Yet among the citizens, at least, the idea was that every person's vote had equal weight with everyone else's. In fact that same principle operated also in certain contexts in oligarchic states—though they defined citizens more narrowly than did the democracies, and they often limited office-holding to even more restricted groups.

Chinese intellectuals operated in a very different environment. The agreed political ideal was the benevolent rule of a wise king surrounded by loyal ministers, though that ideal existed in many varieties, with some putting the emphasis on the king being above the fray, ruling effortlessly by the force of his virtuous example—'doing nothing', even, according to some—while others saw his role in far more interventionist terms. However, even in periods when China was not under unified rule, notably before the founding of the empire by the Qin in 221 BCE, the ideal was not explicitly challenged. Debate tended to centre on who could fulfil that role of the wise ruler, not just who had the force to rule but who had the legitimacy to do so.

In the Warring States period there were different seats of power, though most of the states in question were far larger than the classical Greek city-states. Yet as in Greece, so too in China before the unification, intellectuals could and did travel from one state to another, to gain an audience. But the prime audience whom those Chinese intellectuals, from Confucius onwards, generally targeted were the kings or their ministers themselves. As I have mentioned on several occasions before, many Chinese saw influencing government as their foremost ambition. There is a long tradition of philosophers not just advising, but reprimanding, rulers. Although control of those in power was not exercised by democratic process—by removing them at the next election—considerable attention was paid to curbing arbitrary autocrats. One aspect of the responsibility of leading intellectuals was that they recognized their obligations to restrain those in authority, even at considerable risk to themselves.

The welfare of 'all under heaven' was the supreme goal—for intellectuals as well as for rulers. Political authorities for their part intervened, as again I have repeatedly illustrated, in most areas of life, not just in the regulation of social relations, but in fields as diverse as astronomy and agriculture. But as in Greece, so too in China, it is not that the political circumstances determined the intellectual outputs, for there is also an important influence in the reverse direction, with the intellectuals themselves contributing a great deal to the construction and legitimization of the political ideal.

Our historical survey carries several implications and suggests several problem areas for the admittedly very different global political situation we face today. I shall first consider some points that concern the relationship between science and society, and then turn to make some comments on the strengths and the weaknesses of the political institutions that we rely on in the modern world, both national and international ones.

First, the interaction between society in general and the political authorities in particular on the one hand, and scientific research on the other, is as problematic in the twenty-first century as it has ever been, indeed all the more problematic given the exponential growth of science. As many commentators have pointed out, a significant proportion of scientific research since the Second World War has been driven by military interests, both directly in research into new weapons of war, and indirectly when research in space exploration (for instance) is conducted with an eye to its military implications. When not financed by War Departments, science has often been geared to commercial interests, where both questions as to the subjects to be studied and those to do with how to make use of the insights gained are heavily influenced by profitability.

Many of today's scientists have expressed their concern at this situation. There are active groups, in most developed countries, who address the question of the social responsibilities of science. In part this may be a defensive reaction, by those worried at the damage done to the image of science by its association with the development of weapons of mass destruction, let alone by such calamitous mistakes as those at Chernobyl and Bhopal. Many scientists serve on important committees advising governments on such subjects as mad cow disease, about GM foods, about human genome research, about cloning and about Star Wars, the strategic defence initiative. Yet their input has not always measured up to the problem. They have often misjudged the situation and underestimated its gravity, and public suspicion of expert scientific advice can be almost as great as public suspicion of politicians. Governments sometimes seem more concerned with their own images, with what to say about their policies, than with actually taking steps to meet the problems. However, there are of course exceptions—advisers who do an excellent job summarizing the present state of knowledge, indeterminate as that often is. The Royal Society, for instance, publishes helpful newsletters on its policies on the controversial issues of the day.

Yet others of their colleagues are just as determined to go ahead with their research, however unpopular it may make them in certain quarters. They often use the craven argument that if they do not do the work someone else will, implicitly recognizing the dubious nature of the research in question and underlining the problem of ensuring that scientists take collective responsibility for their work. Someone else, the argument continues, will then get the credit for some discovery and the profit from exploiting it. Alternatively, doubtful projects are defended by the plea that the end justifies the means—an argument that has antecedents that go all the way back to the justification of human vivisection for anatomical research in Ptolemaic Alexandria.

Questions of morality are sidelined in the process. Yet they surely have to be addressed, for as many recent experiences show, we cannot allow the momentum of the scientific juggernaut to carry it just anywhere it likes. There are, indeed, two overlapping types of problems, to do with research itself and to do with the installations in which it is exploited. In the latter case, it is a question of insisting first on the paramount importance of safety—against those who would short-circuit such considerations in the name of profitability (whether or not they admit that that is why they are short-circuiting them). It is evidently useless to impose sanctions on firms *after* some disaster has occurred or great environmental damage has been caused. There are far too many ways in which they can simply evade their responsibilities—by going out of business if need be. Rather the point at which control has to be exercised is not after some calamity such as Bhopal, but when permission was being sought to build such a factory in the first place, let alone to do so in a densely populated area—and then to do so with appallingly inadequate safety measures.

Some governments or their agencies or their officials show less than due determination in the face of the seductive arguments of powerful multinational corporations concerning the supposed great benefits that will accrue from giving them their head—and that is before we come to the problem of resisting old-fashioned, but still all too common, bribery and corruption targeted at individuals in positions of influence.[1] As for

---

[1] See Neild 2002. Foster 2001 offers an analysis of the factors influencing the corrupt behaviour of politicians in the UK, including such considerations as the size of the government's majority (cf. Leigh and Vulliamy 1997). More recent cases of corporate misdeeds in the USA—the Enron and World.com debacles—have seriously undermined public faith that big companies can be trusted to report their own finances honestly and transparently.

the similar problems that arise from governmental installations themselves, evidently existing international agencies are at present totally inadequate to deal with the issue. I shall be coming back to that. Meanwhile we have to register that nowadays our capacity to wreck the environment—whether wilfully or merely inadvertently—goes beyond any conceivable ancient imagining and has grown quite out of step with measures for monitoring and control.

The issues concerning what research should be off limits are sometimes easier—but only where the commercial pressures are less, when there is some doubt about the profitability of an end-product. But the key question is, of course, who should decide, and on what basis, that certain types of investigation should be banned—and who then has the responsibility of implementing those decisions? Does not any interference in scientific research savour of Big Brother? Can we not leave it to the good sense of the scientists themselves to monitor the ethical issues raised by their own research? The idea that all new knowledge, however it is obtained, is good has a powerful rhetorical pull. But clearly we cannot let that argument through: nor, when their own interests and ambitions are at stake, are scientists any more capable of clear-headed altruistic judgement than the rest of us—though that is of course not to say that they are less capable.

I cited just now ancient Greek human vivisection—a gruesome example that has had all too many echoes in recent decades. Experiments on humans for medical research have been carried out in the twentieth century not just by the Nazis (though never as systematically as by them). As for genetic manipulation, programmes involving the selective breeding of what were represented as superior specimens combined with the enforced sterilization or euthanasia of the deformed or the mentally ill go back to Georges Vacher de Lapouge in the 1890s (Lapouge 1896, 1899) and received at least a partial endorsement from two French Nobel prizewinners in the aftermath of the First World War (Charles Richet 1919, and Alexis Carrel 1935, cf. Carol 1995). Enforced sterilization of the mentally ill was adopted by several states in the USA in the period 1907–13 and in a number of European countries—Switzerland, Sweden, Norway, Denmark—in the 1920s (Traverso 2003 examines the antecedents to the Nazis' policies). There the ancient Greek model that lies in the background was Plato's recommendations concerning the breeding of the three distinct classes that were to constitute his ideal state, the 'golden', 'silver', and 'bronze' elements that were to be kept segregated and whose reproduction was to be controlled on eugenic principles.[2]

These examples serve to remind us that when real or imagined scientific interests conflict with moral principles, it is the interests that have to yield. If it is then objected that there is no valid way of deciding on the moral principles themselves, we must agree that such decisions are difficult—especially so when the implications of research are hard to predict or anticipate—but not agree that they cannot be made.

As with the general issues of morality discussed in the last chapter, it is a question, first, of making the most of those cases where there is little or no disagreement, at least on the general principles, and then of using them as a basis for judgement in more difficult cases. That human life is a value is not in question: nor is there any doubt on the principle that no medical intervention should be undertaken without the informed consent of the patients themselves. There are, to be sure, disagreements about what 'informed' consent implies. Again the argument about the morality of abortion is an argument about when a fertilized egg becomes a new human being, and, as Aristotle would have insisted, the answer to that is never going to be precise (even though the law will need to identify an exact period to draw the line between legal and illegal terminations of pregnancy). Rather, it will be a matter of an upper and a lower bound. Moreover, as the abortion argument also illustrates, rival principles are often in stark conflict with one another. The intransigent by definition will not be willing to join a consensus.[3] Yet that does not mean that we can allow attempts to find an informed consensus to be derailed by those expressions of intransigence.

Scientists themselves have a particular responsibility to analyse and explain the possible implications of new research. The more we learn about the development of the human embryo, the better informed our decisions about the implications of abortion at different stages of pregnancy. The more we discover about cloning, the clearer we can be about its possible benefits and dangers. It is not that scientific understanding provides the resolution to the moral problem, but it surely constitutes a

[2] Plato, *Republic* 414b ff., where he recognizes that lies (Socrates calls them 'noble' ones) have to be used to persuade people to accept these policies, even though he usually sets such a high value on truth-telling.

[3] This point was forcefully made by Mary Warnock, who chaired the committee that advised the British government on human fertility and embryology from 1982 to 1984, leading to the Act of 1990 (see Warnock 1985 and Warnock 1998: 50 ff.).

necessary condition for a well-informed resolution. Those whose interests and careers are at stake need to be especially self-critical: but then
just as Aristotle pointed out that we all have to know where our weaknesses of character lie, so one may add that we all have a responsibility
to examine the bases of our moral assumptions, and the influence
of possible rationalizations on the reasoning we use to justify our
decisions.

This has already taken us into the more general political questions
that form the central topic of this chapter. Here the paradox is that there
is far more agreement nowadays than in earlier centuries at least on the
name of the most satisfactory political constitution, that is democracy—though of course not all modern regimes, not those ruled by jun-
tas or dictators at least, even pay lip-service to that ideal. However, that
agreement on what the ideal should be called is not matched by a corresponding consensus on how democracy should work in practice, nor by
a corresponding concern as to how far actual practice lives up to that
ideal.[4]

'Democracy' may seem to be in the ascendant across the world, especially with the decline of Communism in Eastern Europe. More and
more countries have multi-party elections. They have that amount of
say in who governs them and that ensures a minimum degree of
accountability. Those points may be accepted. But my chief concern
relates not to the score, of how many political regimes across the world
are nominally democratic, versus how many are not, but rather with the
problems of modern democracy itself. Let me say straight away, however, that I see no *alternative* to democracy in some form, even though
I see a desperate need first to recognize its weaknesses and to work to
counter them, and then to extend the notion of arriving at a consensus
on the international level.

The first major difference between *all* modern and some ancient
democracies stems from a difference in scale. Ancient Greek city-states
had, by modern standards, tiny populations. Their democracies were
participatory, not representative. It was not a matter of a citizen voting
once every four or five years for someone to represent them at local or
at national level in the decision-taking bodies. Rather, the citizen body
en masse assembled to take all the important decisions themselves.

---

[4] Dunn 1992 provides an overview of the current issues set in a well-informed historical
framework.

They then implemented them. If they decided to go to war, they were the ones who did the fighting. In classical Greek antiquity there were no regular mercenaries who could be paid to do the fighting for you. Those who took the decisions, by majority vote, had to deal with the consequences themselves, in the military, the political, the economic, and administrative domains.

The first problem that faces modern democracies relates to the question of just how representative they are, how well the views of the majority are reflected in the decisions taken. The extent of the participation in the political process on the part of the ordinary mass of the citizen body is minuscule by ancient standards. Many eligible voters do not vote: many eligible to be included on the electoral roll do not exercise that right and drop out of the statistics. It is true that in a state such as Athens, those who lived in the more remote parts of Attica were at a definite disadvantage compared with those who lived in Athens itself—for whom attendance at the assembly was far easier. Nevertheless Cleisthenes' reforms ensured that each tribe had representation in the city, as well as in the two other main areas into which Attica was divided, the country and the seashore. Besides, participation in the political process was far more intense than in any modern state.

In the USA the turnout even at a presidential election is now rarely more than 40 per cent. Those who actually voted for George W. Bush amounted to no more than some 15 per cent of those on the electoral roll. In Britain the turnout at the polls when Blair was re-elected in 2001 was less than 60 per cent, and the vote his party collected just 24 per cent of the roll.[5] In some modern states, Australia, Belgium, Greece, Italy, the solution to voter apathy is to make voting in elections compulsory—not that it is ever possible to ensure 100 per cent turnout. That may engender a certain resentment, but it may be that that is a small price to pay to obviate the distortions of a poor turnout.

[5] In the 1997 election that brought Blair to power, the turnout had been higher, at 71.4% of the electoral roll, with Labour gaining 45% of the votes cast, or some 32% of the total roll. In the French presidential elections in April–May 2002, the turnout while less than usual for France was far higher than in the US presidential elections. On the first round there were 72% voting, in the second 80%. However, many who intended to vote for Lionel Jospin in the second round, but who supported one or other of the many other original candidates in the first, found, to their consternation, that the second round was not a contest between Chirac and Jospin, but between Chirac and the ultra-right-wing Le Pen. A single transferable voting system would remedy such a situation, but no politician of any standing in France suggested that that was the solution. As the experience of all three countries, France, the UK, and the USA, shows, those who get elected by one system are very reluctant to propose any fundamental change to it, however necessary it may seem, once they are in power.

If we ask why, in modern democracies, voters do not go to the polls, and why a further substantial element of the population does not bother to ensure that they are included on the electoral roll, the answers are no doubt complex. First it is easy to assume that a single vote, your own, will make no difference—forgetting that the more widespread that view is, the more fallacious the conclusion. Then there is widespread cynicism about the behaviour of politicians once elected. They are thought of as remote from their constituents, unconcerned with their interests, keen only to further their own careers, when not positively corrupt. Those such as Bok (2001) who have investigated the attitudes and performance of both Senators and members of the House of Representatives in the USA have argued that the common stereotype of feckless and irresponsible politicians is a travesty. Yet that does not affect the point that that remains the stereotype.

This problem is compounded by a further factor. While considerable numbers of citizens pay no attention to what is done in their name, those who do take the trouble to participate in the political process are, by that very fact, disproportionately well represented. This is so especially if they organize lobbies, or even engage professional lobbyists, to press their point of view with elected politicians. One might ask where the harm in that is. Surely this is a legitimate mode of advocating a case, and in a way just an extension of the scrutiny of politicians that takes place at election time. If there are some who do not take the trouble to present an opposing case, then the remedy is in their own hands, and no one should protest if meanwhile the advocates of a particular cause have a free hand.

There is of course some force in that defence of existing practice. Yet it can be argued against that, that the interests of rich and powerful corporations and of other pressure groups have had a distorting effect on political decisions.[6] Since candidates have come to rely more and more on support from such sources to fund their own electoral campaigns, they have become more and more vulnerable to pressure to advocate the causes their sponsors support. The sponsors themselves, to be sure, expect some return on what they may see as an 'investment' in sup-

---

[6] According to Bok 2001: 60, some $US100 million were spent on a national campaign to block the health care reforms proposed by the Clinton administration. This 'generated enough confusion', in Bok's words, 'to persuade many legislators that it was safe to oppose reform', even though polls showed that there was overwhelming popular support for change when the reforms were first introduced.

porting a particular politician whose performance they can monitor, checking how he or she voted on each and every issue, whether or not it impinges on their special interests. Candidates in marginal seats are very conscious that a loss of even a small number of votes may well cost them their re-election.

But if we can diagnose some of the sources of the malaise of modern democracies, and principally (1) voter apathy and (2) the distorting effects of pressure groups, that does not mean that there is any preferable alternative to *some* form of democratic system. In modern states there can clearly be no return to participatory democracy on the Greek model. The principles of one person one vote, the right of all citizens to participate, have to be the foundation of such a system. But here too it seems advisable that the notion of a 'right' should be replaced, rather, by one of a responsibility, of an obligation to perform the role of citizen.

Before I make some further comments on the current malaise, we have still other aspects of the problems to consider. So far my remarks have concerned each individual nation-state. But the problems of international relations, and of the international political dispensation, are very much more severe, for two principal reasons. First the translation of democratic principles onto the international scale is fraught with difficulty, and secondly such international agencies as currently exist have no independent power base that enables them to implement the decisions that they take. To put it bluntly, they are impotent in the face of any unwillingness to accept those decisions on the part of the superpowers, or rather in particular of the one remaining superpower, after the demise of the USSR, namely the USA.

UNO operates, to be sure, on the principle of one nation, one vote. But to count China as one, and Luxembourg as one, is evidently open to fundamental objections. Nor would it be easy to justify—even if it were practicable—weighting each nation's vote proportionately with its population. As it is, there are features of the UN constitution that do not correspond to what an ideal democratic set-up would present, notably in the distribution of permanent seats on the Security Council. That, at present, clearly reflects the outcome of the Second World War. At the same time, the principal problem stems from the refusal of any nation to surrender any part of its sovereignty, for the sake of the greater good that the collectivity might represent. Such a surrender is secured only with great difficulty and with great reluctance in the European Union, where however it is covered by the treaty of Rome that set the EU up. The UN Charter makes no such provision for the ceding of individual states' rights. All participant nations have signed up to its declarations of intent, but they now seem quite inadequate to keep global peace.

But if the structure of UNO and its agencies is open to question, a far worse problem relates to the issue of implementing such decisions as it and they reach. What is needed here is far stronger bodies that are directly accountable to the UN itself, rather than to its constituent nation-states, to carry out, if necessary by military action, what the United Nations has agreed.

It is true that some of the agencies, WHO, and IFAD especially, have had some success both in their educational programmes and in dispensing medical and other aid. The International Court of Justice in the Hague does provide a framework in which to deal with disputes between nations and since July 2002 we now have an International Criminal Court, set up—in the teeth of the opposition of the USA—to cover crimes against humanity. But the ponderousness of the procedures of the original War Crimes Tribunal set up in 1993 in relation to the former Yugoslavia illustrates the problems. By 2002, that had cost an estimated $US900 million. In February 2002, of sixty-six alleged war criminals, a mere eight were serving sentence, while three had completed their sentences. Fifteen were on appeal, five had been found not guilty, three had died, three had had their indictments withdrawn, while twenty-nine still awaited trial. Similarly, six years after the massacres in Rwanda, only eight of the fifty-nine persons arrested have been convicted and the dates of trial for a substantial number (twenty-nine) have yet to be set—and by October 2002 the bill for that tribunal had risen to $536 million. The record to date hardly inspires confidence in the ability of international agencies to deal with what is clearly an ever-increasing problem.

The first problem is that UN resolutions are often blatantly ignored. In the days of the Cold War the use of the veto in the Security Council repeatedly blocked international intervention. Nations still regularly use the argument that the problems in their area are purely an internal matter and therefore none of the business of UNO as such. Israel's 'defensive' moves include outright invasions of neighbouring countries, the Lebanon and the West Bank, and the failure of the USA to counter that argument causes world-wide protest. UN resolutions on the problem are, in those circumstances, usually no more than ammunition for rhetorical arguments, not an effective force for peace in the region.

The two cases of the Korean War and the liberation of Kuwait show that when the USA, in particular, believes its interests are at stake, then there is every chance that decisions taken by the UN collectively will be implemented. But the second invasion of Iraq shows that the USA is prepared to go to war in a coalition where only two other states, the UK and Australia, were also prepared to commit troops. This was in the face of the opposition of France, Germany, Russia, and China and of large segments of the rest of the world including of the populations of the USA and UK themselves. President Bush and others considered the UN was shirking its obligations and argued that resolution 1441 by itself legitimized armed intervention to depose Saddam Hussein. Whatever the rights and wrongs of that argument, the action the coalition took did not have the backing of a further democratically voted mandate.

There is a blatant mismatch between the USA reprimanding the UN for not taking its responsibilities seriously and the same USA adopting policies that positively obstruct the UN and its agencies. The USA has in the past repeatedly failed to pay its full dues to UNO, and both the USA and the UK have withdrawn completely from UNESCO. The USA recently went so far as to renegue on its support for the new International Criminal Court, on the grounds that the convention setting it up does not sufficiently protect US citizens, military or civilian, from the threat of arraignment. The impression that these and other policies make is that the USA will do just whatever it likes and whatever it considers to be in its own narrow interests—fully conscious that the rest of the world is in no position to sanction it for so doing. The USA exports democracy and the principles of accountability, but does not listen to other nations when they express views that are taken to conflict with the USA's own interests.

Yet the price the USA itself thereby pays is to destroy the basis on which international cooperation must be built. Instead of showing leadership from its own position of strength, it plays the role of international bully, not policeman. Just to show it does not pay to disagree with the USA, it even threatened to withdraw aid from those countries that honoured their agreement to the International Criminal Court by duly ratifying its establishment. The rhetoric of the war against terrorism has a fine ring to it—except that one person's terrorist is sometimes another's freedom fighter. From the French Revolution and the

American War of Independence, to the Russian and Chinese revolutions, to the setting up of the state of Israel and Fidel Castro's Cuba, many modern states trace their origins to an armed struggle with earlier regimes in a battle for legitimacy.

In the current political situation that every democracy faces, there is no advantage for any statesman in being an internationalist and often considerable disadvantages. I remarked on how lobbying creates imbalances in the debate on national issues. But the consequences on international ones are far more severe. Who, in the nation-state, is there to represent global or international interests? Nobody gets elected to do just that, and if you do take an internationalist stand, you may be lucky if you are not made to pay for it by losing support from those on whom you *do* depend to get elected, who put you there to look after *their* interests, not those of anyone else.

Green politics have begun to make a difference here, but that must be judged against the background of the norm, of elected representatives expected, even required, to work hard for the interests of individual constituencies, and doing so also for such other interest groups as they may be associated with, the farmers, the fishermen, the road hauliers, the automobile industry, the tobacco industry, the gun manufacturers, or whoever. Thus politicians who try to speak up for the interests of *other* nations risk criticism from closer to home. Yet so far as global issues are concerned, the only hope is that even powerful nations, and pre-eminently the USA itself, should come to see that it *is* in their long-term interests that there should be strong international agencies to ensure peace and stability world-wide. One solution is that there should be a permanent international peace-keeping force, accountable directly to the UN itself rather than to any of its constituent states. But that will certainly not happen without the active support of the USA, and without a massive change of attitude in the voters and the politicians of that country any such proposal looks hopeless.

International political problems cannot be dealt with in isolation from economic ones. Again, the positions adopted by the USA, and to a lesser extent the other members of the group of Seven, are the source of major problems. The rich countries have been enormously successful in growing richer—but only at the cost of the poorer countries becoming poorer and more heavily indebted than ever—both in comparative and sometimes in absolute terms. Where, as Amartya Sen especially has argued (Sen 1981, 1992), world resources are, in general, at present ample for world needs, the basic requirements of food and shelter are often not met, even in countries not torn apart by civil war or invasion, due to massive problems of inequitable distribution. In the consumer-oriented economies of the richer, developed, countries, considerable efforts are expended to *create* needs. Today's perception of a reasonable standard of living equals yesterday's untold luxury. What the citizens of those developed countries expect, even demand,[7] is off the scale of the imagination of poorer nations.

Plenty of decisions continue to be taken, in London, New York, Tokyo, Paris, to exploit mostly other countries' natural resources, their hardwood forests, their mineral wealth, without much thought for what that may do to the environment. A good price has been paid, the argument will go: the rest is their problem. But we all have to realize that damaging *anyone's* environment is a threat to everyone's. We often hear that the case against CFCs, or tobacco, has yet to be proved: so we should do nothing yet. But that will not do. The time for risk-taking is long past. To the argument that we cannot afford to take the steps to implement safer policies, we must answer that we cannot afford *not* to. Time is, emphatically, not on our side.

But if greed lies at the root of the problem, we are not likely to have much chance of success in trying to shift people's attitudes unless we do so in the name of what is in *their self-interest* (though not *just* theirs). The hope must lie not, or not just, in an idealistic appeal to people's altruism, but to their sense that their own egotism does not, and cannot, deliver essential goods, one in particular, call it peace. Once again the historian of the ancient world notices that things have not changed—except that the nature of the weaponry certainly has.

There are two aspects to this, one external and one internal. There can be no lasting peace *between* nations until there is some sense, not that there will be an end to inequality, but at least that there will be some fairer distribution of wealth, a more equitable set of rules for competing.

But *within* many nations there is no peace *now*, between rich and poor, haves and have-nots. It is not just a question of fortress America, embattled against terrorist attack. *Within* America there are hundreds of enclaves that have been turned into mini-fortresses, and so too with Britain, France, Japan, and developing countries too, Mexico, Brazil. The problem goes deeper than those connected with the security of the

---

[7] See Runciman's classic analysis of relative deprivation, Runciman 1966.

playgrounds of the mega-rich. Elsewhere too we are warned: do not stray from the bourgeois suburbs or the campus confines. Do not travel on the subway, or the Underground, or the Metro, after dark, or you may get mugged. Do not walk on the streets: you may get shot at from passing cars (not yet, mercifully, in Europe). As for your children, they have to be protected day and night—from everything from abuse to kidnap.

As the situation deteriorates, there are consequences that even rich individuals and rich nations may come to appreciate to be *against* their interests: indeed they surely *have* to recognize that. The remedy is not to keep increasing the security, but rather to tackle the underlying causes of deep-seated discontent, of misery, and of potential violence. The same applies also to nations. Since September 11, 2001, it is clear that no country, not even the USA, can consider its own territory secure. As for the environment, it is in everyone's interests, for the sake of survival, no less, to come to its defence.

It is clearly intolerable for a tiny proportion of the world's population to live in the greatest luxury while many of the rest have no hope of escape from grinding poverty. There must at the very least be some move towards the equalization of opportunity. The first steps can easily be identified, freedom from hunger, basic health provision, education. The first two are vital for life: the third provides perhaps the best hope for that move towards eventual greater equality.

The diagnosis I have offered of the weaknesses of democracy at both the national and the international level is utterly bleak, and the prognosis almost equally so. It is neither practicable, nor (many would say) at all desirable, to try to turn back to the simpler world of antiquity—neither to the participatory democracy of the ancient Greeks nor to the ideal of benevolent imperial rule of the ancient Chinese. Yet that cannot mean that we just sit back and watch the problems mount and the situation worsen, nor should we ignore what we can learn even from the remote past.

First, there is a massive task of persuasion and of the dissemination of information. Scientists, as I said, carry a heavy load of responsibility to investigate and explain the moral and other implications of the programmes of research that are proposed. With regard to the environment, at least, few now entirely ignore the potential dangers in current trends, even though there are ongoing disagreements both as to the extent of global warming, for instance, and on the factors that contribute to it. Nevertheless if there is some general awareness of ecological issues, there is still an uphill battle to get governments to play their part in helping to control the present situation and reverse current trends. The rejection by the USA of the Rio and Kyoto accords is yet another example of an irresponsible capitulation to commercial and national interests, even though it was claimed that alternative, far weaker, proposals were adequate for the situation.

One must hope first that the voices of socially responsible scientists will carry more weight, and then that those of concerned economists such as Sen will also do so. The universities as a whole, as I argued in Chapter 10, have important responsibilities too, especially as they offer a real potential for change. One of the few slim positive rays of hope lies in the possibility of using and developing the international networks that exist in academic circles to exercise a critical function and bring pressure to bear on governments. But for that the academics themselves have to play a far more active role than they are currently used to. We should all make the most of the internet to exchange information, to educate, and to bring home the urgency of the problems to politicians and administrators, not just at election time but more generally. Indeed this is already beginning to happen—in US and UK elections especially. Yet it is still the case, of course, that access to the web is far from universal, and while the development is to be welcomed, we must recognize that it produces an imbalance in that only a proportion of the total electorate can make use of this means of entering into dialogue with politicians and of probing their policies and attitudes.

The main dangers in the present geopolitical situation are clear, the threat to the environment world-wide, the ways in which increasing inequality fuels the fires of future resentment, the frailty of the geopolitical order. Outside the USA there is the sense that that country is a law unto itself and the world order depends on its perception of its self-interest: inside it, there is a mixture of feelings, upset that the USA's own efforts at keeping the peace are not appreciated, compounded by a new version of the old isolationism. If the rest of the world does not accept US policies, too bad for the rest of the world.[8]

[8] A recent number of *Daedalus* (Winter 2003) devoted to 'International Justice' highlights the problem. The difficulty of providing a theoretical, let alone a practical, basis for the internationalization of justice, and US suspicions of the International Criminal Court, led some contributors to argue bluntly that no attempts can or should be made to curb US power—on which alone, in their view, global order depends.

The weaknesses of our existing political institutions, both national and international, in not even providing an adequate framework for discussion directed at alleviating the problems, those weaknesses must be shown up for what they are. On the national scale there is the failure to engage the electorate and secure their active participation in the political process, as well as the deleterious effects of professional lobbying for commercial and other interests, and the lack of any mechanism to allow for the representation of international interests at the national level. On the world stage, there is the need to cede some measure of sovereignty to international institutions to give them the wherewithal to implement decisions taken by the collectivity of nation-states.

The argument cannot be just an idealistic, moral one, that egotism is to be deplored. Rather, it must also be that altruism and internationalism are now in the interests of *all*. To continue to pursue narrowly national goals and ignore the wider implications should be recognized to lead to disaster, environmental, political, humanitarian. It seems obvious that if we fail to accept that argument, the likely consequences are dire, though I have to end by saying that I am not optimistic that the necessary lessons will be learnt in any other than the hardest way, through the experience of catastrophe. Worse still, events over the last decades in Northern Ireland, in former Yugoslavia, in Rwanda, in Afghanistan, in Cambodia, in the Middle East, show all too clearly that even catastrophe does not necessarily teach good sense.

While democracy is, as I said, the name of what most of the world accepts as the best national political dispensation, its weaknesses must be acknowledged, and so too its current ineffectiveness when translated on to the global scale. In that task of education, the emphasis must be on the analysis of modernity: yet that analysis is best carried out in full recognition of where our current models originated, and of earlier notions, in a less complex world, of how humans should live together. This is not to look back in nostalgia to a past that is well beyond recovery—and that from many points of view no one would wish to recover. It is rather to cultivate a sense that we cannot afford to ignore certain values that were held in high regard, even if those values have to be adapted to our modern situation.

Chief among these are two. First, despite all my criticisms of modern, representative, democracy, there is, as I said, no viable alternative. The principle of accountability is not extended far enough, by which I mean that its reach needs to be internationalized to counteract the interest groups that currently introduce a massive bias in the way in which it works—while the global perspective is under-represented or not represented at all. Yet when all that is said, democracy still provides the only fair, the only just, framework for the conduct of political life. The ancient Greeks are still worth studying for that—for both the positive and the negative models of democratic behaviour and accountability that they provided.

Secondly we should not lose sight of Chinese notions of solidarity. The institutions of imperial rule that were the unchallenged source of legitimate government (and so underpinned the unity) have no modern analogue. But we would do well to reflect on how responsible individuals bore witness to their conception of what served the welfare of all under heaven. We can ponder the role and need for legitimization, even if we have to find alternative sources for it, in the consensus that has to be based on the possibility of equity. Most importantly, in relation to that need for a consensus, the sense of the interdependence of all humans and the principle of collective responsibility for the common welfare surely still have lessons for us today.

Conclusion

I have been teasing out the relevance of ancient cultures for modern dilemmas. This has constantly involved evaluations, moral judgements indeed. The issues include some that go to the heart of the question of how we should live, as individuals, in our own immediate groups, in relation to the wider general community. All description, all history, is evaluative. Yet let me return now, briefly, in conclusion, to some reflections on the pitfalls and the prizes in the investigation of ancient societies and to the question of how history of science can help to throw light on ongoing philosophical problems.

The distance that separates antiquity from ourselves can be seen as at once an obstacle and an opportunity. We should never underestimate how difficult it is to recover ancient aims, goals, preoccupations, and expectations. But while both in those respects, and in terms of what they considered they knew already, their starting points were so different from ours, there is still a sense in which their ambition to understand, and their endeavours to carry their contemporaries with them, are analogous to those we engage in ourselves. The hermeneutic tasks increase the further back in time we go—that is where the particular obstacles lie—but they are not such as to block every effort at interpretation. The opportunities are a matter of the insights we can gain into the different forms those ambitions took and the different styles of understanding that were cultivated. In the process we can become more aware of the limitations of our own preconceptions, the narrowness of our own values, and the potential inadequacy of our institutions to deal with the exponentially increasing problems of the modern world. To be sure, we do not have to study ancient cultures to achieve that self-awareness: but I would claim that it is one way to do so.

Many have come away from the historical encounter with ancient societies with a strong sense of how each was the prisoner of its own value systems and political prejudices, and of how what was claimed as objective knowledge of the external world was merely the reflection of ideology. Those reactions have some validity, but first we have to recognize that the ancients too were quite capable of self-criticism, and secondly we must bear in mind the extent to which the same points apply also to ourselves. We have no need to endorse the view that *all* assertions of objectivity are ideological. However, the claim that all observations are theory-laden admits of degrees, but of no exceptions. We delude ourselves if we think that we escape, with our modern science, and with our own historical descriptions.

The economies of ancient societies, their technologies, their political institutions, their educational ones, their values, all contributed to differentiating the enquiries that were undertaken. But none of these individually, nor all of them jointly, can be said to have determined thought. We saw reason to deny that different ancient investigators were faced with different worlds, or that their reasoning was governed by different formal logical laws—even though different informal rules of communicative exchange applied in different contexts. Considerable differences in world-views are found, as between different ancient societies and also within them. But there are recognizable points of contact between what they were views of. Different styles of enquiry were constituted by preferred modes of argument and different preoccupations and methods. These reflect, and help in creating, differences in perspective. To the objection that we cannot independently have access to what they were perspectives *of*, we can agree but add that multiple perspectives do allow us to establish both those differences and the relevant points of contact.

Our studies of the ancient world can be brought to bear on three main issues in the philosophy and history of science. First we found no grounds, in the materials we considered, for accepting the postulate of strictly incommensurable systems of belief. There are indeed major differences in the basic concepts that different investigators used, and in how they defined the problems they were interested in. But while these presented, and continue to present, great obstacles to understanding, they did, and do, not totally defeat interpretation—by them or by us. The notion of the possibility of two natural languages that are mutually completely unintelligible and across which no communication can be made is a philosophical speculation for which there is no empirical evidence.

So taken in the strictest sense the notion of incommensurable systems of belief is too strong. So too the disputes between correspondence and coherence theories of truth and between realism and relativism or constructivism depend in both cases on overdrawn dichotomies. Evidently neither correspondence nor coherence versions of truth will do. But the actual appeals to different procedures of warranting that we find can be cited to ground a more complex account of that notion. The mistake is to demand a single theory of truth, across every type of context in which it may be relevant to raise questions of reliability or justification. Which modes of verification are appropriate will always be a tricky matter of judgement, but that is not to say that internal consistency will by itself be adequate, let alone that received ideas on appropriateness, whatever they may be, are to be accepted without further scrutiny.

Evidently also one form of naive realism falls with the fall of the correspondence theory of truth. Again some modes of relativism are subject to similar objections to those I have just mentioned against the coherence theory, namely that there are other constraints on theories besides internal consistency and agreement with what is currently accepted. What remains truistically true is that scientific theories are the products of the individuals or groups that propose and maintain them. Meanwhile on the realism side of the controversy what remains true is that the investigators themselves proceeded as if the constraints on their enquiries included more than just their own or their contemporaries' current assumptions. They no doubt sought to be persuasive: but they also aimed to establish what is the case, and they used a variety of empirical means and arguments to do just that. The question was always how reliable they were, how robust were the results obtained, and those results that survived one set of tests or scrutinies might always need to be revised in the light of others. The historical study of ancient enquiries here too suggests complexities that defeat the neat abstractions that philosophical analysis would seek to impose.

The reflections in my final three chapters apply similar historical perspectives to certain aspects of our modern plight. The argument of Chapter 10 was that our institutions of higher education would do well to regain some of the strategic ambitions that animated their predecessors before the rise of narrowly utilitarian, vocational, training. Universities have a special responsibility for criticism and they should not be afraid to stand up for the values of pure, disinterested, research. In the discussion of the notions of human nature and human rights, in

Chapter 11, I suggested that the specifically Western origins of those ideas cast a long shadow over their use and that some of their invocations in modern rhetoric are unselfcritical, half-baked, indeed bordering on the incoherent. In a global perspective the emphasis should be as much on what we *owe* to our fellows—our responsibilities—as on what we can *demand* from them—our rights. My reflections on the institutions of democracy, in Chapter 12, focused on some of their weaknesses in nation-states, and the yawning gap left by their ineffectiveness on an international level. To say that there are no easy solutions is a grotesque understatement. We need to muster all the resources for criticism and analysis that we can, including those from reflections on the past. We have to cut through the rhetoric that allows the one remaining super-power to preach the virtues of democracy for other states, while paying scant attention to the opinions of other nations in the forum of international debate.

In each study I realize that I am open to the charge of excessive idealism. What hope is there that any of these arguments will cut any ice with any of today's hard-bitten politicians or policy-makers? What can reverse, what can make any impact on, today's rampant egotism? To that I have two counters. The first reiterates the point that, practical or not, there is an argument from justice and equity that we should not ignore. Considerations can always be invoked to suggest that what is perceived to be right is too difficult to implement, or too difficult to do so now: but that does not detract from the perception that it *is* right. Doing something to redress the appalling inequalities between rich and poor states, between multinational corporations and primary producers, between the massively advantaged and the preternaturally deprived, surely counts as one such example.

But then the second argument does not just rely on idealism but appeals to the *self-interest* of the privileged. They—we—certainly desire security, freedom from the threat of terrorist, or just ordinary, violence. But there can be no durable peace, no real security, no stability, even, unless something is done about some of the key factors that stoke the aggression and violence, not least the sense of the gross unfairness of unequal resources and opportunities that I have just mentioned. It is in the interests of the rich themselves that this should be done, that as a first step the present trends of increasing inequality should be reversed, that we should all be seen to be working towards that end, to restore hope where at present there is none. We naturally condemn those who take the law into their own hands, from muggers to suicide bombers. But that should not stop us thinking hard about why they did what they did, including about the causes both of their desperation and of their fanaticism.

What are the chances of such an argument from self-interest carrying sufficient weight in the face of mindless materialism and greed? I shall not venture an answer, but end merely by remarking that, whatever the prospects of success, the analysis needs to be carried through. This is just a special, and a specially difficult, case of what this whole book has been about, in its endeavours to explore the lessons to be learnt, for our modern predicaments, from questionings and reflections that stem from the study of the ancient world.

GLOSSARY OF CHINESE AND GREEK TERMS

Chinese

ba	胈	naked
bai	白	white
bei	誖	inconsistent
bencao	本草	herbals
bian	辯	dispute
bienao	鼈臑	pyramid with right triangular base and one lateral edge perpendicular to the base
bu	步	pace (measure of length)
bu ran	不然	not so
cheng	誠	sincere
chi	赤	red
chong	蟲	'insect'
chu	畜	domestic animal
di	狄	(name of tribe)
di li	地理	terrestrial organization
dongwu	動物	animal ('moving thing')
duan	端	starting point, principle
fa jia	法家	'legalists'
fang	倣	imitate
fei	非	(is) not, wrong
feng	鳳	phoenix
gan	肝	liver-function
gangji	綱紀	guiding principles
gu	故	thus, therefore, cause
guo	猓	(name of tribe)
hei	黑	black
huang	黃	yellow
hui	虫	'insect'

jia	家	family, lineage, sect
jian ai	兼愛	concern for everyone
jing[I]	精	inherent characteristics
jing[II]	經	canon
junzi	君子	'gentleman'
ke	客	guest
kongyan	空言	abstract speech
lei	類	category
li[I]	里	'league'
li[II]	理	pattern, order
li[III]	禮	rites
liao	獠	(name of tribe)
lifa	曆法	calendar studies
lipu	曆譜	calendars and chronologies
long	龍	dragon
lü	率	ratio
luan	亂	confusion
luo[I]	玀	(name of tribe)
luo[II]	倮	hairless
luo[III]	臝	hairless
mou	侔	parallelizing, equating
mu	獏	(name of tribe)
niao	鳥	bird
pi	辟	illustrate, compare
qi[I]	氣	breath, energy
qi[II]	齊	homogenize
qilin	麒麟	fabulous creature
qing[I]	青	green
qing[II]	情	feelings
quan	犬	dog
ran	然	so
ren[I]	人	human
ren[II]	仁	humaneness
ri	日	sun
shen	神	spirit, demonic
sheng	生	life
shi[I]	是	is, right, this

shi^{II}	豕	pig
shi^{III}	士	officials, gentlemen retainers
shi^{IV}	詩	*Odes*, poetry
shi^V	使	tell, command, a reason
shigu	是故	for this reason
shigui	蓍龜	milfoil and turtle shell divination
shou	獸	quadruped animal
shu^I	書	*Documents*, book
shu^{II}	庶	ordinary
shu shu	數術	calculations and methods
shu yue	術曰	the method states
shui	水	water
tian	天	heaven
tiandi	天地	heaven and earth
tianwen	天文	heavenly patterns
tianwen suanfa	天文算法	astronomy and mathematics
tong^I	同	equalize
tong^{II}	通	make to communicate
tui	推	infer, induce
wanwu	萬物	the myriad things
wei	位	position
wei shi	為是	deem to be so
wuxing	五行	the five phases
xian	獫	(name of tribe)
xing	性	character
xingfa	形法	study of significant shapes
xun	獯	(name of tribe)
yang^I	陽	sunny side of hill/positive principle
yang^{II}	羊	sheep
yangma	陽馬	pyramid with rectangular base and one lateral side perpendicular to the base
yao	猺	(name of tribe)
yi	義	uprightness, righteousness
yin	陰	shady side of hill/negative principle
yin shi	因是	rely on as so
yu	魚	fish
yuan	援	adduce, draw an analogy

yue	月	moon
yueling	月令	monthly ordinances
yun	狁	(name of tribe)
za zhan	雜占	miscellaneous prognostic procedures
zhen	真	true
zhengming	正名	rectification of names
zhi[I]	直	correct, straight
zhi[II]	豸	footless reptile
zhi[III]	知	knowledge
zhiwu	植物	plant ('stationary thing')
zhou jun	州郡	provinces and commanderies
zi ran	自然	spontaneous

Greek

aitiai	αἰτίαι	causes, explanations
akribes	ἀκριβής	exact
aletheia	ἀλήθεια	truth
alethes	ἀληθής	true
anankaion	ἀναγκαῖον	necessary
anthropos	ἄνθρωπος	human
apodeixis	ἀπόδειξις	demonstration, proof
astrologia	ἀστρολογία	study of the heavens: astrology
astronomia	ἀστρονομία	study of the heavens: astronomy
chloros	χλωρός	'green', fresh
diagramma	διάγραμμα	diagram, proof
doxa, doxai	δόξα, δόξαι	seeming/opinion
eidos	εἶδος	form, species
eikones	εἰκόνες	images
einai	εἶναι	to be, being
entoma	ἔντομα	insects
epagoge	ἐπαγωγή	induction
epikleros	ἐπίκληρος	heiress
eristike	ἐριστική	disputatious reasoning
genos	γένος	genus, group, family

hairesis	αἵρεσις	sect, choice
helios	ἥλιος	sun
homoiotetes	ὁμοιότητες	similarities
ichthus	ἰχθῦς	fish
leukos	λευκός	bright, white
logos	λόγος	word, account, argument
malakia	μαλάκια	'softies', cephalopods
malakostraka	μαλακόστρακα	soft-shelled, crustacea
malakoteron	μαλακώτερον	looser
manthanein	μανθάνειν	learn
mathematike	μαθηματική	'mathematics'
mathematikos	μαθηματικός	'mathematician' astronomer/astrologer
melas	μέλας	dark, black
metabasis tou homoiou	μετάβασις τοῦ ὁμοίου	transition to the similar
metis	μῆτις	cunning intelligence
muthos	μῦθος	story, fiction, myth
nomos	νόμος	law, custom, convention
on, ontos	ὄν, ὄντως	being, really/truly
ostrakoderma	ὀστρακόδερμα	'potsherd-skinned', testacea
ousia	οὐσία	being, reality, substance
parabolai	παραβολαί	comparisons
paradeigma	παράδειγμα	example, paradigm
para phusin	παρὰ φύσιν	contrary to nature
pepsis	πέψις	concoction
phronesis	φρόνησις	practical reasoning
phusike	φυσική	study of nature
phusiologos	φυσιολόγος	student of nature, natural philosopher
phusis	φύσις	nature
pithanologia	πιθανολογία	plausible talk
pseudes	ψευδής	false
selene	σελήνη	moon
to ti en einai	τὸ τί ἦν εἶναι	essence

NOTES ON EDITIONS

Chinese

With some exceptions to be mentioned, ancient Chinese texts are cited according to standard editions, for example those of the Harvard-Yenching Institute series (HY) or the University of Hong Kong Institute of Chinese Studies series (ICS)

Erya (爾雅) in the ICS edition, Classical Works 16 (1995).

Gongsun Longzi (公孫龍子) in the ICS edition (1998).

Guanzi (管子) in the Zhao Yongxian edition, reprinted in the *Sibu beiyao* series (Shanghai, 1936).

Hanfeizi (韓非子) in the edition of Chen Qiyou (Shanghai, 1958).

Hanshu (漢書) in the edition of Yan Shigu, *Zhonghua shuju* (Beijing, 1962).

Hou Hanshu (後漢書) in the *Zhonghua shuju* edition (Beijing, 1965).

Huainanzi (淮南子) in the edition of Liu Wendian (Shanghai, 1923).

Jiuzhang suanshu (九章算術) in the edition of Qian Baocong, *Suanjing shishu* (Beijing, 1963).

Liji (禮記) in the ICS edition (1992).

Lunheng (論衡) in the edition of Liu Pansui (Beijing, 1957).

Lunyu (論語) in the ICS edition, Classical Works 14 (1995).

Lüshi chunqiu (呂氏春秋) in the edition of Chen Qiyou (Shanghai, 1984).

Mengzi (Mencius) (孟子) in the HY series, Supplement 17 (Beijing, 1941).

Mozi (墨子) in the HY series, Supplement 21 (Beijing, 1948).

Shangshu (尚書) (*Shujing,* 書經) in the ICS edition, Classical Works 9 (1995).

Shanhaijing (山海經) in the ICS edition (1994).

Shiji (史記) in the *Zhonghua shuju* edition (Beijing, 1959), cited by *juan,* page, and where necessary column number.

Shuo yuan (說苑) in the ICS edition (1992).

Suanshushu (算數書) from the *Zhangjiashan han mu zhu jian* edition (Beijing, 2001).

Sunzi (孫子) in the edition and translation of R. Ames, *Sun-tzu: The Art of Warfare* (New York, 1996).

Xunzi (荀子) in the HY series, Supplement 22 (Beijing, 1950), cited by *pian* and line number.

Yantielun (鹽鐵論) in the ICS edition, Philosophical Works 14 (1994).

Zhanguoce (戰國策) in the ICS series (1992).

Zhoubi suanjing (周髀算經) in the edition of Qian Baocong, *Suanjing shishu* (Beijing, 1963).

Zhuangzi (莊子) in the HY series, Supplement 20 (Beijing, 1947), cited by *pian* and line number.

Greek and Latin

I cite the major Greek and Latin authors by standard editions, for example the fragments of the Presocratic philosophers according to the edition of H. Diels, revised by W. Kranz, *Die Fragmente der Vorsokratiker*, 6th edn. (Berlin, 1952), the works of Plato according to Burnet's Oxford text, the treatises of Aristotle according to Bekker's Berlin edition. Greek mathematical texts (Euclid, Archimedes) and Ptolemy are cited according to the Teubner editions. Greek and Latin medical texts are cited, for preference, according to the *Corpus Medicorum Graecorum* (*CMG*) and *Corpus Medicorum Latinorum* (*CML*) editions, and failing that, for the Hippocratic treatises, I use E. Littré (L), *Œuvres complètes d'Hippocrate* (Paris, 1839–61). Abbreviations for Greek works are those in the *Greek–English Lexicon* of H. G. Liddell and R. Scott, rev. H. S. Jones with Supplement (Oxford, 1968). Thus Simplicius, *In Cael.*, refers to Simplicius' work *In Aristotelis De Caelo Commentaria*, ed. J. L. Heiberg (*Commentaria in Aristotelem Graeca*, vol. vii) (Berlin 1894).

Modern

All modern works are cited by author's name and year of publication. Full details are to be found in the References.

With the exception of Confucius and Mencius, all Chinese names and words are transliterated according to the Pinyin convention. Homophones are distinguished by superscript Roman numerals.

REFERENCES

ANDERSON, B. R. O'G. (1991), *Imagined Communities* (1st pub. 1983), rev. edn. (London).

ANGLE, S. C. (2002), *Human Rights and Chinese Thought* (Cambridge).

ANNAS, J., and BARNES, J. (1985), *The Modes of Scepticism* (Cambridge).

ATRAN, SCOTT (1990), *Cognitive Foundations of Natural History: Towards an Anthropology of Science* (Cambridge).

——(1994), 'Core Domains versus Scientific Theories: Evidence from Systematics and Itza-Maya Folkbiology', in Hirschfeld and Gelman (1994: 316–40).

——(1995), 'Causal Constraints on Categories and Categorical Constraints on Biological Reasoning across Cultures', in Sperber, Premack, and Premack (1995: 205–33).

AUSTIN, J. L. (1962), *How to Do Things with Words* (Oxford).

BALDRY, H. C. (1965), *The Unity of Mankind in Greek Thought* (Cambridge).

BARNES, BARRY (1973), 'The Comparison of Belief-Systems: Anomaly versus Falsehood', in Horton and Finnegan (1973: 182–98).

——(1974), *Scientific Knowledge and Sociological Theory* (London).

——and BLOOR, D. (1982), 'Relativism, Rationalism and the Sociology of Knowledge', in Hollis and Lukes (1982: 21–47).

BARNES, J. (1990), *The Toils of Scepticism* (Cambridge).

——BRUNSCHWIG, J., BURNYEAT, M., and SCHOFIELD, M. (eds.) (1982), *Science and Speculation* (Cambridge).

BARTH, F. (1975), *Ritual and Knowledge among the Baktaman of New Guinea* (Oslo).

——(1987), *Cosmologies in the Making* (Cambridge).

BASCOM, W. (1969), *Ifa Divination* (Bloomington, Ind.).

BAUER, J. R., and BELL, D. A. (eds.) (1999), *The East Asian Challenge for Human Rights* (Cambridge).

BERLIN, BRENT (1992), *Ethnobiological Classification* (Princeton).

——BREEDLOVE, D. E., and RAVEN, P. H. (1973), 'General Principles of Classification and Nomenclature in Folk Biology', *American Anthropologist*, 75: 214–42.

——and KAY, P. (1969), *Basic Color Terms: Their Universality and Evolution* (Berkeley).

BIARDEAU, M. (1957), 'Le Rôle de l'exemple dans l'inférence indienne', *Journal asiatique*, 245: 233–40.

BLOOR, D. (1976), *Knowledge and Social Imagery* (London).

BOK, D. (2001), *The Trouble with Government* (Cambridge, Mass.).

BOK, S. (1978), *Lying: Moral Choice in Public and Private Life* (Hassocks).

BOURGON, J. (1997), 'Les Vertus juridiques de l'exemple: nature et fonction de la mise en exemple dans le droit de la Chine impériale', *Extrême-Orient Extrême-Occident*, 19: 7–44.

BOWEN, A. (2001), 'La scienza del cielo nel periodo pretolemaico', in S. Petruccioli (ed.), *Storia della Scienza* (Rome), vol. i, section 4, ch. 21, 806–39.

BOWKER, G. C., and STAR, S. L. (1999), *Sorting Things Out: Classification and its Consequences* (Cambridge, Mass.).

BOYER, P. (1986), 'The "Empty" Concepts of Traditional Thinking', *Man*, NS 21: 50–64.

——(1990), *Tradition as Truth and Communication* (Cambridge).

BRAY, F. (1997), *Technology and Gender: Fabrics of Power in Late Imperial China* (Berkeley).

BRONKHORST, J. (2002), 'Discipliné par le débat', in L. Bansat-Boudon and J. Scheid (eds.), *Le Disciple et ses maîtres* (Paris), 207–25.

BROWN, C. H. (1984), *Language and Living Things: Uniformities in Folk Classification and Naming* (New Brunswick, NJ).

BROWN, D. (2000), *Mesopotamian Planetary Astronomy-Astrology* (Groningen).

BULMER, R. (1967), 'Why is the Cassowary not a Bird? A Problem of Zoological Taxonomy among the Karam of the New Guinea Highlands', *Man*, NS 2: 5–25.

BURNYEAT, M. F. (1982), 'The Origins of Non-deductive Inference', in Barnes et al. (1982: 193–238).

——(ed.) (1983), *The Skeptical Tradition* (Berkeley).

——(1994a), 'Enthymeme: Aristotle on the Logic of Persuasion', in D. J. Furley and A. Nehamas (eds.), *Aristotle's Rhetoric: Philosophical Essays* (Princeton), 3–55.

——(1994b), 'Did the Ancient Greeks Have the Concept of Human Rights?', *Polis*, 13: 1–11.

CALAME, C, (1999), 'The Rhetoric of *Muthos* and *Logos*: Forms of Figurative Discourse', in R. Buxton (ed.), *From Myth to Reason?* (Oxford), 119–43.

CAREY, S. (1985), *Conceptual Change in Childhood* (Cambridge, Mass.).

——(1995), 'On the Origin of Causal Understanding', in Sperber, Premack, and Premack (1995: 268–302).

——and SPELKE, E. S. (1994), 'Domain Specific Knowledge and Conceptual Change', in Hirschfeld and Gelman (1994: 169–200).

CAROL, A. (1995), *Histoire de l'eugénisme en France: la médecine et la procréation XIXe–XXe siècle* (Paris).

CARREL, A. (1935), *L'Homme, cet inconnu* (Paris).

CHEMLA, K. (1988), 'La Pertinence du concept de classification pour l'analyse de textes mathématiques chinois', *Extrême-Orient Extrême-Occident*, 10: 61–87.

——(1990a), 'Du parallélisme entre énoncés mathématiques', *Revue d'histoire des sciences*, 43: 57–80.

——(1990b), 'De l'algorithme comme liste d'opérations', *Extrême-Orient Extrême-Occident*, 12: 79–94.

——(1992), 'Résonances entre démonstration et procédure', *Extrême-Orient Extrême-Occident*, 14: 91–129.

——(1994), 'Nombre et opération, chaîne et trame du réel mathématique', *Extrême-Orient Extrême-Occident*, 16: 43–70.

——(1997), 'Qu'est-ce qu'un problème dans la tradition mathématique de la Chine ancienne?', *Extrême-Orient Extrême-Occident*, 19: 91–126.

——(forthcoming), 'Generality above Abstraction', *Science in Context*.

CHENG, A. (1997), 'La Valeur de l'exemple: "Le Saint confucéen: de l'exemplarité à l'exemple"', *Extrême-Orient Extrême-Occident*, 19: 73–90.

CHENG, C.-Y. (1997), 'Philosophical Significance of Gongsun Long: A New Interpretation of Theory of *Zhi* as Meaning and Reference', *Journal of Chinese Philosophy*, 24: 139–77.

CLASSEN, C. J. (ed.) (1976), *Sophistik*, Wege der Forschung 187 (Darmstadt).

CONKLIN, H. C. (1955), 'Hanunoo Color Terms', *Southwestern Journal of Anthropology*, 11: 339–44.

CONNELL, S. E. (forthcoming), *Aristotle, On the Generation of Animals* (Cambridge).

CROMBIE, A. C. (1994), *Styles of Scientific Thinking in the European Tradition*, 3 vols. (London).

CSIKSZENTMIHALYI, M., and NYLAN, M. (forthcoming), 'Constructing Lineages and Inventing Traditions through Exemplary Figures', *T'oung Pao*.

CULLEN, C. (1993), 'A Chinese Eratosthenes of the Flat Earth: A Study of a Fragment of Cosmology in *Huainanzi*' (1st pub. *Bulletin of the School of Oriental and African Studies*, 39 (1976), 106–27), rev. in Major (1993: 269–90).

——(1996), *Astronomy and Mathematics in Ancient China: The Zhou bi suan jing* (Cambridge).

——(2000), 'Seeing the Appearances: Ecliptic and Equator in the Eastern Han', *Studies in the History of Natural Sciences*, 19: 352–82.

——(forthcoming), *The Suan shu shu: A Provisional Edition*.

CUNNINGHAM, A., and WILSON, P. (1993), 'De-centring the "Big Picture": The *Origins of Modern Science* and the Modern Origins of Science', *British Journal for the History of Science*, 26: 407–32.

DAMEROW, P. (1996), *Abstraction and Representation: Essays on the Cultural Evolution of Thinking*, trans. R. Hanauer (Dordrecht).

DAVIDSON, D. (2001*a*), *Essays on Action and Events* (1st pub. 1980), 2nd edn. (Oxford).

——(2001*b*), *Inquiries into Truth and Interpretation* (1st pub. 1984), 2nd edn. (Oxford).

——(2001*c*), *Subjective, Intersubjective, Objective* (Oxford).

DAWSON, R. (1994), *Sima Qian: Historical Records* (Oxford).

DELPLA, I. (2001), *Quine, Davidson. Le principe de charité* (Paris).

——(ed.) (2002), *L'Usage anthropologique du principe de charité,* Philosophia Scientiae 6.2 (Paris).

DENNETT, D. (1991), *Consciousness Explained* (Boston).

——(1996), *Kinds of Minds* (London).

DESCOLA, P. (2002), 'L'Anthropologie de la nature', *Annales*, 57.1: 9–25.

DETIENNE, M. (1972/1977), *The Gardens of Adonis*, trans. J. Lloyd (of *Les Jardins d'Adonis* (Paris, 1972)) (Hassocks).

——(1967/1996), *The Masters of Truth in Archaic Greece*, trans. J. Lloyd (of *Les Maîtres de vérité dans la Grèce archaïque* (Paris, 1967)) (New York).

——and VERNANT, J.-P. (1978), *Cunning Intelligence in Greek Culture and Society*, trans. J. Lloyd (of *Les Ruses de l'intelligence: la mètis des grecs* (Paris, 1974)) (Hassocks).

DIKÖTTER, F. (1992), *The Discourse of Race in Modern China* (London).

DJAMOURI, R. (1993), 'Théorie de la "rectification des dénominations" et réflexion linguistique chez Xunzi', *Extrême-Orient Extrême-Occident*, 15: 55–74.

DOROFEEVA-LICHTMANN, V. (1995), 'Conception of Terrestrial Organization in the *Shan hai jing*', *Bulletin de l'École Française d'Extrême Orient*, 82: 57–110.

——(2001), 'I testi geografici ufficiali dalla dinastia Han al dinastia Tang', in S. Petruccioli (ed.), *Storia della Scienza* (Rome), vol. ii, section 1, ch. 16, 190–7.

DOUGLAS, MARY (1966), *Purity and Danger* (London).

——(1970), *Natural Symbols* (London).

DUMMETT, M. (2000), *Elements of Intuitionism* (1st pub. 1977), 2nd edn. (Oxford).

DUNBAR, R. I. M. (1995), *The Trouble with Science* (London).

DUNN, J. (ed.) (1992), *Democracy: The Unfinished Journey* (Oxford).

DURKHEIM, E., and MAUSS, M. (1901–2/1963), *Primitive Classification*, trans. R. Needham (of 'De quelques formes primitives de classification', *L'Année sociologique*, 6 (1901–2), 1–72) (London).

DWORKIN, R. (1978), *Taking Rights Seriously* (London).

ELLEN, R. (1993), *The Cultural Relations of Classification* (Cambridge).

——and REASON, D. (eds.) (1979), *Classifications in their Social Context* (New York).

ELMAN, B. (2000), *A Cultural History of Civil Examinations in Late Imperial China* (Berkeley).

EVANS-PRITCHARD, E. E. (1956), *Nuer Religion* (Oxford).

FARQUHAR, J. (1994), *Knowing Practice: The Clinical Encounter in Chinese Medicine* (Boulder, Colo.).

FERNANDEZ, J. W. (1982), *Bwiti: An Ethnography of the Religious Imagination in Africa* (Princeton).

FEYERABEND, P. K. (1975), *Against Method* (London).

FODOR, J. A. (1983), *The Modularity of Mind* (Cambridge, Mass.).

FORRESTER, J. (1996), 'If p, then what? Thinking in Cases', *History of the Human Sciences*, 9, 3: 1–25.

FOSTER, C. D. (2001), *The Corruption of Politics and the Politics of Corruption* (London: Public Management and Policy Association).

FREDE, M. (1985), *Galen: Three Treatises on the Nature of Science* (Indianapolis).

FURTH, C. (1999), *A Flourishing Yin: Gender in China's Medical History, 960–1665* (Berkeley).

GASSMANN, R. H. (1988), *Cheng Ming. Richtigstellung der Bezeichnungen. Zu den Quellen eines Philosophems im antiken China. Ein Beitrag zur Konfuziusforschung*, Études asiatiques suisses 7 (Berne).

GELLNER, E. (1973), 'The Savage and the Modern Mind', in Horton and Finnegan (1973: 162–81).

——(1985), *Relativism and the Social Sciences* (Cambridge).

GOLDSCHMIDT, V. (1947), *Le Paradigme dans la dialectique platonicienne* (Paris).

GOODMAN, N. (1985), *Ways of Worldmaking* (Indianapolis).

GOODY, J. (1977), *The Domestication of the Savage Mind* (Cambridge).

GRAHAM, A. C. (1978), *Later Mohist Logic, Ethics and Science* (London).

——(1981), *Chuang-tzu: The Seven Inner Chapters* (London).

——(1989), *Disputers of the Tao* (La Salle, Ill.).

GRANET, M. (1934a), *La Pensée chinoise* (Paris).

——(1934b), 'La Mentalité chinoise', in M. Lahy-Hollebeque (ed.), *L'Évolution humaine des origines à nos jours*, vol. i (Paris), 371–87.

GRICE, H. P. (1957), 'Meaning', *Philosophical Review*, 66: 377–88.

——(1968), 'Utterer's Meaning, Sentence-Meaning and Word-Meaning', *Foundations of Language*, 4: 225–42.

——(1975), 'Logic and Conversation', in P. Cole and J. L. Morgan (eds.), *Syntax and Semantics 3: Speech Acts* (New York), 41–58.

GUTHRIE, W. K. C. (1962), *A History of Greek Philosophy*, i: *The Earlier Presocratics and the Pythagoreans* (Cambridge).

——(1969), *A History of Greek Philosophy*, iii: *The Fifth-Century Enlightenment* (Cambridge).

HAACK, S. (1996), *Deviant Logic, Fuzzy Logic: Beyond the Formalism* (Chicago).

—— (1998), *Manifesto of a Passionate Moderate* (Chicago).

HACKING, I. (1975), *The Emergence of Probability* (Cambridge).

—— (1992), ' "Style" for Historians and Philosophers', *Studies in History and Philosophy of Science*, 23: 1–20.

HALL, D. L., and AMES, R. T. (1987), *Thinking Through Confucius* (Albany, N.Y.).

HANKINSON, R. J. (1995), *The Sceptics* (London).

HANSEN, C. (1983), *Language and Logic in Ancient China* (Ann Arbor).

—— (1985), 'Chinese Language, Chinese Philosophy and "Truth" ', *Journal of Asian Studies*, 44: 491–517.

HARBSMEIER, C. (1989), 'Marginalia Sino-logica', in R. E. Allinson (ed.), *Understanding the Chinese Mind* (Oxford), 125–66.

—— (1998), *Science and Civilisation in China*, vii/1: *Language and Logic* (Cambridge).

HARPER, D. (1999), 'Warring States Natural Philosophy and Occult Thought', in Loewe and Shaughnessy (1999: 813–84).

HECQUET-DEVIENNE, M. (1993), 'La Pensée et le mot dans les "Réfutations sophistiques" ', *Revue philosophique de la France et de l'étranger*, 183: 179–96.

HEINIMANN, F. (1945), *Nomos und Physis* (Basel).

HINTIKKA, J., GRUENDER, D., and AGAZZI, E. (eds.) (1981), *Theory Change, Ancient Axiomatics and Galileo's Methodology* (Dordrecht).

HIRSCHFELD, L. A., and GELMAN, S. A. (eds.) (1994), *Mapping the Mind: Domain Specificity in Cognition and Culture* (Cambridge).

HOLLIS, M., and LUKES, S. (eds.) (1982), *Rationality and Relativism* (Oxford).

HOLTON, G. (1986), *The Advancement of Science and its Burdens* (Cambridge).

—— (1993), *Science and Anti-Science* (Cambridge, Mass.).

HORTON, R., and FINNEGAN, R. (eds.) (1973), *Modes of Thought* (London).

HØYRUP, J. (2002), *Lengths, Widths, Surfaces: A Portrait of Old Babylonian Algebra and its Kin* (New York).

HSU, E. (2002), *The Telling Touch* (Habilitationschrift, Sinology, University of Heidelberg).

HUANG YI-LONG (2001), 'Astronomia e astrologia', in S. Petruccioli (ed.), *Storia della Scienza* (Rome), vol. ii, section 1, ch. 13, 167–70.

HULL, D. L. (1965), 'The Effect of Essentialism on Taxonomy: Two Thousand Years of Stasis', *British Journal for the Philosophy of Science*, 15: 314–26. 16: 1–20.

—— (1991), 'Common Sense and Science', *Biology and Philosophy*, 6: 467–79.

HULSEWÉ, A. F. P. (1955), *Remnants of Han Law*, i: *Introductory Studies* (Leiden).

HUNN, E. S. (1977), *Tzeltal Folk Zoology* (New York).

IERODIAKONOU, K. (2002), 'Aristotle's Use of Examples in the *Prior Analytics*', *Phronesis*, 47: 127–52.

INAGAKI, K., and HATANO, G. (1993), 'Young Children's Understanding of the Mind–Body Distinction', *Child Development*, 64: 1534–49.

JARDINE, N. (1969), 'A Logical Basis for Biological Classification', *Systematic Zoology*, 18: 37–52.

—— and SIBSON, R. (1971), *Mathematical Taxonomy* (London).

JEYIFOUS, S. (1986), 'Atimodemo: Semantic Conceptual Development among the Yoruba', Ph.D. diss., Cornell University.

JOHNSTON, I. (2000), 'Choosing the Greater and Choosing the Lesser: A Translation and Analysis of the Daqu and Xiaoqu Chapters of the *Mozi*', *Journal of Chinese Philosophy*, 27: 375–407.

—— (forthcoming), *Gongsun Longzi*.

KALINOWSKI, M. (forthcoming), 'Technical Traditions in Ancient China and *Shushu* Culture in Chinese Religion', Proceedings of the International Conference on Chinese Religion and Society, Hong Kong, May 2000 (Hong Kong).

KARMILOFF-SMITH, A. (1996), *Beyond Modularity* (Cambridge, Mass.).

KERFERD, G. B. (1981), *The Sophistic Movement* (Cambridge).

KNOBLOCK, J. (1988–94), *Xunzi: A Translation and Study of the Complete Works*, 3 vols. (Stanford, Calif.).

—— and RIEGEL, J. (2000), *The Annals of Lü Buwei* (Stanford, Calif.).

KNORR, W. R. (1981), 'On the Early History of Axiomatics: The Interaction of Mathematics and Philosophy in Greek Antiquity', in Hintikka, Gruender, and Agazzi (1981: 145–86).

KUHN, T. S. (1970), *The Structure of Scientific Revolutions* (1st pub. 1962), 2nd edn. (Chicago).

KUSCH, M. (2002), *Knowledge by Agreement* (Oxford).

LACKNER, M. (1993), 'La Portée des événements: réflexions néo-confucéennes sur "la rectification des noms" (*Entretiens* 13.3)', *Extrême-Orient Extrême-Occident*, 15: 75–87.

LAKOFF, G., and JOHNSON, M. (1980), *The Metaphors we Live by* (Chicago).

LAMB, T., and BOURRIAU, J. (eds.) (1995), *Colour: Art and Science* (Cambridge).

LANJOUW, J., et al. (eds.) (1961), *International Code of Botanical Nomenclature* (Utrecht: International Bureau for Plant Taxonomy).

LAPOUGE, G. VACHER DE (1896), *Les Sélections sociales* (Paris).

—— (1899), *L'Aryen, son rôle social*, Cours libre à l'Université de Montpellier 1889–1890 (Paris).

LEACH, E. R. (1961), *Rethinking Anthropology* (London).

LEIGH, D., and VULLIAMY, E. (1997), *Sleaze: The Corruption of Parliament* (London).

LENNOX, J. G. (2001), *Aristotle's Philosophy of Biology* (Cambridge).

LEVI, J. (1993), 'Quelques aspects de la rectification des noms dans la pensée et la pratique politiques de la Chine ancienne', *Extrême-Orient Extrême-Occident*, 15: 23–53.

LEVINSON, S. C. (1983), *Pragmatics* (Cambridge).

LÉVI-STRAUSS, C. (1962/1966), *The Savage Mind* (trans. of *La Pensée sauvage* (Paris, 1962)) (London).

——(1962/1969), *Totemism*, trans. R. Needham (of *Le Totémisme aujourd'hui* (Paris, 1962)) (London).

LÉVY-BRUHL, L. (1923), *Primitive Mentality*, trans. L. A. Clare (of *La Mentalité primitive* (Paris, 1922)) (London).

LLOYD, G. E. R. (1979), *Magic, Reason and Experience* (Cambridge).

——(1983), *Science, Folklore and Ideology* (Cambridge).

——(1990), *Demystifying Mentalities* (Cambridge).

——(1991), *Methods and Problems in Greek Science* (Cambridge).

——(1996a), *Adversaries and Authorities* (Cambridge).

——(1996b), *Aristotelian Explorations* (Cambridge).

——(1997), 'Les Animaux dans l'antiquité étaient bons à penser', in B. Cassin and J.-L. Labarrière (eds.), *L'Animal dans l'antiquité* (Paris), 545–62.

——(1999), 'Humains et animaux: problèmes de taxinomie en Grèce et en Chine anciennes', in C. Calame and M. Kilani (eds.), *La Fabrication de l'humain dans les cultures et en anthropologie* (Lausanne), 73–91.

——(2002), *The Ambitions of Curiosity* (Cambridge).

——(forthcoming), 'Was Misunderstanding Inevitable? Ricci and the Problem of Cross-Cultural Interpretation', in Zhang Longxi (ed.), *Ricci and After*.

——and SIVIN, N. (2002), *The Way and the Word* (New Haven).

LOEWE, M., and SHAUGHNESSY, E. L. (eds.) (1999), *The Cambridge History of Ancient China: From the Origins of Civilization to 221 B.C.* (Cambridge).

LONG, A. A., and SEDLEY, D. N. (1987), *The Hellenistic Philosophers*, 2 vols. (Cambridge).

LORAUX, N. (1978/1993), 'On the Race of Women and Some of its Tribes: Hesiod and Semonides' (1st pub. as 'Sur la race des femmes et quelques-unes de ses tribus', *Arethusa*, 11 (1978), 43–87), in *The Children of Athena*, trans. C. Levine (of *Les Enfants d'Athéna* (Paris, 1981)) (Princeton), 72–110.

LOVEJOY, A. O. (1936), *The Great Chain of Being* (Cambridge, Mass.).

LUHRMANN, T. (1989), *Persuasions of the Witch's Craft* (Oxford).

——(2000), *Of Two Minds: The Growing Disorder in American Psychiatry* (New York).

LYONS, J. (1995), 'Colour in Language', in Lamb and Bourriau (1995: 194–224).

MacIntyre, A. (1970), 'The Idea of a Social Science', in Wilson (1970: 112–30).

—— (1981), *After Virtue* (London).

—— (1988), *Whose Justice? Which Rationality?* (London).

Major, J. S. (1993), *Heaven and Earth in Early Han Thought* (Albany, NY).

Malotki, E. (1983), *Hopi Time: A Linguistic Analysis of the Temporal Concepts in the Hopi Language* (Berlin).

Matilal, B. K. (1971), *Epistemology, Logic and Grammar in Indian Philosophical Analysis*, Janua Linguarum Series Minor 111 (The Hague).

—— (1985), *Logic, Language and Reality* (Delhi).

Mayr, E. (ed.) (1957), *The Species Problem*, American Association for the Advancement of Science Publications 50 (Washington, DC).

—— (1969), *Principles of Systematic Zoology* (New York).

—— (1982), *The Growth of Biological Thought* (Cambridge, Mass.).

—— (1988), *Towards a New Philosophy of Biology* (Cambridge, Mass.).

Mendell, H. (1998a), 'Reflections on Eudoxus, Callippus and their Curves: Hippopedes and Callippopedes', *Centaurus*, 40: 177–275.

—— (1998b), 'Making Sense of Aristotelian Demonstration', *Oxford Studies in Ancient Philosophy*, 16: 161–225.

Métailié, G. (2001a), 'Uno sguardo sul mondo naturale', in S. Petruccioli (ed.), *Storia della Scienza* (Rome), vol. ii, section 1, ch. 20, 255–63.

—— (2001b), 'Uno sguardo sul mondo naturale', in S. Petruccioli (ed.), *Storia della Scienza* (Rome), vol. ii, section 1, ch. 48, 536–48.

Mohanty, J. N. (1992), *Reason and Tradition in Indian Thought* (Oxford).

Mollon, J. (1995), 'Seeing Colour', in Lamb and Bourriau (1995: 127–50).

Moore, O. K. (1957), 'Divination—a New Perspective', *American Anthropologist*, 59: 67–74.

Mueller, I. (1981), *Philosophy of Mathematics and Deductive Structure in Euclid's Elements* (Cambridge, Mass.).

Needham, J. (1956), *Science and Civilisation in China*, ii: *History of Scientific Thought* (Cambridge).

Needham, R. (1972), *Belief, Language and Experience* (Oxford).

—— (1980), *Reconnaissances* (Toronto).

Neild, R. R. (2002), *Public Corruption: The Dark Side of Social Evolution* (London).

Netz, R. (1999), *The Shaping of Deduction in Greek Mathematics* (Cambridge).

Neugebauer, O. (1957), *The Exact Sciences in Antiquity* (1st pub. 1952), 2nd edn. (Providence, RI).

—— (1975), *A History of Ancient Mathematical Astronomy*, 3 vols. (Berlin).

—— and Sachs, A. (1945), *Mathematical Cuneiform Texts*, American Oriental Series 29 (New Haven).

NYLAN, M. (1992), *The Shifting Center: The Original 'Great Plan' and Later Readings*, Monumenta Serica Monograph Series 24 (Nettetal).

—— (2001), *The Five 'Confucian' Classics* (New Haven).

O'NEILL, O. (1989), *Constructions of Reason: Explorations of Kant's Practical Philosophy* (Cambridge).

—— (2002), *A Question of Trust*, Reith Lectures 2002 (Cambridge).

PARK, G. K. (1963), 'Divination and its Social Contexts', *Journal of the Royal Anthropological Institute*, 93: 195–209.

PELLEGRIN, P. (1982), *La Classification des animaux chez Aristote* (Paris).

—— (1986), *Aristotle's Classification of Animals*, rev. trans. A. Preus (of Pellegrin 1982) (Berkeley).

PORZIG, W. (1934), 'Wesenhafte Bedeutungsbeziehungen', *Beiträge zur Geschichte der deutschen Sprache und Literatur*, 58: 70–97.

PRAWITZ, D. (1980), 'Intuitionistic Logic: A Philosophical Challenge', in G. H. von Wright (ed.), *Logic and Philosophy* (The Hague), 1–10.

PRIEST, G., and ROUTLEY, R. (1989), 'Systems of Paraconsistent Logic', in G. Priest, R. Routley, and J. Norman (eds.), *Paraconsistent Logic: Essays on the Inconsistent* (Munich), 151–86.

PUTNAM, H. (1975a), *Mathematics, Matter and Method, Philosophical Papers*, vol. i (Cambridge).

—— (1975b), *Mind, Language and Reality, Philosophical Papers*, vol. ii (Cambridge).

—— (1983), *Realism and Reason, Philosophical Papers*, vol. iii (Cambridge).

—— (1999), *The Threefold Cord* (New York).

QIAN BAOCONG (1963), *Suanjing shishu* (Beijing).

QUINE, W. VAN O. (1960), *Word and Object* (Cambridge, Mass.).

RAPHALS, L. (1998), *Sharing the Light: Representations of Women and Virtue in Early China* (Albany, NY).

RASHDALL, H. (1936), *The Universities of Europe in the Middle Ages*, ed. F. M. Powicke and A. B. Emden, 3 vols., 2nd edn. (Oxford).

RAWLS, J. (1971), *A Theory of Justice* (Oxford).

READ, S. (1988), *Relevant Logic* (Oxford).

—— (1994), *Thinking about Logic* (Oxford).

REDING, J.-P. (1985), *Les Fondements philosophiques de la rhétorique chez les sophistes grecs et les sophistes chinois* (Berne).

RICHET, C. (1919), *La Sélection humaine* (Paris).

ROBINSON, R. (1941/1953), *Plato's Earlier Dialectic* (1st pub. 1941), 2nd edn. (Oxford).

ROCHBERG, F. (1988), *Aspects of Babylonian Celestial Divination*, Archiv für Orientforschung 22 (Horn).

—— (forthcoming), *The Heavenly Writing: Divination and Horoscopy in Mesopotamian Culture* (Cambridge).

ROGET, P. M. (1962), *Roget's Thesaurus*, new edn. rev. and modernized by R. A. Dutch (1st pub. 1852) (London).

RORTY, R. (1991), *Objectivity, Relativism and Truth* (Cambridge).

RUNCIMAN, W. G. (1966), *Relative Deprivation and Social Justice* (London).

SAPIR, E. (1949), *Selected Writings of Edward Sapir in Language, Culture, and Personality* (Berkeley).

SCHOFIELD, M. (1999), *The Stoic Idea of the City* (1st pub. 1991), 2nd edn. (Cambridge).

SCHWINGES, R. C. (1992), 'Student Education, Student Life', in H. de Ridder-Symoens (ed.), *A History of the University in Europe*, i: *Universities in the Middle Ages* (Cambridge), 195–243.

SEARBY, P. (1997), *A History of the University of Cambridge*, iii: *1750–1870* (Cambridge).

SEARLE, J. R. (1983), *Intentionality* (Cambridge).

SEDLEY, D. N. (1982), 'On Signs', in Barnes et al. (1982: 239–72).

SEN, A. (1981), *Poverty and Famines: An Essay on Entitlement and Deprivation* (Oxford).

—— (1992), *Inequality Reexamined* (Oxford).

SIMPSON, G. G. (1961), *Principles of Animal Taxonomy* (New York).

SIVIN, N. (1995*a*), *Science in Ancient China: Researches and Reflections*, vol. i (Aldershot).

—— (1995*b*), *Medicine, Philosophy and Religion in Ancient China: Researches and Reflections*, vol. ii (Aldershot).

SPERBER, D. (1975), *Rethinking Symbolism*, trans. A. Morton (Cambridge).

—— PREMACK, D., and PREMACK, A. J. (eds.) (1995), *Causal Cognition: A Multidisciplinary Debate* (Oxford).

—— and WILSON, D. (1986), *Relevance: Communication and Cognition* (Oxford).

STADEN, H. VON (1982), 'Hairesis and Heresy: The Case of the *Haireseis iatrikai*', in B. F. Meyer and E. P. Sanders (eds.), *Jewish and Christian Self-Definition*, vol. iii (London), 76–100, 199–206.

—— (1989), *Herophilus: The Art of Medicine in Early Alexandria* (Cambridge).

STANFORD, P. K. (1995), 'For Pluralism and against Realism about Species', *Philosophy of Science*, 62: 70–91.

STERCKX, R. (2002), *The Animal and the Daemon in Early China* (Albany, NY).

SUPPES, P. (1981), 'Limitations of the Axiomatic Method in Ancient Greek Mathematical Sources', in Hintikka, Gruender, and Agazzi (1981: 197–213).

TAMBIAH, S. J. (1969), 'Animals are Good to Think and Good to Prohibit', *Ethnology*, 8: 423–59.

—— (1973), 'Form and Meaning of Magical Acts: A Point of View', in Horton and Finnegan (1973: 199–229).

—— (1990), *Magic, Science, Religion and the Scope of Rationality* (Cambridge).

TRAVERSO, E. (2003), *The Origins of Nazi Violence* trans. J. Lloyd (of *La Violence nazie* (Paris, 2002))) (New York).

VANDERMEERSCH, L. (1993), 'Rectification des noms et langue graphique chinoises', *Extrême-Orient Extrême-Occident*, 15: 11–21.

VERNANT, J.-P. (1972/1980), 'Between the Beasts and the Gods', trans. J. Lloyd (of 'Introduction' to M. Detienne, *Les Jardins d'Adonis* (Paris, 1972)), in *Myth and Society in Ancient Greece* (New York), 143–82.

VEYNE, P. (1988), *Did the Greeks Believe in their Myths?*, trans. P. Wissing (of *Les Grecs ont-ils cru à leurs mythes?* (Paris, 1983))) (Chicago).

VICKERS, B. (ed.) (1984), *Occult and Scientific Mentalities in the Renaissance* (Cambridge).

VOLKOV, A. (1992), 'Analogical Reasoning in Ancient China: Some Examples', *Extrême-Orient Extrême-Occident*, 14: 15–48.

—— (1996–7), 'The Mathematical Work of Zhao Youqin: Remote Surveying and the Computation of π', *Taiwanese Journal for Philosophy and History of Science*, 5.1: 129–89.

—— (1997), 'Zhao Youqin and his Calculation of π', *Historia Mathematica*, 24: 301–31.

WAGNER, D. (1979), 'An Early Chinese Derivation of the Volume of a Pyramid: Liu Hui, Third Century A.D.', *Historia Mathematica*, 6: 164–88.

WARDY, R. B. B. (2000), *Aristotle in China: Language, Categories and Translation* (Cambridge).

WARNOCK, M. (1985), *A Question of Life: The Warnock Report on Human Fertilisation and Embryology* (Oxford).

—— (1998), *An Intelligent Person's Guide to Ethics* (London).

WHORF, B. L. (1967), *Language, Thought and Reality*, ed. J. Carroll (1st pub. 1956), repr. (Cambridge, Mass.).

WILLIAMS, B. (2002), *Truth and Truthfulness: An Essay in Genealogy* (Princeton).

WILSON, B. R. (ed.) (1970), *Rationality* (Oxford).

WINCH, P. (1970), 'Understanding a Primitive Society', in Wilson (1970: 78–111).

XI ZEZONG and PO SHUJEN (1966), 'Ancient Oriental Records of Novae and Supernovae', *Science*, 154: 596–603.

YATES, R. D. S. (1994), 'The Yin-Yang Texts from Yinqueshan: An Introduction and Partial Reconstruction, with Notes on their Significance in Relation to Huang-Lao Daoism', *Early China*, 19: 75–144.

YAVETZ, I. (1998), 'On the Homocentric Spheres of Eudoxus', *Archive for History of Exact Sciences*, 52: 221–78.

ZADEH, L. (1987), *Fuzzy Sets and Applications: Selected Papers by Lofti A. Zadeh*, ed. R. R. Yager et al. (New York).

ZIMMERMANN, F. (1992), 'Remarques comparatives sur la place de l'exemple dans l'argumentation (en Inde)', *Extrême-Orient Extrême-Occident*, 14: 199–204.

INDEX